RAPE AND INEQUALITY

Volume 148, Sage Library of Social Research

RECENT VOLUMES IN
SAGE LIBRARY OF SOCIAL RESEARCH

RAPE AND INEQUALITY

Julia R. and Herman Schwendinger

Volume 148
SAGE LIBRARY OF
SOCIAL RESEARCH

SAGE PUBLICATIONS
Beverly Hills / London / New Delhi

For information address:

SAGE Publications, Inc.
275 South Beverly Drive
Beverly Hills, California 90212

SAGE Publications India Pvt. Ltd.
C-236 Defence Colony
New Delhi 110 024, India

SAGE Publications Ltd
28 Banner Street
London EC1Y 8QE, England

Printed in the United States of America

Library of Congress Cataloging in Publication Data

Main entry under title:

Schwendinger, Julia R.
  Rape and inequality.

  (Sage library of social research ; 148)
  Bibliography: p.
  1. Rape—United States   2. Sexism—United States.
3. Violence—United States.   4. Victims of crimes—
United States.   5. Rape—United States—Prevention.
I. Schwendinger, Herman.   II. Title.   III. Series.
HV6561.S37   1983   364.1'532'09   82-24092
ISBN 0-8039-1967-0
ISBN 0-8039-1968-9 (pbk.)

FIRST PRINTING

CONTENTS

ACKNOWLEDGMENTS

We were fortunate to have received help and support from many people over the years — from the birth of the idea to the full maturity of this book. In particular, we want to thank all the rape victims who opened their hearts and revealed their memories to us at a time when sharing one's rape experience was not at all common. Thanks also to Bay Area Women Against Rape, from whom we learned much in the early years.

A number of persons reviewed the manuscript in its various forms and stages of development. For their encouragement and positive criticism on the earliest version, when we were still in Berkeley, we wish to thank Oleta Kirk Abrams, Pauline Bart, Tommie and Michael Hannigan, Freada Klein, Robin Mc Duff, Michael Ort, and Leni Schwendinger. We appreciate the support from Dragan Milovanovic, who offered helpful comments after we moved to New York. Sally Luther, who set her own work aside and painstakingly critiqued an early version, deserves special mention. In addition, portions of some of the chapters have been previously published in CRIME AND SOCIAL JUSTICE and in CRIME AND DELIN-QUENCY. We are indebted to Tony Platt, Paul Takagi, and Sarah Dike, the editors of these journals, for their acknowledgment of the worth of our work in its developmental stages.

With regard to the final manuscript, special thanks are due to Virginia Engquist Grabiner for her incisive critique and editing help. For their generous help with indexing and proof-reading, we are grateful to Joan Casamo and Gail Imai. Finally, we cannot say "thank you" enough to Eleanor Leacock and David Greenberg for their careful reading and suggestions on the final manuscript.

INTRODUCTION

Prior to the 1970s, rape was not only tabooed as an activity but also as a subject of comment and target of social change. Breaking the taboo, Julia R. Schwendinger was one of the original founders of the first rape crisis center within the United States and abroad, Bay Area Women Against Rape (BAWAR).[1] However, preceding BAWAR, there was a small committee to fight rape within the Berkeley Women's Health Collective in 1970 (Schwendinger and Schwendinger, 1978). It was here that the idea of a 24-hour hotline and the belief that victims needed alternative services to the criminal justice, hospital, and the mental health institutions, were born. BAWAR's vision of services incorporated these ideas and implemented them along with direct counseling, public education, and rape prevention activity. The tiny handful of women involved in both of these organizing efforts was composed of political activists and militant feminists who also saw themselves as advocates of rape victims in the established institutions.

When BAWAR was formed, in early 1972, it engaged the police and hospitals militantly, although its claim to the advocacy role was first laughed at. Its members were looked upon as usurpers by the criminal justice personnel. Doctors at the hospital were outraged that lay women had the nerve to tell them their medical practices were harmful, and they rejected positive suggestions to improve their treatment of rape victims. In fact, the original women in BAWAR wanted to change much more than the health and the criminal justice institutions. They wanted to politicize women and bring about more basic changes in relations between the powerful and the oppressed. Speaking out about rape, teaching women that collectively they could fight male domination, and forcing the hospital and police to change their treatment of rape victims whether they wanted to or not was quite an accomplishment.

While she was active in the Women's Health Collective, Julia Schwendinger was a graduate student at the Berkeley School of Criminology at the University of California. After she had decided on a dissertation subject, the library was one of her first stops as she tried to learn more about a generally hushed-up topic: *rape*. The excellent main library at the University boasted a single subject matter card, *The Rape of Lucrece,* and the law library contained only a handful of narrow legalistic articles. Since that time, however, numerous theories and descriptions, articles and books have been written on the subject.

But the approach presented in this book is radically different. It differs from that of other studies of rape by dealing with larger social factors that have, on the whole, been overlooked. While not ignoring culture as an important contributing variable, this work emphasizes socioeconomic factors and their relationship to the causes of rape throughout history. Set in an international and historical context, it ties rape into the development of sexual inequality which has occured in certain societies and not others. It shows that violence against women is not universal but that when it takes place it has unique causal characteristics in each socioeconomic formation. These characteristics have nothing to do with the instincts for power and aggression that are alleged to be naturally inherent in men.

Our differences with previous approaches to the subject suggest the organization of the material, which is in four parts. In Part I, Critique of Existing Explanations, we describe the types of sexual behavior included in our analysis and we critique popular, legal, and scientific myths about rape. The first two chapters also acknowledge the contributions made by antirape groups in debunking such myths and defending victims. But they point out that preventing rape requires broader political action based on valid theories of causal relationships.

The third chapter, "Forms of Rape," describes types of sexual crimes that must be explained theoretically and establishes a context for what is to come. A macroscopic focus is emphasized from the start. While most studies limit themselves to individualistic rapes and microscopic situations, the arena of study is broadened to include rape that is officially instituted for torturing and terrorizing conquered populations and political dissenters. Since members of military forces and civil servants, including the police, perpetrate the acts we call institutionalized rapes, these people are not deterred legally. A consideration of sexual harassment is also included in this chapter. On the other hand, the rape of men is not included, although we consider this form of rape important.

To set off our own theoretical ideas, which build slowly from Part Two onward, we then offer two chapters that critically analyze the theories predominating among criminologists, sociologists, and feminist authors. Some theories, such as interactionist theories, have been explicitly stated in recent works; others, such as Freudian theories, are often used implicitly. We begin this critical analysis in Chapter 4 by discussing androcentric (male-centered) theories, which are often thinly disguised legalistic explanations that establish a "scientific" premise for blaming the female victim. Generally, these theories take male supremacist standards of behavior for granted and may even, at times, be adopted, by female authors.

Chapter 5 goes into major feminist theories. We show that these theories break sharply with androcentric perspectives but that they have not completely escaped reliance on very basic theoretical postulates developed by traditional scholars. These basic postulates are subjected to a critical evaluation, and serious questions are raised about their scientific validity. Feminists have turned our attention to the larger issues and contexts of rape that no traditional scholars have genuinely addressed. Simultaneously, however, some of them have also obscured these larger issues and relationships by attributing them to sexual deprivation or an eternal war between the sexes.

In criticizing these feminist theories, our aim is to provide information and evidence that will further the search for truth about the foundations of violence against women. Contradictions between the views of different feminists are brought to light and examined. The oppression of women needs to be approached freely, from many points of view, to create the most powerful political challenge.

Part II, Rape Laws and Private Property, is a comparative analysis of the origins of rape laws. Its purpose is not to be a definitive history, or "herstory," of the law; rather, it deals with current political and economic issues that determine outlooks on how to prevent and control rape. Chapters 6 and 7 scrutinize the currently fashionable idea that rape laws protect men and their private property rather than women. It has been noted that there are two main positions on the conception of the rape law. Some writers reduce modern rape laws to laws that merely protect male property, while others discount these laws as inconsequential because their implementation in favor of women is inadequate. We grant that rape laws have been shaped by chauvinist standards and that they are not enforced properly. On the other hand, we suggest a more complicated and more appropriate way to look at legal developments. First, the notion of private property itself is examined as a changing phenomenon that arose under particular economic conditions in which material surpluses, accumulated by individual men or patrilineal estates, contributed to social class formations and sexual inequality. To show how property relationships are connected to these laws, we describe the formal proscriptions against rape, from customary practice among people subsisting in a "hunting and gathering" society through slave, feudal, colonial, and metropolitan capitalist societies. The gradual disappearance of an important feudal doctrine, the doctrine of coverture, is used to *contradict* the idea that the laws in question continue to protect *male* property.

In Part III, An Explanation of Rape, we argue against generalizations about the universality of sexual inequality and male violence against women. The chapters in this part are historical and empirical. While some of the historical aspects of rape and rape law are covered in preceding chapters, in this part of the book the history of rape is differentiated from the history of Man. We argue against the universality of rape and propose that although every mode of production (together, of course, with other historical conditions) creates its own crimes, rape may or may not be one of them. To describe this history we rely once again on anthropological research.

Chapter 8 takes on the well-known universal "war between the sexes," bringing out contradictory evidence found in both feminist and nonfeminist anthropological studies. Gentle tribes, such as the Tasaday, Arapesh, Montagnais, and others are described. Using Eleanor Leacock's material on the Montagnais bands, we illustrate the sexist relationships that were imposed by European colonizers and their religious, political, and economic institutions.

In Chapter 9 we show that rape, sexual inequality, and socioeconomic relations are interrelated. Within the context of modes of production and their articulation with each other, woman's status is affected by property relations and her participation in social production. In Chapters 10 and 11 we show that the development of rape in a society is related to the degree to which violence is generalized in other aspects of life. Using the Human Relations Area Files, which index primary anthropological reports on precapitalist formations, we provide evidence that exploitative modes of production culminating in precapitalist class societies produce greater sexual inequality and violence in general.

In Chapters 10 and 11, the focus on rape, which characterizes the preceding chapters, is broadened to include other forms of violence. Rape is no longer considered apart from other forms of violence against women or isolated from the general level of violence in society. From a macroscopic point of view, rape does not exist in a social vacuum merely because it is an individual crime. It is dynamically related to constellations of harmful practices that vary from one society to another.

Part IV, Priorities for Rape Prevention, deals with violence in general, suggesting connections between this broader phenomenon and sexual violence and then making some suggestions for rape prevention. In Chapter 12, we deal with the social mechanisms, operating in societies dominated by the capitalist mode of production, that make violence against women appear to be derived spontaneously from the "nature of man."

Chapters 13 and 14 take up the ideological, political, and economic patterning of rape and its motivational characteristics. These chapters also note research showing that raped wives who had independent labor market status were assertive and effectively prevented future attacks by their husbands, and that social learning of violent behavior takes place in the home, among peers, and from exposure to the media. Obviously, these relationships point to the need for the broader prevention strategies that support sexual equality at home and in the labor market and that work against cultural influences inculcating violent behavior toward women. These chapters also point to the enormous escalation of rape in wartime and the concentration of rapists in communities persistently affected by racism, underemployment, and disorganization. The harsher penal sanctions proposed by so-called law and order policies are rejected because they lead to further lawlessness and disorder.

We believe that rape can be partially deterred in specific localities and among particular persons by popular self-defense strategies and the swift apprehension and conviction of rapists. However, for the United States as a whole, rape cannot be prevented substantially without a continuing struggle for equality by independent women's groups, significant changes in the conditions that affect the most oppressed segments of the American population, and a determined opposition to war.

Note

1. For a history ("herstory") of the rape crisis center movement, see Mary Ann Largen (1981).

PART I

CRITIQUE OF EXISTING EXPLANATIONS

CHAPTER 1

THE MANTLE OF MYTH

Fear on the street has become a commonplace of the American city scene. How does a woman react to stares, sexual invitations, and wolf whistles? Often she lowers her eyes and quickens her step — a smile or hesitation might invite danger. Some women are flattered but most have a growing sense of powerlessness, fear, and anger.

Added to these widespread concerns is the mistrust, instigated by traditional beliefs, of blameless rape victims. Cynics openly declare that it is impossible to rape a woman without her willing consent. But we will show that their accusation has no basis in reality. When raped women desperately need unqualified emotional support, this mythical notion breeds suspicion and slander. Furthermore, there is a striking number of other myths, and their repeated expression hangs like a shroud over the victim.

Ideas can be powerful and mythologies are potentially harmful. Beliefs in Aryan superiority and German antisemitism reinforced hatred of the Jewish people, providing fuel for the never-to-be-forgotten holocaust. Countering harmful ideas can therefore be important, even though thoughts must operate together with other social forces in determining behavior.

Since valid material helps protect the integrity of victims, let us debunk a few of the many popular myths about assault victims, including those created by social scientists.

Myths About the Impossibility of Rape

Questions that are asked about molestation often contain these popular myths. Not long ago, for instance, questions of this kind were expressed in an American talk show broadcast over the radio in the San Francisco Bay Area. In the broadcast, listeners were encouraged to telephone their own questions about the subject of sexual assault to a moderator and three members of a women's antirape group, the panel of experts on the show. What questions and what myths did they talk about?

The first person who telephoned was a man who did not believe that a woman could actually be molested if she was unwilling to engage in sexual intercourse. The voice was that of a mature adult. He said: "Hello. You have someone on the program who has been talking to you whose name is Maria, don't you? I want to talk to Maria."

His tone became fatherly and condescending. He asked: "How are you tonight, Maria? Do you *actually* believe there is such a thing as rape?"

Maria, who had been a rape victim herself, sounded nervous as she answered. She said: "Yes, there is such a thing; and the idea that rape is impossible is one of the myths we have to deal with."

"I feel that there's no such thing as rape," the man answered, and he proceeded to try to tell Maria that violation is impossible because it is easily resisted. "In fact," he added, "I have taught my three daughters self- protection. Anyone can learn to use the knee and how to use the side of their hand to chop at the Adam's apple."

Before discussing the validity of the caller's opinions, it should be noted that he is not alone in this belief. A wide variety of persons share his opinion.

Under different circumstances, facetious remarks may dress up the equivalents of this man's assertions. For example, some say: "A woman with her skirt up can run faster than a man with his pants down." The same idea is clearly expressed when someone says, "Frankly, I can't see how any woman who doesn't *want* it can be raped."

This belief is expressed by doctors, defense lawyers, district attorneys, and police officers. Often, when pressed, a professional appears to make a more complicated analysis, couching this commonplace belief in scientific jargon. When so altered, it suggests: "Rape is impossible when all other things are equal." This cryptic sentence however, differs only in its implication that assault occurs under typical circumstances, allowing the victim an element of choice. Because she had a choice, she is morally responsible for submitting to the rapist. Consequently, the phrase "when all things are equal" connotes, in this context, certain allegedly normal conditions that justify the condemnation of the victim.

Anthropologist Margaret Mead (1969) suggests one of these so-called normal conditions when she says, "By and large, within the same homogeneous social setting an ordinarily strong man cannot rape an ordinarily strong healthy woman." By implication, an average woman who says she was raped by an average man is lying. She could not have been molested without consenting willingly.

Morris Ploskowe (1962), author of *Sex and the Law,* also brings in the attributes of strength and well-being. He claims: "Rape cannot be perpetrated by one man alone on an adult woman of good health and vigor." He backs up his claim with statements by medico-legal "experts."

It is readily understandable why common sense would indicate that rape is impossible without willing consent. Persons who have not experienced rape tend to compare it to their own sexual intercourse, which is usually based on voluntary participation rather than force. But to make the simple comparison between a typical act of rape and a typical act of sexual intercourse is to transform an ugly act into a thing of beauty.

The "other things" indicated by Mead and Ploskowe are neither "ordinary" nor "equal." For example, the single largest group of rape victims is composed of female young adults, age 16 to 24; these women are indeed representatives of the prime age group from the standpoint of health and vigor. Nevertheless, many women in this group are actually molested in spite of active resistance which endangers their lives.

Case in point: A recent victim in San Francisco, a 19-year-old Japanese woman who came from Tokyo as an exchange student, was attacked by a rapist with a knife. When he tried to kiss her, she struck back, biting him on the tongue. This bite provoked the attacker into a furious assault; he stabbed the woman fifteen times. A veteran sex-crime inspector said he had never known a victim to survive such a brutal and vicious knifing.

Consequently, deriving typical rape conditions from the health and vigor of participants can be misleading. Of greater importance is the frequent occurrence of other factors, such as the victim's paralyzing fear, the suddenness of the rapist's attack, and the possibility of injury or death, which may lead to an inability to resist.

Rape-induced paralysis closely parallels *tonic immobility* or *animal hypnosis*. Tonic immobility often results as an animal's response to a predator, say psychologists Susan D. Suarez and Gordon G. Gallup, Jr. (1979: 315), who compare the paralysis of sexual assault victims with the immobility of animals under attack: "Since fear, overtones of predation, contact, and restraint are common denominators to rape and the induction of tonic immobility, and because the reactions by rape victims are often [identical] to behaviors shown by immobilized animals, it is concluded that tonic immobility and rape-induced paralysis represent the same phenomena." Suarez and Gallup point out that this phenomenon may account for the lack of resistance on the part of victims: "Retrospective reports from many victims indicate that the lack of movement during rape may be due to the victim being in a state of tonic immobility. Statements such as 'my body felt paralyzed' or 'my body went absolutely stiff' are quite common and analogous to the profound motoric inhibition and periods of muscular rigidity evidenced by animals following manual restraint."

A simple analogy may further highlight the fallacy of equal forces in many rape situations. Opposing armies strategically seek the element of surprise to add to their impact. A parallel exists when a woman is violated after being forcibly overcome by an unexpected attacker.

Case in point: In this illustration Carolyn, a 19-year-old woman was babysitting for a family in their house. The rapist broke in by climbing through a window. The shocked victim was caught completely unawares. She said, "I was sitting in the living room but he came in through a bedroom window. He walked up very quietly and grabbed me from behind."

Although he had a knife, she screamed and struggled with him. He threatened her, bound and gagged her, beat her up, and raped her. Then he finally left by the window after she promised not to call the police. "What," we asked her, "was the first thing you did afterward?" She answered, "I went to look in the mirror to see if I was really alive."

There are also victims who give unwilling consent. They do this because they are fully aware of the futility and dangers of active resistance when the odds against them are overwhelming.

Case in point: Ann. On a Friday afternoon Ann stopped in at a bar a block from her house in Oakland to have a drink. Two young men whom she recognized from her neighborhood asked her to join them. They talked for a couple of hours and seemed "friendly and nice." When they invited her to have another drink in their house, she accepted.

Another forty-five minutes of talk ensued. "Then, suddenly," she said, "as if by a signal, one of them grabbed me and the other started to tear my clothes off. They threatened to take me to San Francisco."

"Go get the gun from my bedroom drawer," snarled the one who owned the house to his companion.

She was so frightened that she said she would give them anything if they would not hurt her — that she would not report them - and that they would still be friends.

A person can be terribly frightened at the threat of violence. Further, it is useful to keep in mind here that the rapist's motives are not soley sexual. Rape often involves a desire to subjugate a person forcibly regardless of whether the victim is a man, woman, or child. In rape, sexual motives are usually interwoven with aggression, sadism, and contempt (Davis, 1968; DeFrancis, 1969; Tormes, 1968). This crime may also be motivated by racial bigotry, national chauvinism, and other supremacist ideologies.

Under these conditions there are not many options available to the potential assault victim. The lack of choices and the contemptuous attitude of the aggressor clearly and vividly illustrate how rape and making love are opposite acts. Presumably, in an *ideal* lovemaking situation the woman has the real choice of not engaging in a sexual act. In reality, of course, the choice involves some constraint in the situations of many women, because refusal may represent social or economic risks that they are not ready to take. But, in rape, instead of any choice, physical force is *always* present or implied.

In some cases a woman on the street is unexpectedly grabbed by the throat from behind and brutally pushed to the ground. In others, a woman is dehumanized and issued a command: "Be quiet and you won't get hurt!" "Lie down, and don't make a sound or I'll kill you!"

Usually the urgency of this command is accented with a knife, gun, another weapon, or a threat. Such threats may be directed at the woman's life, her children, or a companion. The authoritarian tone, the shock and surprise at the command, the weapon, and the force ordinarily reduce the balance of power to very unequal proportions. In short, Mead, Ploskowe, and the man who telephoned the radio program are either misleading or simply wrong on factual grounds. We have repeatedly found too many circumstances in which force or the threat of force has been sufficient to secure *unwilling* consent from a woman.

Consequences of the Myth

Widespread belief in this myth has cruel consequences. Among them is that a woman can be "twice victimized," first by the rapist and then by other persons who humiliate and mistreat her. These others feel that she willingly consented and only later had second thoughts about it.

Case in point: Jo Ellen. "My experience with the doctor was much worse than with the police," she said. "My doctor said he didn't believe in rape if a girl really wanted to resist it.

He performed a little trick with me holding a cup and showing that if I moved it around he couldn't put a stick in it." To the doctor, the cup symbolized her vagina and the stick was a penis.

She hesitated before continuing, a tight expression settling over her face as she relived the insulting moment from her past. Finally, she went on: "He scoffed at me. He gave me no medication of any type."

Oleta Kirk Abrams, co-founder of Bay Area Women Against Rape (BAWAR), tells a similar story; however, her tale indicates the fatal flaw underlying the illustration. The story begins with a young woman and her male companion, who were having a drink in a tavern. The man recognized a police officer who entered and invited him to sit at their table. A conversation about assault incidents ensued, and, at one point, the officer stated that if a woman struggled hard enough it would be impossible for her to be raped. The woman at the table strongly disagreed.

To back up his claim, the policeman handed her a large glass. He suggested that she move it rapidly about while he would attempt to insert his billie club into it. After demonstrating how hard this task could be, he suggested that she try it and gave her the club. She picked up the club and rapped him sharply across the arm; he released the glass and drew back in surprise. *She then placed the club into the glass effortlessly.* The reversal, which now made the glass accessible, more nearly approximated the power relations involved in many rape situations.[1]

The doctor and the policeman are not the only misinformed persons who have used a phallic symbol and a moving cup to illustrate the impossibility of rape without willing consent. The assault victim who presses legal charges against her attacker may encounter similar illustrations in the courtroom.

Defense attorneys have employed this demonstration to indicate that a healthy woman not wishing sex will *resist it to the utmost* with the result that intercourse will not occur. To win this kind of contest, the rape victim must act like a contender for a boxing title who does not let her fans down; it must be clearly demonstrated that she did not throw the fight. Obviously, under these conditions, an absence of cuts and bruises is tellingly noted by the defense attorneys. This lack of physical evidence is used to "prove" the innocence of the accused rapist; moreover, the "proof" is reportedly "demonstrated" by maintaining that it is the woman who has the moral responsibility to prevent rape by resisting the rapist to the utmost.

Rape laws have reflected the Victorian expectation that a woman should resist as long as she has the power to do so. In one Wisconsin decision, it was stated that the woman must "exert the utmost power in the protection of herself. . . . There must be the utmost vehement exercise of every physical means and faculty within the woman's power to resist the penetration of her person and this must be shown to persist until the offense is consummated" (1938, 288 Wisc. 235. 280 N.W. 357).

The Wisconsin law has been changing. Most of the forcible rape laws in the United States are no longer so rigid. In clear reaction against such requirements in the law, it was decided in a California case that "the female need not resist as long as either strength endures or consciousness continues. Rather, the resistance must be proportional to the outrage, and the amount of resistance necessarily depends upon the circumstances such as the relative strength of the parties, age, condition of the female, uselessness of resistance, and the degree of force manifested, which rule in some jurisdictions is expressly adopted by statute" (1935, 10 Ca. App. 2nd 538).

But the stipulation that "the resistance must be proportional to the outrage" retains the sexist imprint of the mythical impossibility of rape. In addition, it implicitly assumes that rape situations encourage deliberative responses on the part of the victim, permitting her realistically to calculate her moves. This assumption flies in the face of the elemental features of too many sexual attack situations which, to say the least, afford little opportunity for deliberation. Also, as indicated, an overwhelming sense of fear may in some cases inhibit any impulse to show physical resistance regardless of emotional revulsion to the rapist's demands.

Consequently, if the *threat* of force or violence by a man is sufficient to secure unwilling consent from many women, then any absolute requirement in law for a show of physical resistance must go against the woman's legitimate rights in this matter. Recognizing this unfairness in the law, women mounted a great struggle in California, and the California rape law was amended. It now states that rape can occur "where [the woman] is prevented from resisting by threats of great and immediate bodily harm, accompanied by apparent power of execution." Unfortunately, the revised statute is still hampered by qualifying conditions, such as "great bodily harm," that can be interpreted unjustly. (Who will decide what degree of bodily harm is great?) The law's clear demand for some physical resistance, in any jurisdiction where it still stands, requires a woman to endanger her life or risk losing her rights later in a trial.

This loss of legal rights is mentioned by Suarez and Gallup (1979: 318). In their view, nonresistance may perform an adaptive function: "Adopting a motionless posture during rape can serve at least three immediate functions: 1) sexual arousal of the rapist may be prevented and the attack therefore aborted, 2) amount of bodily harm resulting from beating precipitated by struggling is minimized, and 3) the victim can take advantage of an opportunity to escape from or subdue the rapist if he becomes distracted." In this connection, a further point is made: "It seems ironic that victims should be legally penalized for exhibiting a reaction which has such obvious adaptive value and may be firmly embedded in the biology of our species."

A businessman may forcibly resist theft of his property. But no law *demands* this kind of personal resistance as a condition for the lawful protection of his property rights. Women's rights, on the other hand, seem to be another matter.

"Asking for It" and "Uncontrollable Passions" Myths

One of the more common myths about the molestation victim is that she was "asking for it." To support this myth, various assumptions are brought into play when the woman's behavior is evaluated by others. It is commonly assumed, for instance, that a woman bears the responsibility for rape if she stimulates the man sexually. Allegedly he is not responsible, because, once aroused, a male can no longer control his sexual urge.

When translated into criminological jargon, this myth defines sexual assault as a *victim-precipitated* crime. From this standpoint, it is assumed that there is something in the behavior of assault victims or in their psychological makeup that differentiates them from nonvictims. Under ordinary conditions, women as catalytic agents may typically be seen as wearing something rapists consider provocative, or their willingness to make a friendly response to a strange man's conversation is interpreted as an invitation.

This way of thinking rarely questions the oppressive sexist norms that regulate the everyday activities of women. In this context, furthermore, the burden of responsibility for maintaining these restrictive norms is placed on the woman alone; her rejection of the norms is interpreted as a sexually exploitable opportunity. For example, Menachem Amir, an Israeli criminologist and author of *Patterns in Forcible Rape,* is a strong proponent of the victim-precipitation idea. He says that the victim's behavior is not even as important as "the offender's interpretation of her actions" (Amir, 1971: 261).

From this point of view, a woman's acceptance of an automobile ride or an invitation to dinner, or her entering an apartment alone with a male may be misunderstood by the alleged rapist or intentionally rationalized as a sign of a woman's consent. Indeed, the logical conclusion of this idea is that a woman can be seen as inviting attack by her very presence or by any response she might make. In this Alex in Wonderland scene, she may really mean "yes" when she says "no," according to the rapist's "interpretation of her actions." Therefore, at the heart of this idea are male-supremacist *expectations* and *prerogatives* not "uncontrollable passions."

The myth about uncontrollable passions is closely allied with the common belief in victim-as-precipitator. A common way of stating this myth is: "She led him on and he couldn't help it." Like a source of energy, all that is needed is a flame to ignite it and the uncontrollable act explodes.

For example, returning to the radio talk show, one caller, a young woman this time, asked a question and offered a seemingly disconnected assertion. She asked: " I want to know, what 'turns a man on'; you know what I mean? What turns on the majority of men?" After posing this common question, she made a surprising statement: "I'm sure," she said, "you've heard that the women outpopulate the men?"

It should be emphasized that her query dealt with the causes of sexual assault; therefore, whatever "turns a man on," in this context, precipitates forcible rape. The question further assumes that something about the woman's behavior causes the molester to select *her* as his victim.

Finally, the caller's assertion ("women outpopulate men") implies that an imbalance in sexual populations is related to this crime. There is an assumption here that men are basically animals, driven insane by biological needs. These naturalistic notions bear some analysis.

One theory suggests that an imbalance in the two sexual populations *increases* the incidence of rape. This increase is thought to occur if either sex outnumbers the other. The presence of a greater proportion of women indicates that they will naturally compete all the harder for sexual mates, thus ensnaring men with their highly provocative sexual behavior. A greater proportion of men, on the other hand, reportedly produces intensely frustrated males who forcibly seize the mates of others or brutally attack single women. In either case, given the scarcity of one sex, these banal naturalistic premises assume that the members of the other sex will act the part of amoral beasts.

In scientific circles, a theory of this kind, the "sex ratio theory," was developed by Hans von Hentig (1951). Not surprisingly, this male scholar viewed the problem solely from the standpoint of *male* sex starvation. That is, he proposed that a greater proportion of men would generate a greater incidence of sexual assault. Studies mentioned below have tested this theory and have failed to find systematic evidence of its explanatory value.

In Denmark, Kaare Svalastoga (1962) found evidence for this theory when rural and urban areas were compared, but the theory was not supported at all when cities were examined. In addition, he found a great difference in rates of rape in cities with the *same* sex ratio.

Menachem Amir (1971: 68) also tested von Hentig's hypothesis, using Philadelphia data, and found no statistically significant patterns that confirmed it. In fact, some of his data contradicted this theory entirely.

Legalization of Prostitution Myth

Finally, a popular myth proposed by some seeking a simple solution to the problem concerns the relations between prostitution and sexual attack. In a letter to Bay Area Women Against Rape, one person wrote, "We lived in the Reno, Nevada, area before moving to Los Angeles. In Nevada there is legal prostitution, and I cannot remember reading about any rapes. Do you believe that legal prostitution will reduce rape attacks in California?" (Incidentally, the letter writer was not aware of the fact that Las Vegas, Nevada, which is located in a county that has legalized prostitution, has one of the highest rape rates in the United States.)

Popular myths suggest that the number of attacks would decrease if prostitution were legal and controlled. However, the evidence shows that this is false. Three cities that had allowed open prostitution actually experienced a *decline* in all sexual crimes, including rape, after prostitution was prohibited. In Gary, Indiana, there were 81 complaints of sex crimes in 1947 and only 69 in 1949, when houses of prostitution were closed. In Terre Haute, Indiana, the closing of the vice district in 1943 was measured against reports of aggravated assaults that included sex crimes. A three-year record showed 36 aggravated assaults occurred in 1942, but the number dropped sharply to 14 in 1943. In 1944 there were only 4 reported rapes. The third case involved Honolulu, Hawaii, where prostitution was big business. For the eleven months prior to September 1944, the month in which all houses of prostitution were closed, there had been 29 rapes and 559 other sex crimes. The record for the following eleven months showed a decline to 22 rapes and 404 other sex crimes (Kinsie, 1950: 250-252).

Behind this myth is the false notion that violation is essentially a crime of sexual passion which can easily be prevented by commercial forms of sex.[2] But commercialized sex objectifies women as mere things and reduces sexual relationships to cash values. Under these conditions, moral relations corrode and power determines sexual conduct.

These myths make wrong assumptions about the legal issues of resistance and consent and about the causal conditions of sexual assault. They constitute misinformation that contributes nothing positive toward understanding the existence of rape.

Notes

1. This story was related in a personal interview. A "true rape" here means one that actually occurred.

2. If rape were simply an act of frustrated sexual passion, the trends in the three cities cited in the text would have been in the opposite direction. Kinsie (1950:250) overgeneralizes psychiatric relations, but the following statement is otherwise worthy of note: "The sexual psychopaths who are responsible for most sex crimes do not as a rule patronize prostitutes, nor are they apt to be concerned in any way with prostitution activities." Also see Alan J. Davis (1968:15). We have previously mentioned the power and dominance factors in the rape of women; these also appear in the homosexual rape of men in prisons. According to Davis: "It appears that need for sexual release is not the primary motive of a sexual aggressor . . . A primary goal of the sexual aggressor, it is clear, is the conquest and degradation of his victim."

CHAPTER 2

A VICTIM SPEAKS OUT

Counting the "little rapes" — the sexual passes by Uncle Charlie, or lascivious invitations suggested in the streets — most American women have experienced frightening sexual incidents.[1] In the United States, "rape and the fear of rape," according to Susan Griffin (1971: 27), "are a daily part of every woman's consciousness." How does the victim feel when the rape is just about to take place? What are her thoughts while this mind-chilling attack is in progress? If she survives to tell about it, what are her feelings afterward?

Sexual crimes of violence may not leave their victims physically damaged. Although the rape victim often sustains minor physical injuries, the emotional damages she suffers are, by far, the more universal of the two. Dr. William J. Washington, Jr. (1972: 26), after a study of sex assault cases at the District of Columbia General Hospital, said: "It is my firm belief that the psychological trauma is frequently of greater severity than the physical event."

Charlene Lanza, a public health nurse who was one of the pioneers in counseling rape victims, collaborated with Dr. Washington and agrees with his statement. She reports that, "the most common injuries are emotional." But, she significantly adds, "the threat of physical injury adds to the emotional impact" (1974: 26).

Besides being an act of violence, rape temporarily destroys the victim's sense of self-determination and undermines her integrity as a person. Despite these effects, however, a generation of rape victims has started to speak out.

Nancy Rider is a rape victim. She and her husband Don came to our house in Berkeley, California, one afternoon to talk about the rape and the feelings they experienced. With their permission, we taped the interview.

Abduction and Rape

Nancy was returning from junior college one balmy July evening just at the fall of darkness. She had walked past a skating rink a short distance from her home when a strange man jumped out of a parked car, pinned her against a tall fence, and threatened her with a knife. As she described her terror, she recalled the weakness and vulnerability of her position. She spoke of the circumstances that were ideal for the rapist.

With a touch of shyness, Nancy looked at Don for support and then said: " I didn't react fast enough to get away and when I did realize what was happening I looked up and down the street and there was nobody in sight. Not a car in sight. The apartments across the street were empty. [Housing redevelopment was going on.] And I was about half a block from any other apartments."

Sensing the self-blame in Nancy's statements about not reacting rapidly enough, we assured her that she had quickly examined her surroundings for possible help.

But Nancy was equally prompt in her reply. " Yes. I know," she said. "But I didn't physically struggle, which became an issue later as far as the police were concerned."

Nancy's statements also reflected her fear of physical injury or even death at the hands of the rapist. She spoke earnestly about her strongest feeling during the incident.

" I was very afraid of him because of the fact that he seemed very tense and out of control. In talking to him, I tried not to antagonize him to the point where he would attack me with his knife."

To maximize her terror and unquestioning obedience, the rapist held a knife to the side of her face as he pushed Nancy into his car. She noted his extreme nervousness and, in fear for her life, she tried to talk to him; but he would not answer.

"He didn't talk to me," she observed. "He had certain things that evidently he planned to say, but he didn't react or respond to anything that I said."

Don, her husband, couldn't resist saying something at this point. "That louse," he said, "he had it all planned out."

While tying her hands and feet together, the rapist made menacing remarks stressing that Nancy's life was at stake if she did not obey his commands. Her feelings of fear and helplessness were increased by the rapist's ominous statements.

The rapist forced Nancy down brutally in the back of his car, threw a tarpaulin over her, and drove off. To ensure his control over her, he threatened to slash her legs if she made an outcry. All thoughts of escape vanished. She felt completely helpless.

"There was nothing I could do, that I could see any point in doing," she said. "I kept trying to look to see where he was going, but I couldn't see anything. Anytime I moved at all he started threatening me — it was even getting so that it was hard for me to breathe."

The rapist drove to a secluded area where the forcible rape took place. The first thing he did was bark out a command.

"When he stopped the car, he ordered me to take my pants off, but my hands were tied and he started making sort of other kinds of threats then. He was going to punch me in the stomach or something. But he put down the knife, at least, so he wasn't directly threatening me with it, anymore."

Remembering the humiliation of the experience, Nancy continued. "I still felt too helpless to do anything," she murmured. "So he yanked off my pants himself and after that he raped me."

Nancy reported that the rapist took a long time. He was having difficulty getting an erection to penetrate her. He did not kiss or stroke her nor did he make any attempt to force her to stimulate him. He seemed sexually incompetent and ignorant, and he blamed *her* for his inability. Comical? Bizarre? No. It's always the woman who is blamed. If he had been more sophisticated, he might have added a Freudian twist and blamed his own mother, too.

What happened next reveals the impossible attempts by the rapist to normalize his relations with Nancy. Nancy talked about his change in mood afterwards. "So then, after he got finished, [he untied me and] I got dressed. Instead of pushing me in the back seat, he said, 'You can sit in front now.' By this time," she commented, "he was being quite cordial to me. He was also much less nervous than he had been."

The rapist's plans seemed to call for a young, passive victim, and he had a scenario into which the rape was supposed to fit. The cast of this scenario emerged from the statements he made while driving the car.

Nancy remembered: "He said things like, 'What is your father going to think of this?' and 'Is your father rich?' and when he was going through this thing he didn't seem to believe that I wasn't as young as he seemed to be fantasizing. Later, he even asked me if I was a virgin, after I had told him I was married."

When the rapist was referring to Nancy's father, or whatever her father represented to him, Nancy felt that she was simply an object; her only reason for existence was to obey commands. Speaking in a flat tone, Nancy said: "I was pretty unimportant; I was a thing."

After the rape ended, the rapist seemed undecided about what to do with Nancy next and at one point said, "I ought to throw you out right here." When he reached the main highway, however, he declared: "I'm going to San Francisco, so I'll drop you off in Oakland, where you can get a ride."[2]

During the drive to Oakland, the rapist went through Nancy's purse. To forestall an arrest, he threatened to retaliate violently if she reported him to the police.

"He took my purse and he went through it. I had a ten-dollar bill and a one-dollar bill; and then he also took my library card with my name and address on it. And he said: 'If anyone comes after me, I'll come back and get you.' It was as though he thought that by saying that, he'd protect himself completely."

But Nancy had plans of her own. Having been unable to escape the rape, she was going to do everything in her power to have him arrested if she got out of her nightmare alive. First she concentrated on characteristics of her assailant for future identification. Then, since she was somewhat dazed and having trouble recalling his face clearly or even remembering the clothes he was wearing, she decided to memorize details about his car:

"The car was the only thing that I could focus in on, and I noticed the kind of car it was, and was determined to get the license number. So when he dropped me off, I just stood there hoping that he would drive past me and I could get it.

I had noticed that there were two women standing not too far away, and I thought, he can't do too much, with them in sight like that. But he noticed that I was standing there. He immediately jumped out of the car, menacing me and he started screaming something at me!

So, I started walking past the car, and as I got to the other side of it, I read the license number and kept on walking over to where those people were; and he rushed back to his car and sped away."

As it happens, Nancy's reactions proved to be excellent survival techniques. Because of her levelheadedness and in spite of the barrage of threats, she was not injured physically. The police followed up on her evidence about the car and the rapist was caught. But she reported emotional reactions that surfaced when contacting police and hospital personnel.

Police and Hospital Contacts

After her frightening experience with the rapist had ended, Nancy still had to deal with a number of practical and emotional problems. She did not immediately report the incident to the police. Instead she phoned Don, who picked her up and drove her home.

In our interview, Nancy reflected on her ambivalence with regard to the police: "I had read articles recently about what happens when you go to the police, and how it turns out, and I was somewhat hesitant about going through that. But I knew that with his license number they could most likely track down the guy, and I wanted them to do that, so that he wouldn't be doing it again. I was also somewhat afraid that he was going to come around since he had my house key."

After a period of hesitation, Nancy finally called the Women's Center in Berkeley, where she was advised to contact the police immediately. The police directed her to the emergency clinic at a local private hospital.

She went to the hospital, where she waited for almost an hour for a medical examination. While waiting, a police officer asked her numerous questions about the rape, filling out a detailed official form on the spot. Since she had to wait in an area that provided passage between the examination room and the waiting room, the interrogation was conducted in public, under very disturbing circumstances.

Nancy described what it was like in the hospital: "Nobody was standing or sitting right around us, but a lot of people were milling about and running in and out. There were a lot of piercing screams in the background, and all sorts of other weird things. I didn't know what was going on."

But a very strange thing did go on. Nancy became the center of attention for a group of bored police officers. Nancy: "Several other cops were around for different reasons and they just kind of got in on the questioning while they were there." Don: "I think they all got off on it. I really do." Nancy: "And the one who was filling out the forms kept asking specific questions about the sexual acts involved. And like he didn't ask once, he asked half a dozen times."

When Nancy was eventually admitted for the examination, she found the doctor's treatment to be impersonal and perfunctory. "I got the distinct impression too," she said, "that nobody was impressed because I wasn't hysterical enough, I didn't look beaten up and because I was in control of myself. For that reason nobody was particularly solicitous of me or supportive in any way, really. . . . So after I'd been waiting for a while, finally I got taken back into the examination room. And I even had to wait quite a while after that. When the doctor finally came, he just sort of breezed in and was fairly brisk. He didn't offer me tranquilizers which I certainly could have used by then — although maybe I wasn't showing it outwardly."

Don immediately agreed with this. "She was showing it to me. I could see it. She wasn't breaking down and crying, but I know Nancy. She was pretty freaked." As she continued to describe her unpleasant experience at the hospital, the reasons for her shabby treatment were partly revealed. She was being responded to as a police witness rather than a hospital patient. "The doctor," she reiterated, "gave me a rather cursory examination very quickly. And then he started asking me a lot of questions." These questions concerned elements of the crime, of importance to the police.

At this point, we inquired whether, in the interest of Nancy's medical condition, the doctor offered any information about the prevention of pregnancy or venereal disease. Nancy reported that no such information was provided.

Nancy and her husband were then taken to the police station to answer *further* questions. At 2:00 a.m. they left the station and returned home. She told us what happened next: "We stayed up after that, talking most of the night. I didn't have anything to calm me down. We decided we were going to take the next day off." "Next morning we went down to Kaiser Hospital[3] for tranquilizers. I was still pretty upset. I waited for about an hour there in the drop-in clinic for those drugs — and I was crying. I had not cried, in fact, the whole time until then. Just the period of waiting in Kaiser, I think, was too much for me. So I burst into tears."

Then Nancy's luck improved. The doctor in this hospital focussed on her and her problems rather than legal issues. Nancy brightened up as she said, "She [the doctor] just gave me the tranquilizers I asked for and sort of asked me, 'Well, what are you going to do from here? How are you going to deal with this?' The tone of her questions asked: 'What difference is this going to make to you? What are you going to do?' I started thinking about this. I hadn't thought about that kind of thing before. That was a helpful thing for her to say. 'Cause I realized that I couldn't let it make me stay home all the time with my doors locked. I wasn't going to be able to go on taking tranquilizers everyday forever to keep me from being upset."

Nancy was on her way to coping successfully with her bitter experience. One of the effects of a crisis is that it alters people's perceptions and creates a need for changing their own lives. In Nancy's case it rocked her out of her complacency. She told us what she did: "I went back to work the next day. Oh, I realized that for a long time I had been feeling terribly discontented at work and the rape kind of gave me the impetus to go back and say that I only wanted to work half-time. It had that kind of effect on me. I had been kind of drifting along. I had been doing it without any idea about what I was going to be doing in the future. I just kept going everyday."

Nancy's reflections after the rape crisis put her more in touch with herself and how she was living.

Other Victims' Feelings

Let us now analyze certain emotions Nancy experienced, especially since her psychic reactions occur frequently among victims. Particular sequences of emotions in rape are related to the type and duration of the entire episode. For example, forcible rape may occur as a series of events or it may be over and done right after an initial assault. In Nancy's case a number of related actions occurred before, during, and after the rape. These included the assault, the kidnap/car ride, the rape itself, and her transportation back from the actual scene of the crime. Each of these events evoked certain feelings.

Nancy reported that the strongest feelings she had *during* the incident were fear and helplessness. Several authors of studies developing the theme of the victim's feelings have found that the feeling of fear is almost universal during the rape.

Many raped women report that the sexual aspect of the rape is of less concern to them than the fear of dying.

Aphanasis, or "the fear of annihilation," is caused by certain trauma. L. Keiser (1968) notes that the duration of this extremely intensive fear varies with the type of trauma. For example, it lasts several seconds in a rear-end collision; in a mugging, much longer, but still less than one minute. For the rape victim, it is much, much longer.

Psychiatrist Carroll M. Brodsky (1976: 45) has estimated that for his rape-victim patients this fear lasted on the average from two to five minutes. This apparently small period of time can seem an eternity to the woman who is simultaneously experiencing a sexual assault and the fears of injury or death.

But Nancy also had many fears before and after the rape. Because of the obvious danger and because the rapist used terror as an additional weapon, there were signs of Nancy's fear *before* the rape actually took place. Various statements signify her fear: "He asked, 'Did I value my life?' . . . the knife was sharp . . . I could just lie here and bleed and nobody would see me."

The victim's fears can range from fear of imminent death to a fear of retaliation in the future if she survives the attack and if she later exercises any of her rights regarding prosecution.

A second ordeal following the rape is triggered by a sense of self-blame for what happened. Rape victims generally share an early individualistic reaction: "Why *me?* instead of "What made him do it?" Even though the second question may later be asked, most women learn to turn blame inward against themselves and not outward against others or society. When asked about her guilt feelings after the rape, Nancy summed them up as a "feeling that somehow it's your fault for not doing something about it in the first second."

In addition to a lasting fear and self-blame, there was a more diffused damage to Nancy's ego. Nancy said that immediately after the rape she was overwhelmed with self-recrimination: "Mostly I was casting around for a reason for the rape. I was inclined to blame myself. We were looking around for who was to blame. The thing I thought about the next day or two was criticizing myself for not having been quick enough to do something about it in the first second, which was really the only time I could have done anything. . . . It's a very hard thing to get over. The feeling that somehow it's your fault. I struggled very hard with that especially the next few days."

For Nancy, this was a long speech, but she continued: "For one thing, it's a police attitude that if you didn't struggle, then somehow you were inviting the whole thing. And although nobody exactly says anything, you definitely get the feeling from the way they react to you. The whole thing was very unhelpful . . . The nature of the experience itself makes you feel that way too. Somehow, if you'd thought of the right thing to say or do somehow you could have prevented it. But that's just not the way things are."

Here Nancy's misgivings are understandable, and they should be interpreted sympathetically. The reasons many women internalize blame and the reasons they are vulnerable to rape are closely related. Women, from childhood, learn to be supportive of other people, and in the socialization process they are oriented toward marriage and children. Girls learn early in life to protect and nurture other children and men; they thereby acquire habits that will carry over into the future to benefit their sons and husbands. Part of this nurturance is geared to appreciating and helping others. Since they are encouraged to devote themselves to the welfare of others, women acquire personal qualities that make them easy targets for unprincipled and predatory males.

If she has a compassionate and trusting nature, a woman who is the "mark" (intended victim) of a rapist with a slick "con" (story) is usually slow to perceive his intention as rape. She may not alter her submissive demeanor until it is too late. How can a woman make a hair-trigger response in the first few seconds when she has learned to be trusting and not to make snap judgments? Her response may be delayed because, traditionally, a woman's role is to be protected and to accept men as her protectors. As a feature of this role, a woman receives neither training nor practice in physically defending herself;

ordinarily she is expected to defend herself only verbally. Often a woman tries to talk her way to freedom even though she is relatively immobilized by her fears and when she no longer has any doubt that she is the victim of a rapist, she may not even scream or struggle to escape. Therefore, this concatenation of the potential for lethal danger, her images of herself, the stigma attached to rape, the emotional uncertainties of the situation, and the rapist's exploitation of her responses creates ambivalence.

In many parts of society, female socialization is dominated by standards that engender contradictory modes of behavior. Contradictions instantly appear in a rape confrontation. Girls must not be noisy, impolite, or aggressive, but they should scream and struggle when being sexually attacked. How can such a forceful reaction come about when, from childhood on, women are discouraged from rough physical contact?

Because of her contradictory experiences, the victim-to-be may hesitate. Rape victims' responses are frequently delayed and ineffectual. The "mark" makes a familiar response — she tries to talk her way out of the problem. Crippled within these familiar reaction patterns, it is not surprising for a victim whose verbal defenses fail to feel afterwards that she may have done something that provoked the rape. This may be coupled with the sense that she also did not do anything to prevent it. Unfortunately, rape is an act for which society has uniquely prepared many women to be the victims; yet, the sexist moral codes of the same society results for some in a false sense of guilt.

Although the majority of women finally learn to cope, some suffer a period of shock, confusion, nervousness and depression. Nancy showed many signs that she had suffered from these reactions: "I felt *too helpless* to do anything." "I *couldn't remember* what clothes he was wearing." These comments illustrate the inhibition engendered by shock. At the hospital she heard screams and saw people running in and out, but she was too confused to "know what was going on." She and her husband were too nervous and upset to sleep, so she went to another hospital for tranquilizers after the first one had failed to supply them on the initial visit.

Nancy's depression manifested itself in cry. ig at the hospital. In the period after the rape, she told a rape-victim advocate that she was sometimes too depressed in the morning to get out of bed. Such feelings must have intensified when she started developing vaginal symptoms and thought she had gonorrhea.

Depending on circumstances, the intensity of the victim's feelings will vary. Brodsky notes that the reaction to being raped at work is more intense (because the work-place is considered a safe zone) and the reactions include shock and feelings of being deceived and tricked. Brodsky (Walker: 43) says: "Work was a safe place. One did not go to work fearing attack. The victim did not take the special precautions nor was she as vigilant as she would have been in a high risk setting." On the other hand, there also appears to be less self-blame in the work situation. Burgess and Holmstrom (1976: 32) indicate that children have the greatest difficulty coping and adapting after a rape. Children cannot leave the family to escape a rapist who is a family member. Besides this, the rest of the family is often nonsupportive, blaming the child to avoid the involvement of authorities and their potential threat to family stability.

For certain personalities, Nancy's coping mechanisms can also be seen as rather typical. She did not respond by immediately screaming and struggling with her assailant. Instead she tried to talk to him. Many women respond with verbal abilities that are well developed and that have been encouraged by their parents and others. Only a small percentage of women in our research and in a Philadelphia study actually screamed, although screaming has a discouraging effect on the rapist under circumstances in which someone is likely to hear the outcry.[4]

Taking these coping mechanisms and the negative self-image together, it is obvious that Nancy's feelings were mostly turned inward.

There is, however, a more positive side to Nancy's emotions and actions. After the initial shock, she showed great strength. As indicated, she memorized the license plate number and an accurate description of the kidnap car. Then she called the police and went through the trial. She also made important decisions about not hiding behind locked doors and living on tranquilizers every day for the rest of her life. After the interview she joined Bay Area Women Against Rape so that she could help other women who were exposed to the same damaging experience.

One decade has elapsed since Nancy joined the antirape movement that pioneered an aggressive stance for dealing with damaging experiences such as hers. Joining the struggle against violence against women, antirape programs formed in more than 600 U. S. and Canadian communities.

It is a fact that individual women do prevent rape. The number of attempted rapes generally exceeds the number of completed rapes, according to victimization studies. Sometimes as many as six rapes out of ten are attempted but not completed. In an effort to defend themselves further, women like Nancy have demanded better street lighting, organized escort services, and posted street sheets listing the *modi operandi* (MOs) and descriptions of local rapists. Sharing their experiences, learning self-defense — where to hit and run, how to use keys and whistles as defensive weapons — may have provided useful tactics for individual women. Supporting the idea of self-defense, William Sanders (1980: 74) notes, "Just about *any* resistance had some effectiveness" in preventing rape.[5] Studies also show that because of women's movement pressure, training of sex-crime investigators has improved police response to rape victims (Sanders, 1980; LaFree, 1979; McCahill, Meyer and Fischman, 1979). Furthermore, using their creativity, women have come a long way from the first rape speak-out. While visiting different campuses, we find *Take Back the Night Marches* to protest rape; we note feminist groups sponsoring campaigns against sadistic pornography and working toward encouraging popular justice groups, and neighbors performing local surveillance to supplement inadequate police protection. All this education and practice has probably made a difference in improving the safety of the individual woman.

But there are still larger issues involved. The level of criminality may become more vicious as resistance increases. Furthermore, while some women become better at avoiding molesters, other women who must be in unsafe places (out of doors at night) or women who are past their prime at defending themselves are chosen by rapists seeking more vulnerable targets. Therefore, attackers may be foiled on two or three occasions, but the incidence of sexual assaults remains high because rapists finally succeed when attempts are repeated often enough. Finally, married women are especially vulnerable to rape by violence-prone husbands. The women who stopped the violence among Diana Russell's (1982) wife-rape cases may have been more assertive women. How can married women learn to use assertive strategies safely, and can assertiveness provide an invisible shield for women raped by men who are not their husbands? We deal with such questions in the last chapter.

The following chapter emphasizes broader conditions ignored by people who are organizing crime-fighting policies. The remainder of the book addresses itself to the more basic causes of rapes, the overall incidence of which may well be intractable to individual self-defense solutions. Approached this way, controlling this crime requires larger changes in social policy. After a decade of antirape activities, rates have not come down. It is now time to think much more deeply about the *forms of rape* and their *social foundations* rather than individual strategies alone.

Notes

1. The "little rapes" are discussed in Medea and Thompson (1974: 49ff.)
2. San Francisco is across the bay from Oakland, where the rape took place.
3. A private insurance group hospital.
4. See, for example, Comment (1968: 295).
5. For a study of rape avoidance strategies, see Pauline Bart and Patricia O'Brien (1980).

CHAPTER 3

FORMS OF RAPE

Rape is expressed in various social, economic, and political contexts. Consequently, not all rapes can be fittingly classified as "street crimes" or "common" crimes. Although much has been written about these street crimes because they are prohibited by law, we shall see that rape can result from immoral methods that are not considered illegal in most countries. Also, the most brutal sexual violence has been repeatedly adopted as a policy of terror by commanding officers or government bureaucrats in certain countries, regardless of the criminal law.

Since the social context of rape varies enormously, we devote this chapter to some of the circumstances in which it occurs. We discuss the more familiar forms of rape as well as instances of sexual extortion. We also focus on the extreme forms of sexual violence that are condoned, at least informally, by some established authority. In the next two chapters we then review current theories and see what forms of rape they take into account when they attempt to explain sexual violence.

Individualistic Rapes

Individualistic rapes include gang rapes, felony rapes, and one-on-one assaults that usually victimize individual women who are not related to the rapist.[1] Under ordinary circumstances, these so-called street crimes are the most frightening to the general public and therefore are the most likely to receive the attention of local feminist activists, police, and social service agencies. Moreover, the choice of victim in these crimes seems, at times, to be a matter of chance, dependent entirely on sheerly tactical conditions; for example, the unexpected availability of a defenseless victim coupled with an opportunity for committing the crime without detection.

Does this mean that these rapes are totally spontaneous? Are they committed perhaps by psychotic strangers with uncontrollable urges who leap from the shadows upon lone women? These questions evoke pictures of the rapist running planlessly amok, images of a potential rapist fitfully ruminating when along comes Ms. Sexy Female and, at that instant, reason departs and he explodes.

Research, however, shows that psychotic strangers and explosive events do not dominate rape occurrences. The facts show that many rapes are committed by acquaintances and relatives and that the majority of rapists are not psychotics, even though some of them are. Furthermore, the motives of most rapists do not involve uncontrollable passions at all. Instead of being spontaneous events, most rapes exhibit forethought and planning.

Menachem Amir (1971: 142), in a study of 646 police reports of rape in Philadelphia, estimated that 71 percent of these rapes were planned, 11 percent were partially planned, and only 16 percent appeared to be "explosive" events.

Furthermore, it can be assumed that many of Amir's so-called explosive events were *felony rapes,* involving criminals who raped women in the course of committing another crime, such as burglary. The felony rape suggests an unplanned crime but one that is largely due to rational and opportunistic motives rather than irrational compulsions.

Another conception of individualistic rape that has wide currency emphasizes the role of the seductive female, "the foxy lady," who excites men *purposely* and then denies them sexual intercourse. One version of this victim-precipitated rape contains a sadomasochistic woman. Desirous of a violent sexual encounter, she first seduces the male and then, when his emotions are peaked, suddenly rejects further sexual advances. Her partner becomes enraged; he attacks and forces her into submission.

There is also little support in scientific research for victim precipitation. If a rape is planned beforehand (and, as noted, the overwhelming majority *are*), its outcome cannot be genuinely caused by seductive stimulation and explosive frustration. On the other hand, planning itself is not the only contradiction; there are unplanned rapes that also contradict victim precipitation. The previously mentioned felony rape, for instance, usually involves total strangers, and in these cases seduction by the victim is quite unlikely.

Individualistic rapes, however, are more complex than the myths suggest. Rapists approach the victim in various ways. Although force is invariably employed as an immediate or last resort, rapists may at first use deceitful methods to set up the victim. The rapist may meet the victim out of doors but, by force or cunning, alter the circumstances, transferring her indoors where the rape will actually take place. In approximately half of the cases considered by the Philadelphia police reports study, it was found that the victim encountered the rapist out of doors while walking on the street, strolling in the park, standing in front of a bar, or waiting for a car or a bus. Conversely, the rape may begin indoors. Other cases discussed by Amir (1971: 139) were initiated in the rapist's or the victim's home or temporary residence, in a bar, or at a party.

Many rapists approach their victims with the short con, or the *short-run* confidence game. Ann, whose case was described in Chapter 1, was conned, by two local men, out of her neighborhood bar.[2] A short con may begin when the rapist meets his victim in a bar or at a party. Often the appearance of the conman is calculated to allay suspicion; he may be well dressed and a smooth and convincing talker, or he may be unconventionally dressed, befitting the norms of the intended victim.

Numerous short cons can be documented from our interviews with victims. Short cons take place when the attacker meets the victim and asks for a service: "Have you got a match?" "Can you give me and my brother a ride to the hospital?" Alternatively, the rapist might, at first, offer a service:

"I'll drive you home from the party." "The landlord wants me to look at a leak in the plumbing in your apartment." If she responds positively, the woman is immediately involved in a lengthier interaction and the actual rape may begin.

But the attack may not follow the response immediately. The conning rapist, for instance, may "play" with the victim, much like a cat with a mouse, before he is ready to pounce. They may talk, drink, or drive until he feels safe and ready.

The rapist with a *long con* may lead the mark into a series of separate encounters involving social and sexual relations; but, when trust is developed, he rapes her. Joan Konig, not her real name, is an attractive woman in her late twenties with brown curly hair and a generally restrained manner. She dated a man, enjoyed herself, and after seeing him once or twice slept with him. She accepted when he asked for another date. He took her to a remote area where he suggested they swim nude. Having learned to trust him, she agreed. At this point, the relationship changed. He beat her up, tortured and humiliated her, and raped her repeatedly over a period of several hours.

In another long con, the rapist was an official in a civil rights organization where his victim, Rhonda, worked. He had tickets, he said, and made a date with Rhonda for the following Saturday night to attend a lecture by a famous civil rights leader whom she wanted to hear. After he picked her up, he drove to his apartment, claiming to have forgotten something. Cautious by nature, Rhonda hesitated to go in. After coaxing her inside, he locked the door and raped her. After the rape he said, "Clean yourself up and I'll take you home." Rhonda commented wryly, "He never intended to take me to the lecture."

On the other hand, some rapists use the *sudden attack* method and immediately employ force to subdue the victim.[3] Two other cases in our interviews of rape victims illustrate the sudden-attack rape. Nancy, whose case was described at length in Chapter 2, was attacked by a strange man who leaped from a parked automobile and forcibly kidnapped her at knifepoint. Elizabeth, an English major at the University of California, Berkeley, had been walking to her apartment at 8:30 or 9:00 p.m. when she heard someone running up behind her.

Almost instantly she was seized by the neck and dragged into a vacant schoolyard.

Whatever else characterizes the rape, there is almost always (except in the gang rape) an attempt to carry out the act in privacy or seclusion. Some of this situational detail, which is described in publications by social scientists and journalists, suggests that rapists are acutely aware of the legal implications of their assaults. Partly to avoid legal sanctions, they engage rationally in numerous deceitful maneuvers, surprise attacks, and calculating attempts to escape public exposure. The victim is also aware that rape is a crime and may memorize the offender's appearance or license plate to optimize his arrest.

Hence, on at least one level, what is to be learned from a situational analysis is that most of the individualistic forms of rape, even rapes by strangers, are rational events. Second, they usually reflect the respective parties' opposing interests and practical concerns about legal sanctions. Regardless of their initial motivations, rapists generally know that they cannot roam the city and rape women at will or with impunity.

These, then, are some of the situational variations that are found whenever rape involves obviously punishable events. Such variations, however, contrast sharply with the modi operandi of the other forms of rape.

Sexual Extortion

Sexual extortion is not generally included in theories of rape that are limited to the legal definitions of this crime.[4] However, this extortion is a form of coercive sex, and it complicates and broadens the search for the causes of rape because it is forced without physical violence or a threat of this violence.

Sexual harassment is often linked to extortion whenever it is perpetrated by men who can affect an important aspect of a woman's life. Harassment frequently includes many of the more subtle forms of sexism that occur at places where women work; consequently, in her book *Sexual Shakedown: The Sexual Harassment of Women on the Job,* Lin Farley (1978:14) defines sexual harassment as "unsolicited nonreciprocal male behavior that asserts a woman's sex role over her function as a worker." Very few women report or complain of harassment on their jobs, because resistance involves humiliation and economic penalties. Women who complain are ridiculed and, since they are usually harassed by managers or other high-ranking men, risk being fired. If sex is stipulated as part of a new job and a woman refuses, the chances are that she will not be hired.

Therefore, before taking action — either complaining or quitting — a working woman is also forced to calculate the risks to her independence and livelihood. Farley (1978: 23) says: "To make a decision women must weigh in the balance economic necessity, prospects for other jobs, a good recommendation rather than a poor one, the chances of being fired, the attitudes of husband, friends, lovers or parents, interest in the job and rate of pay, the number of times the abuse has been experienced and countless other factors." If her job is a good one, she risks sliding down to a less desirable one. If she cannot find suitable new work, she forfeits unemployment payments because she left the job "voluntarily."

Partly because of the risks of reporting, little is known about the incidence of sexual harassment. It is likely, however, that sexual acts extorted from women numerically exceed forcible rape. No government statistics are available on a national basis; however, a questionnaire published by *Redbook* (1976: 149), a national magazine, had more than 9,000 respondents. The majority felt that sexual harassment was a serious problem; 90 percent of the respondents had one or more experiences on their jobs.[5] Though this study was not based on a random sample, it suggests that the problem is significant for many women.

Regardless of the risk, some women do complain, but they do so informally. One congressional aide told a congresswoman that she had to date "that dirty old man" [a congressman] twice a week to keep her job. This congresswoman was further informed that, in order to get a job, "kinky sex" was demanded of certain women employees. The congresswoman also discovered that women were asked, as a job requirement, if they engaged in oral sex.

Women may come up against such work requirements in institutions with either high or low prestige, in traditional and nontraditional occupations. About 20 employees on Capitol Hill alone reportedly complained that sex is an expected part of their jobs. Although usually such complaints are made only to one's closest circle of friends, most of the twenty spoke out despite their fears of "severe job repercussions." They were interested in developing a grievance procedure to protect their economic security.

Occupational coercion to provide sex on demand is also revealed by women employed in nontraditional jobs. Bitzy Gomez is a truck driver who handles big rigs. After ten years of fighting off passes in the sleeper compartment of tractor-trailer rigs, Gomez formed the Los Angeles Coalition of Women Truck Drivers in 1976 to defend working women against both unions and employers who regard them as prostitutes. Approximately 100 women responded to an advertisement for a coalition. Gomez reported that all the women were faced with job discrimination in finding work and sexual abuse when they were on the job.

More explicit economic motives for harassment may be involved here. Sexual harassment may be motivated by the desire to discourage women who are competing for men's jobs. Gomez added that some union locals will not allow women to join because their members see women as competition. According to Gomez, women on a road test often find that it becomes a "sleeper test." After you drive 20 miles out of town the man giving the test tells you to "put out or get out."

A further example is sexual extortion by police. There are obvious parallels here to the extortion experienced by women truck drivers. In the District of Columbia, policewomen have complained of sexual harrassment by male officers who frequently outranked the women. The women said the male officers punished those who did not submit to sexual advances and that rewards, in the form of better assignments and better treatment, were given to those who did submit.

Women in other occupations — stenographers, waitresses, singers, actresses, jockeys, and there are more — are also coerced to provide sex on demand. Their bosses in business, bureaucracy, and entertainment are their oppressors. Complaining about "systematic sexual abuse," a group of 35 student actresses and their NOW supporters protested against their acting director in New York City in October 1979. The director, who was their source of training, support, and job offers had reportedly used his position and power to manipulate them into engaging in sex with him. The women organized, shared their victimization experiences and brought a criminal suit against the director. It was dismissed because they could not prove that physical force was used to compel them to submit to his sexual advances.

Although men with supervisory authority, political power, and economic means have used their power and resources to coerce women sexually, sometimes harassment is indirect. Bitzy Gomez, for instance, contended that many trucking firms try to discourage women truckers by placing them with male partners and using them as "sexual rewards" for the men's good performance records. Management, therefore, encourages sexual abuse in order to maintain highly profitable discriminatory labor markets. Even though management may not abuse the women directly, such policies are responsible for the continuation of this abuse.

Rape in the Family

Among the least protected rape victims are those who are married to their rapists (Russell, 1982). Most states in this country and most other countries have never criminalized wife rape, even though nuclear families provide private situations ideal for the rapist, away from the public and the protection of the women's kin and friends. Too often, marriage relationships are debased by the ideology of male supremacy, an overemphasis on sex, and the economic dependency and powerlessness of married women. In these situations, some men feel their married status gives them license to beat and rape their wives. The ideology of male supremacy may even be internalized by the woman herself or by her relatives, who may blame her or accept such extreme male dominance as unavoidable. Criminal justice representatives, such as police and domestic court judges generally follow a "hands-off," simple "order maintenance" policy (pacifying a violent husband temporarily but offering little help to raped or beaten wives.) Locked in by child-care responsibilities, restricted job markets and a dependent economic and social status, wives in violent homes are captives of brutalizing circumstances.

All rape victims suffer from the emotional impact of being raped, but for obvious reasons, rape affects children most adversely (Gager and Schurr, 1976). Especially when the child is abused by a close relative, such as the father, the emotions are confused, blame is turned inward and self hate often develops. In such a case, there is no one to whom the child can appeal; the molester lives in the same house and abuses the child repeatedly, and frequently other family members turn against her instead of her abuser. "Spouses tend to protect one another. Children are coerced in secrecy by threats, bribes, and other manipulative means," says Joyce Daily (1980), an Arizona Probation Department Worker appointed by the Arizona Supreme Court as a member of the Foster Care Review Board. Sometimes the mother and the father gang up on the child to keep the rapes secret (Daily, 1980: 28-29).

Sexual extortion, wife rape, and child rape are forms of exploitation imposed by some men who have power over the lives of women. To be subject to extortion, women have to be in exploitable or dependent positions in the first place; consequently, certain forms of this violence, such as sexual extortion in the workplace, may be committed more frequently by men who have greater power or wealth at their command. In our society the greatest differences in power and wealth occur in the relations between men and women, social classes, and warring nations. The opportunism and inhumanity inhering in power and wealth, rather than individual sexual desire, are keys to understanding rape, especially the most extreme forms of sexual violence condoned, at least informally, as we shall see, by official policy.

Rape as Economic or Political Policy

Today, rape against certain women is punishable, in most societies, if it is motivated solely by an individual rapist's selfish aims. On the other hand, rape is often *not* punished when it serves special economic and political purposes. When it is an overtly political act, it becomes an instrument for terrorizing a conquered population, dominating a racial group, defiling an enemy, and seeking vengeance. Most of these rapes involve the collusion of authorities and are more extreme. However, by considering these extremes, one can avoid the errors of limiting the analysis of rape and the rapist's motives to legally punishable events and idiosyncratic causes.

The final form of sexual assault to be discussed, takes a yet more disquieting shape. We are reminded of the institutionalized rape of enslaved women by slave owners and of the legal sale of daughters of the poor to wealthy landowners as concubines.

History is stained with other episodes of institutionalized rape. They include rape by soldiers, mercenaries, colonizers and fascists to subdue target populations. Common criminals have forced prostitution on defenseless women in "white slavery." During World War II, German officers established slavebrothels to entertain the Nazi "supermen."

Published accounts have exposed systematic rape by soldiers and police during periods of political repression and war. There are written accounts and verbal narratives about World Wars I and II, the Pakistan-Bangladesh War, Nanking under Japanese occupation, Vietnam under the Thieu regime, El Salvador under the current military junta, and others. The reports tell of women who have been humiliated, raped, and murdered in front of their families and their communities with the tacit or explicit approval of military officers and police. The rapists in these situations were safe from worry about being reported or punished.

In an imperialist war and during surges of counterrevolu-
tionary repression, sexual assaults on individual women are
accompanied by extreme brutality and also by economic
crimes. In World War I, for instance, the German advance
from Liege toward Antwerp was marked by outrages against
the person and the property of women, district by district,
village by village. Arnold Toynbee (1943: 137-138), the late
historian, in his "Violation of Women in War," cites many
cases. He reports:

> At Jouy-sur-Morin two Germans came into a house carrying
> looted bottles of champagne, and violated a girl of eighteen as
> the mother was kept off with the bayonet by each soldier in
> turn; the father was away.
>
> At Mericourt-sur-Somme three German soldiers dragged a
> girl of seventeen into a cellar, violated her in succession, and
> seized all the jewelry and money on her person.

One exceptionally morbid aspect of assaults on women in
wartime is the repeated raping of the same woman. Illustrations
of the effects of these rapes are contained in a 1916 doctoral
thesis, written by a French physician, Rene DuBois, concerning ten obstetrical-rape cases.[6] Dr. DuBois (1943: 101-102)
describes two young girls whose house was invaded by 20
soldiers: "Each girl endured ten consecutive assaults by the
fellow tormenters, after which the conquerors left, leaving
them bleeding there. The eldest, whose case we are discussing,
was sick three months. Her younger sister, 13 years old, pregnant too, could not withstand the shock to which she had been
subjected; she died in July 1915 after several months of
suffering."
The French doctor also considered the medical effects of
other organized forms of consecutive rape. These forms consisted of forcible abduction and internment of groups of women
who were then sexually assaulted by troops of soldiers. This
point is illustrated by a mass assault in September 1914, in one
French district: "The Germans carried off the whole popula-

tion. The men were dispatched to Germany; the women and children were driven like a herd of animals [until] they reached [a village] on November 28 and a sort of cantonment [temporary quarters] was established." DuBois reported further that the women prisoners were locked up in a breeding farm, each in a little cabin built originally for one pig. Each of these women was sexually assaulted every day by members of the squad of hussars.

An acid test of national morality is the treatment of an enemy population by invading armies. Under these conditions, both individualistic and organized acts of rape are known to rise dramatically; but the amount of increase can be determined by official policy. World War II provides examples of notable variations that illustrate official involvement. Where official policy is not supportive of rape, the instances are limited or nonexistent.

The Soviet troops that were part of the second wave to invade Berlin participated in a spontaneous outbreak of rape that was repressed by higher commanders. On the other hand, the first Soviet army units to enter Berlin were elite troops, composed of individuals who took pains to be exemplary soldiers. They celebrated with German anti-Nazis and, after discovering the few Jews who had been in hiding, openly expressed their compassion and joy. A Western study (Ryan, 1966) reports that Berliners, who were in fear of rape and plunder, were surprised at the scrupulous behavior of these shock troops.

But the elite units were soon followed up by others, who were responsible for mopping-up operations. These other soldiers swept through the city on a wild spree, raping women and destroying property at will. German women reported that soldiers entered air raid shelters plundering, raping, and killing some of the women who refused to submit (Ryan, 1966: 484-493). At first, many officers were reluctant to prevent rapes. In one instance, a woman ran into the street, found an officer, and reported that her sister was being raped. The officer did not help her. Instead he replied, "The Germans were worse than this in Russia. This is simply revenge."

In his book *Russia at War,* Alexander Werth (1964: 703) describes the events leading to the massive rape of German women. Throughout the war, Soviet soldiers had been informed of the atrocities committed by Germans against Soviet citizens. In the final years, these soldiers went beyond the borders of the USSR for the first time and witnessed the enormity of the horror inflicted on Russian prisoners of war. They discovered for themselves the crimes against people of other nations, especially Jews, at Maidanek and Auschwitz. The true extent of German atrocities is not yet even known. Estimates indicate that perhaps as many as three million Russian prisoners and six million Jews died because of German maltreatment.

Simultaneously with the soldiers' firsthand discovery of Nazi atrocities, ultranationalist appeals to patriotism and hatred against the German people, which had gradually increased during the war, became crystallized in Soviet posters and communiques. Posters grimly declared, "Red Army Soldier: You are now on German soil; the hour of revenge has struck!" Brownmiller (1975: 65) correctly points out the link between this nationalistic material and attacks on women. One particularly inflammatory communique written by Ilya Ehrenburg (Werth, 1964: 965) declared:

> Germany is a witch. We are in Germany. German towns are burning, I am happy. The Germans have no souls.
>
> Not only divisions and armies are advancing on Berlin. All the corpses of the innocents are advancing on Berlin. The boots and shoes and the babies' slippers of those murdered and gassed at Maidanek are marching on Berlin.
>
> We shall put up gallows in Berlin. An icy wind is sweeping along the streets of Berlin. But it is not the icy wind, it is terror that is driving *the Germans and their females* to the west. 800 years ago the Poles and the Lithuanians used to say: "We shall torment them in heaven as they tormented us on earth" [our emphasis].
>
> Some say the Germans from the Rhine are different from the Germans on the Oder. I don't know that we should worry about such fine points. A German is a German everywhere.

The Germans have been punished, but not enough. The hour
of revenge has struck!

Not only did such communiques whip up indiscriminate
rage against the German people, fascist and nonfascist alike,
but they reduced all Germans to a level of beasts who should be
punished collectively for crimes against humanity.

This nationalistic propaganda campaign backfired, as it
reinforced traditional chauvinism among Soviet soldiers, especially those from Soviet European and Asian communities
where virtually feudal patriarchal attitudes prevailed.

Alexander Werth (1964: 966-968) notes that two days before
the final offensive against Berlin was about to commence from
the Oder bridgeheads, Soviet authorities became alarmed and
suddenly put a stop to the hate campaign against the Germans.
This command decision came too late, however, for many
women and their families. Soviet soldiers attacked German
citizens and destroyed their property. Rapes took place while
the battle for Berlin raged until the Soviet commanders could
restore the troops to discipline. Conspicuously absent from
accounts of the period are command decisions that demanded
swift and severe punishments to terminate the violence against
women more rapidly.

The rapes by Soviet soldiers are on the borderline between
institutionalized and individualistic rape, because this crime
was not officially condoned by military policy but at the same
time was not forcibly repressed at the outset. A different example illustrates the most extreme forms of degradation and brutality that are associated with officially supported rape.
Japanese invaders committed atrocities in the Rape of Nanking, which involved brutally sadistic assaults on the men,
women, and children of a totally undefended city. (Although
the city had been protected by Chiang Kai-shek's Nationalist
forces, they had retreated westward prior to this invasion in
December 1937.)

According to the International Military Tribunal for the Far
East, Tokyo, Japanese soldiers continued to plunder the city
and murder its inhabitants for an entire month and a half after

Nanking had been taken. Women were not spared; young and old were raped. Resistance was met with bayonets and bullets. The tribunal estimates 20,000 such rapes in the first month of occupation (Brownmiller, 1975: 57-62). "Death was a frequent penalty for the slightest resistance on the part of a victim or the members of her family who sought to protect her," the war-crimes tribunal declared. "Even girls of tender years and old women were raped in large numbers throughout the city, and many cases of abnormal or sadistic behavior in connection with the rapings occurred. Many women were killed after the act and their bodies mutilated" (*Judgment of the International Military Tribunal for the Far East,* 1948: 1012-1019).

After examining the testimony of victims and observers, the war-crimes tribunal concluded: "The barbarous behavior of the Japanese army cannot be excused as the acts of a soldiery which had temporarily gotten out of hand when at last a stubbornly defended position had capitulated — rape, arson, and murder continued to be committed on a large scale for at least six weeks after the city had been taken." It also found that the commanders of the Japanese army had either secretly ordered the sacking of the city or willfully allowed it to take place on a systematic basis. At this tribunal, General Matsui, the commander of the Japanese forces, was found guilty of crimes against humanity and sentenced to be hanged.

Rape in wartime reaches its nadir whenever it is used as an instrument of social policy. Because of such complicity by the highest authorities, the magnitude of rape by the German troops in World War II and of the Pak troops in the Pakistani-Bangladesh War is similarly astounding.

Dr. Herman Rauschning reported Hitler as saying that the provision of sexual gratification by force should be one of the main devices of Nazi propaganda (Creel, 1944: 30). Men and women from the "non-Aryan races" were viewed by Nazi officials as less than human, and among the Gestapo methods for dehumanizing women — and by this means also terrorizing their relatives and neighbors — was the victimization of daughters, with the parents bound in a position in which they could watch their children being raped (Creel,1944: 22).

The rapes, murders and sexual sadism of the Nazi shock troops are a matter of historical record. One Nuremburg trial document reads: "In the city of Lvov, 32 women working in a garment factory were first violated and then murdered by German storm troopers." Another statement reads: "Near the town of Borissov in Bielorussia, 75 women and girls attempting to flee at the approach of the German troops fell into their hands. The Germans first raped then savagely murdered 36 of their number."[7]

The Nazi regime institutionalized rape on a large scale and officially victimized the women of conquered populations. George Creel, (1944: 31), author of *Criminals and Punishment,* examined many of the depositions against war criminals taken following the retreat of the German soldiers, noting that "rape is the order of the day in the first stages of every [military] occupation, even the aged suffering violation. "

After a time, however, unorganized rape was frowned upon in some locales and the German command ordered the procurement of women for sexual slavery. Young girls were rounded up by the Gestapo and herded into military slave brothels. According to Cardinal Hlond, the primate of Poland, "On March 16, the Germans organized in Warsaw a wholesale and official abduction of young girls from the Solec district and the streets of the suburb of Czerniakov. Eighty of them were arrested in and outside of their houses, and sent to the hospital of Saint Lazare, where they were examined by military doctors" (Creel, 1944: 31). Following the examination, the healthy girls were put in brothels.

At the Nuremberg trials, Russian testimony revealed: "In the city of Smolensk the German command opened up a brothel for officers in one of the hotels into which hundreds of women and girls were driven; they were mercilessly dragged down the street by their arms and hair."[8] The Nuremberg trials documented numerous other instances of sexual enslavement.

Nor is such institutionalized rape a thing of the distant past. During the Pakistani-Bangladesh War, officials at the highest levels of the Pakistani government also ordered massive use of rape to terrorize and contain a population. From March to

December 1971, nearly 200,000 women were violated by Pakistani soldiers. Wholesale as well as random seizure of women took place. Raping centers were established in military camps on the outskirts of cities. Hundreds of women were imprisoned in these camps, to be systematically assaulted by troops.

The effects of these assaults were similar to those occurring in World War II as well as in other wars. The massive degradation inflicted on Bengali women demoralized them and drove many insane. Rape was especially harmful to the Bengali women because of patriarchal and ethnocentric prohibitions. There are strong sexual taboos affecting future social relations following extramarital associations of any sort by Bengali women; and there are racial differences as well as hatreds between the Pakistanis and the Bengalis. Unwanted pregnancies would provide public evidence of sexual assaults, otherwise kept secret. Because of these factors, rape encouraged numerous suicides (Roy, 1975: 65-72).[9]

But the military use of sexual slavery, a form of rape against the same women repeated time after time, does not exhaust the forms of rape maintained with the complicity of authorities. Women held in captivity by authorities for other reasons have also been repeatedly violated. In *Women of Viet Nam,* Arlene Eisen-Bergman (1974: 60-77) documents and analyzes additional cases of rape as punishment and as politically condoned acts of terror. Many of these acts were committed against women while they were imprisoned.

Special forms of torture were kept in reserve for women. According to Jean Pierre Debris and Andre Menras (1973: 55-56), two Frenchmen imprisoned in Chi Hoa during the Vietnam War, female students had live eels inserted in their vaginas. Other women were interrogated as they stood naked for hours before masked torturers. Fear and torture were added to interrogations as the women refused to "confess" or give names of associates. Lizards were made to crawl all over their bodies. Their nipples were burned with cigarettes. Their pubic hair was set afire. Coca Cola bottles were pushed into their vaginas. And they were raped, especially if they were virgins.

There were nearly 125,000 women in South Vietnamese jails. Some of them, Eisen-Bergman (1974: 98) notes: "were arrested because they rejected the sexual advances of Thieu's soldiers." Others were there because they participated in peace movements or because they had supported the Provisional Revolutionary Government.

In addition to sexual violence by South Vietnamese military and police, Vietnamese women suffered at the hands of American soldiers despite military laws against rape. Sergeant Michael McClusker of the First Marine Division related one instance that was reported in the "Winter Soldier Investigation": "A squad of nine men . . . went into this village. They were supposed to go after what they called a Viet Cong whore. Instead of capturing her, they raped her — every man raped her. . . . The last man to make love [sic] to her, shot her in the head."[10]

Another instance reported in this investigation occurred while SP/4 Joe Galbally, Americal Division, was on patrol. He said: "We entered a [village]. These people were aware of what American soldiers do to them, so naturally they tried to hide the young girls. We found one hiding in a bomb shelter in a sort of basement of her house. She was taken out, raped by six or seven people in front of her family, in front of us, and the villagers. This isn't just one incident; this was just the first one I can remember. I know of ten or fifteen of such incidents at least."[11]

Some American soldiers also used the threat of forced sex as a counterinsurgency weapon. According to SP/5 Don Dzagulones, Americal Division, a woman suspected of being a spy was threatened with rape during her interrogation. When she would not talk, "they threatened to burn her pubic hairs. . . . She caught on fire and went into shock. . . . They gave medics instructions to take her to the hospital under the pretext of being in a coma from malaria."[12]

A *New Yorker* writer, Daniel Lang, has written about a reconnaissance patrol that enslaved a 20-year-old woman, repeatedly raping her over a five-day period; then, on the last day they murdered her.[13] Symbolic of American imperialism in

Vietnam was the woman's body in a rice paddy observed by helicopter gunner Ronald L. Ridenhour, a few days after American troops had swept through the area. Ridenhour said, "She was spread-eagled, as if on display. She had the 11th Brigade patch between her legs — as if it were some sort of display, some badge of honor."[14]

Notes

1. Individualistic rapes are informally committed by individuals or groups, while most of the rapes discussed later in the chapter are supported by institutions such as the military. Individualistic rapes, however, also occur in institutional and noninstitutional contexts.

2. The case illustrations in this chapter are derived from Julia Schwendinger's interviews of rape victims, which were conducted for her dissertation. In these interviews it was found that a woman can be raped by a stranger indoors or outdoors, suddenly or after a short con, with or without planning. Any variation of these conditions can also occur where the rapist is an acquaintance.

3. Similar regularities have been noted by Burgess and Holmstrom, who call the two types "blitz rape" and "confidence rape."

4. This exclusion is related to the criminologist's practice of organizing theory around legal standards such as the criterion of consent in forcible rape. From this standpoint, the act of sexual intercourse retains the appearance of consensual sex because of legal norms, although the consent is not really given freely. Further, on the scale of propriety, morality demands that these women value their sexual autonomy more than their economic welfare or the welfare of their dependents. Consent to sex for economic reasons, for instance, is considered to be based merely on free will, and a woman is expected to resign from her job rather than submit, which many, in fact, do. Such judgments, however, cannot eliminate the element of coercion. A very thin line of legality separates force-and-violence rape from sex based on other forms of coercion.

5. Sexual harassment was broadly spelled out in a questionnaire distributed by the Women's Section of the Human Affairs Program at Cornell University in 1975. The questionnaire called it: "Any repeated and unwanted sexual comments, looks, suggestions or physical contact that you find objectionable or offensive and cause you discomfort on your job." The questionnaire had 155 responses from women who attended a speakout on sexual harassment and from women who belonged to a civil service employees association in Binghamton, New York. Farley (1978: 20) reports that "92 listed sexual harassment as a serious problem; 70% personally experienced some form of harassment, and 56% of these reported physical harassment."

6. Recent research suggests the reason for the frequency of pregnancy resulting from rape. Contrary to earlier beliefs regarding spontaneous ovulation, which is the basis for the rhythm method of contraception, experiments with animals by Drs. Clark and Zarrow have demonstrated that coitus-induced ovulation may occur in a spontaneous ovulator. (It has been assumed that women ovulate spontaneously at mid-cycle.) Clark and Zarrow's finding has been substantiated by five German

gynecologists who have "demonstrated not only that ovulation can occur at any time in the cycle, but also that copulation may initiate it. All the women in these studies have been raped and all were certain as to the date of their last menstruation." Whether the rape-induced ovulation was due to trauma or the intensity of the coitus has not been determined. (See Clark and Zarrow, 1971: 53.)

7. Cited in Brownmiller (1975: 55); originally in *Trial of the Major War Criminals before the International Military Tribunal*. Vol. 7 (1947: 456-57).

8. *Ibid.;* cited in Brownmiller (1975: 55).

9. In one Pak military camp nearly 500 women were kept naked and their hair was cut short to prevent them from using their clothing or hair to strangle themselves.

10. Testimony by Sgt. Michael McClusker (Vietnam Veterans Against the War, 1972: 29).

11. Testimony by SP/4 Joe Galbally (Vietnam Veterans Against the War, 1972: 46).

12. Testimony by Sp/5 Don Dzagulones (Vietnam Veterans Against the War, 1972: 118).

13. Daniel Lang, *New Yorker,* October 18, 1969; cited in Brownmiller (1975: 101-102).

14. Quoted in Brownmiller (1975: 105).

CHAPTER 4

ANDROCENTRIC THEORIES OF RAPE

The forms of rape vary widely; yet some theories deal only with certain kinds of rape and not others. This chapter will discuss two of these, symbolic interactionist and psychoanalytic theories.

Interactionist Theories

Symbolic interaction theories emphasize that social interaction is mediated by signs and symbols, by eye contact, gestures, and words.[1] People observe and interpret each other's actions and react accordingly, and rape can be counted among such reactions. Interactionists, therefore, often consider rape to be caused by the way men and women communicate their attitudes and feelings toward one another.

Victim-precipitation theories are interactionist theories, and they emphasize the rapist's reactions to the victim.[2] According to Menachem Amir (1971: 266, 355, 346), offenders and victims are "mutually interacting partners." Furthermore, the female partner sometimes encourages rape "when [she] uses what could be interpreted as indecency in language and gestures, or constitutes what could be taken as an invitation to sexual relations." Victim precipitation, therefore, refers "to those rape cases in which the victim — actually or so it was interpreted by the offender — agreed to sexual relations but retracted before the actual act or did not resist strongly enough." The victim here is obviously regarded as a significant causal agent.

From this standpoint there is something in the psychological makeup of rape victims that differentiates them from non-victims. Under ordinary conditions, therefore, women as catalytic agents may typically be seen as wearing something rapists consider provocative; their willingness to make a friendly response to a strange man's conversation is interpreted as an invitation of sorts; the acceptance of automobile rides, invitations to dinner, or entering apartments alone with a male may be misunderstood or intentionally rationalized as a sign of their consent.

This way of thinking rarely questions the oppressive sexist norms that regulate the everyday activities of women. In this context, furthermore, the burden of responsibility for maintaining these norms continues to be placed on the woman, because her unwillingness to abide by such norms defines the situation as sexually exploitable. Also, the concept of victim precipitation can be criticized because its defining elements are exactly the same as those chosen by male supremacists, who insist that a victim's right to refuse sex can be ignored because the rapist has the right to force sexual intercourse when she is considered responsible for arousing him sexually.

Such underlying ideas obviously short-circuit the woman's rights; consequently, the notion of victim-precipitation itself is a naive reflection of male supremacist standards. It is a normative explanation that chiefly relies on the rapist's judgments "She was asking for it" or "She did not resist strongly enough" and on his rationalizations "Her behavior was provocative" or "She changed her mind too late." The victim-precipitation theory merely takes such sexist judgments and rationalizations at face value and converts them into a causal explanation of rape.

Symbolic interaction theorists conjure up additional normative relationships. For instance, it is alleged that rapes occur when the victim does not "negotiate" her relationships realistically — she allows the rapist's "framed assumptions" to dominate and fails to communicate her desire not to have sexual intercourse (Goode, 1969). Presumably, under these circumstances, an unambiguous expression of the victim's "real intentions" would have discouraged the rapist from assaulting her in the first place. On the other hand, if the rapist eventually discovers that the victim really does not want sex and then explodes, his attack is defined as a victim-precipitated act.

However, if the rapist honestly misunderstands her intentions throughout the assault, then the theory rests on slightly different assumptions. Under these conditions he remains caught in a web of misunderstandings.

In the case of misunderstood intentions both the rapist and the victim repeatedly interpret each other's behavior incorrectly.[3] The victim takes for granted that the rapist will respect her rejection of his advances. The rapist, on the other hand, interprets the victim's rejection as a mere show of respectability. Finally, believing that her protestations mask a secret desire to submit to a violent male, he single-mindedly acts as if she is consenting.

What can be said about these symbolic interaction theories? When used as a *general* explanation of forcible rape, they make no sense at all.[4] They appear contrived especially when they are applied to rape in wartime or during fascist repression. For example, after studying Pakistani wartime rapes, including rapes of women enslaved in military brothels, K.K. Roy (1975) pointed out that the victims were raped by soldiers who were total strangers. Also, following their capture, many victims struggled with the rapists, seriously and undeniably risking their lives. Roy (1975: 68) insists that the victims cannot by any stretch of the imagination be held responsible for their victimization either consciously or by default: "No events can thus be said to have been precipitated by the victim."

Only when a certain degree of *equality* exists between the rapist and his victim are the theories plausible. Then and only then are the frequently used phrases like "negotiated order," "shared misunderstandings," or "failure to communicate" credible in that the victim presumably has the power to abort the sequence of events leading to the rapist's assault. Under conditions of parity, therefore, it is presumed that if the victim had responded "properly" in both an existential and a moral sense — the rape would not have taken place.

It is true that some dominating males define a woman who acts "improperly" as a "legitimate" victim for an assault. Here, again, however, we are confronted with normative logic that takes sexist standards for granted. If the victim acts "properly" by resisting, these same males may redefine her as a person who "really" wants to be raped; that is, she is "turned on" by violent sex. Why, in light of these alternative possibilities, should either response on the victim's part have causal or moral significance? If we consider the effects of the rapist's belief that he has certain chauvinistic prerogatives, neither response should carry any weight. Rather than the victim's response, it is actually the rapist's supremacist attitudes and behavior that dominate the situation and determine its violent outcome.

It is also true that a forcible rape may be preceded by "misunderstandings" or a "failure to communicate," but are these factors significant causes? Because of the emphasis on parity, the interaction theories tacitly minimize the structural realities of the situation and the power differentials that characterize the overwhelming number of forcible rapes. By maximizing an illusion of equality, these theories mask the degree to which the rapist's chauvinism is still the essential cause, regardless of the "propriety" of the victim's behavior.[5]

Symbolic interactionists painstakingly describe the interpersonal relationships that influence the rapist's definition of the "legitimate victim." To justify his assault, however, the rapist must believe that he has the *right* under these conditions to *force* the victim to submit to his will. Such a belief in the use of force emerges under historically determined circumstances, and no interaction theory alone — no theory that is devoid of reference to these circumstances will help us understand the social foundations of the rapist's motivations.

Similar criticisms can be applied to the use of these normative ideas in legal judgments about the aggressor's versus the victim's rights. Amir (1971: 266) wants to emphasize the causal connection between precipitation and rape "with the aim of educating the law to recognize it too." Such efforts, however, are totally unnecessary. The fact is that criminal justice officials have ignored the victim's rights by certifying this androcentric idea for many years.

Consequently, the legalistic counterpart to these theories is equally objectionable. In September 1975, the California Supreme Court handed down a decision about criminal intent in rape cases. Earlier a trial by jury in Superior Court had found two brothers guilty of various charges. One brother was charged with assault with intent to commit rape and the other with kidnapping, assault, forcible rape, and oral and genital copulation. The Supreme Court justices, however, decided that the guilty verdict was invalid because the Superior Court judge did not instruct the jury properly. The court claimed that the jurors should have been instructed: If you have any doubts, if you think the second defendant *reasonably and generally* believed that the victim had freely consented to the [alleged kidnapping] and the intercourse" (our emphasis), then you should acquit both defendants.[6]

Obviously, the California Supreme Court justices subscribed to the common dictum that when a man misunderstands the intention of the victim, his actions are legal as long as he "reasonably and genuinely" believes that she desires intercourse with a violent male.

Judges in Great Britain march to the same drumbeat. There is a notorious British example of this dictum in legal cases. In 1975, the year the California case occurred, the Law Lords (they are equivalent to the American Supreme Court Judges) ruled 3 to 2 that if a man honestly thought he was acting as the woman wanted, he was innocent of rape no matter how unreasonable his belief (Coote and Gill, 1975).

This ruling involved the case of Director of Public Prosecutions (*DPP*) v. *Morgan,* wherein an RAF Sergeant, William Morgan, had invited three junior aircraftsmen to his home to have intercourse with his wife. Anna Coote and Tess Gill (1975: 7), two experts on women's rights in British law, reported: "He told them she might struggle but that they should not take her seriously, since she only pretended to resist in order to increase her own excitement. Mrs. Morgan, was not, in fact, a willing party to the attack, but the aircraftsmen claimed they believed she was." The aircraftsmen were convicted of rape and sentenced to three years in prison; Mrs. Morgan's husband received seven years for aiding and abetting the crime. They appealed to the Law Lords who upheld the convictions because it was felt that no jury would have accepted their story in preference to Mrs. Morgan's. However, the Lords also ruled that men could properly defend themselves in court by claiming that they *honestly believed* in the woman's consent, even though their belief might seem unreasonable. If the air-craftsmen's belief that Mrs. Morgan wanted violent sex had been more credible, the Lords would have dismissed the con-victions on the grounds that the men did not intend to rape her.

This ruling has been supported in England by the Women's Rights Committee of the National Council for Civil Liberties. Patricia Hewitt (1975), General Secretary of the National Council, says: "A genuine belief in the woman's consent (whether based on reasonable grounds or not) should be ac-cepted as a defence in rape trials."

Coote and Gill (1975: 27) also write: "Despite the difficul-ties it might raise, we support the Law Lord's ruling in (*DPP*) v. *Morgan* because we endorse the principle that a person should not be convicted of a serious crime which he did not intend to commit. We agree that in exceptional cases it might be possible for a man to hold a genuine belief, based on unreasonable grounds, that a woman consented. In a case of this kind, what counts, in our view, is not what he *should* have thought, but what he *actually* thought at the time. If there was no guilty intent in his mind, then he should not be convicted."

We disagree with this stand on criminal intent because it ignores the ideological construction of criminal motives. Crim-inal intent is not frozen in ice; nor does a person have to believe that his act is legitimate to be relieved of criminal responsibility. A defense favored by Nazi criminals such as Adolph Eichman was that they honestly believed that they were acting properly;

they obeyed the state. Nevertheless, their professed motives did not shield them from responsibility for crimes against humanity. Moreover, because they were found guilty of disregarding higher ideals, the standards of obedience underlying their professed motives were morally discredited.

In this particular case, the fundamental issue, in our opinion, is whether the criterion of criminal intent should hold a rapist responsible for any willingness to ignore the protestations of a victim on the basis of chauvinistic standards. The basic issue in (*DPP*) v. *Morgan* is not whether the men honestly believed that Mrs. Morgan wanted violent sex but whether they had any right to predicate that belief on Mr. Morgan's words. Even if they honestly believed Mr. Morgan, they should have been held criminally responsible for their act because they warranted their belief on his authority alone and refused to take Mrs. Morgan's protestations at face value.

Legally, the victim is the *only* person whose consent matters, and the law has the responsibility to establish the prima facie grounds on which knowledge about this consent should be obtained. The law in this regard should outstrip customs based on male supremacy. However, it cannot accomplish this end by simply emphasizing the formal requirements for criminal intent without first discrediting the repugnant principles and standards used by rapists to define their acts as legitimate.

Psychoanalytic Theories

A small number of rapists are psychotic, and their crimes can be especially terrifying and dangerous. However, psychoanalytic theories view *most* rapists as emotionally disturbed individuals (Groth, 1979). According to these theories, such men may have acquired an intense hatred of women during childhood or have undergone experiences that triggered their latent homosexual tendencies. Rape, then, among other things, is inflicted when men are obsessively motivated by hatred of women and a desperate need to convince themselves of their own masculinity.

Freudian theory has claimed a scientific expertise in regard to sexual relationships. One would assume, therefore, that it is especially useful in identifying the causes of sexual crimes. Certain aspects of this theory that deal with mechanisms of defense appear helpful for understanding why some men displace anger and frustration (arising from loss of status on the job or at home) toward their wives. However, scientific research has not treated other Freudian assumptions about violence kindly. Despite its enormous popularity among middle-class Americans and professionals, certain parts of this theory, which attribute violence to "psychopathic" or "latent homosexual" tendencies, have had little or no verification.[7] The concept of psychopathy is hardly employed today by criminologists, and even scholars who favor other elements of Freudian theory conclude that "there is no objective evidence supporting the Freudian theory of homosexuality" (Kline, 1972: 282).

The contradictions to Freudian expectations emerging from research in the recent decade are considerable. Today, Dr. Murray L. Cohen and Richard Boucher (1972: 255) say: "The sexual offender may be passive and inhibited or active and assertive, gentle or violent, religious or irreligious, masculine or effeminite. He may hate his mother, love his mother, or be ambivalent about her. He may have had a repressive sexual development or he may have been overstimulated."

Nevertheless, the systematic failure to obtain rigorous proof has not stemmed the tide of psychoanalytic explanations for rape. In Ann Burgess and Lynda Holmstrom's (1974: 26) work, for instance, the aggressive rapist is said to be motivated by his desire to inflict pain and by his destructive wishes. He is angry at all or certain kinds of women, and the rape is a displacement of this emotion toward the victim. In this development "a real heterosexuality existed only in fantasy and homosexuality was intensely repressed." The rapist, when examined psychoanalytically, reveals serious personality disorders.

Psychoanalytic ideas are also central to the sociological concept, "the subculture of violence," which is applied to rapists by Amir and given credence by Brownmiller.[8] This subculture is allegedly created by men who live in similar areas and who resort to violence as a solution to their sexual ambivalence and disorders. Thus, for instance, it is said that such a subculture exists in black ghettos where "mother-dominated families" stimulate latent homosexual tendencies in male children. Amir (1971: 330-331) states: "The Negro male's aggressive sexuality seems to be more problemmatical due to the strong need to overcome problems of masculinity and sexual identity."

But, again, research has raised doubts about the validity of the subculture of violence theory (Ball-Rokeach, 1973, 1975; Magura, 1975). Moreover, empirical studies have never demonstrated that the Americans, Russians, Germans, Japanese, Pakistanis, and so on essentially raped women in wartime because of mother-dominated families or homosexual tendencies. Such a demonstration, in our opinion, will never be forthcoming, because there are too many rapes committed by men from national groups that epitomize very traditional family relations. In these groups, women are subjugated by stable patriarchal forms of domination and are not socialized into "mother-dominating" patterns.

To make matters worse, academics use concepts of sexual repression, sexual ambivalence, and "mother domination" as magical touchstones that explain everything so long as it is considered deviant. Such notions are so taken for granted that social scientists are hardly aware of how inconsistent their application to deviant behavior has become.[9]

The androcentric assumptions underlying these Freudian ideas are also striking. The psychoanalytic emphasis on irrational and unconscious personality processes implicitly minimizes the rational connections between violence and male supremacy, or between violence and other supremacist doctrines learned in our society. Thus, even though supremacist doctrines about male, racial, and national groups have justified violence for thousands of years, psychoanalytic theories implicitly maintain that it is not these doctrines that foster violence. On the contrary, it is the *anxiety and ambivalence about one's masculinity* that cause violence. Hence it is concluded that if *female status* undermines male supremacy, then the male children in our culture will be driven to violence because of their sexual anxieties when they get older.[10] (The converse of this theory, the stereotype that all men are naturally aggressive, is central to the next chapter.)

Obviously the view that female status undermines masculinity rejects the possibility (a possibility we believe is true) that an egalitarian trend among the sexes will accompany the social and ideological changes that will lessen interpersonal violence. Nevertheless, in place of such possibilities and despite the lack of scientific proof, higher status and autonomy for women are said to increase the potentiality for criminal violence, delinquency, and cultural aberrations.[11]

Clearly, then, in addition to their androcentric bias, interactionist and psychoanalytic theories have provided normative and unscientific guides to rape. The interactionists emphasize rational behavior but ignore power differentials and determinants of rape that go beyond isolated interpersonal conditions. Psychoanalysis, on the other hand, vastly overemphasizes the number of rapes due to personality disorders. Simultaneously, it offers causal notions that have become part of conventional wisdom about rape regardless of empirical validity. The facile use of these notions has trivialized the causes of violence against women and sexual inequality.

Notes

1. For a trenchant critique of symbolic interactionism, see Richard Lichtman (1970).

2. William Sanders (1980) provides another type of interactionist theory, which does not rely on victim-precipitation assumptions.

3. Margaret Mead (1969: 208) implies an interactionist theory when she states: "Rape does occur in modern societies, where there are many levels and sections with different social mores, in which some members of both sexes are utterly unable to interpret the behavior of members of the other sex who come from a different setting."

4. They also make little sense in light of the fact that the overwhelming majority of rapes, because they are planned, partially planned, and felony-related, do not involve a rapist's ignorance of the victim's objections.

5. The explanation of the immediate symbolic relationships, therefore, must focus on the sexist structuring of interpreted meanings even if this structure is realized situationally through voluntaristic behavior.

6. The California Supreme Court reversed the convictions of rape and kidnapping but affirmed the judgments in other respects (*People* vs. *Mayberry,* 15 Cal.3d 143.)

7. Some scholars, such as the philosopher of science Ernest Nagel (1959: 55), contended some time ago that Freudian theory as a whole has received the Scottish verdict: *not proven.* Today there are works indicating that some Freudian propositions have been sustained while others have not (see Fisher and Greenberg, 1977). However, with regard to "psychopathology," a category used frequently by psychoanalysts to explain criminal behavior, we even find Fisher and Greenberg's (1977: 410) positive estimations to be unconvincing. Surveys scrutinizing decades of research findings have not supported Freudian theories of criminal behavior (see Schuessler and Cressey, 1950). The term "psychopathic personality" has been called a "scrapbasket to which is relegated a group of otherwise unclassified personality disorders and problems" (Preu, 1944: 922-937; also, Ullman and Krasner, 1969). Citing, among others, Hulsey Cason's (1943, 1946) careful studies of the (inadequate) correspondence between offender traits and psychopathic categories, Donald Cressey (1974: 160) concludes, "the concept *psychopathic personality* is as useless in the interpretation of criminal behavior as was the older concept *moral imbecile* which has been completely discarded by scholars in this field."

8. This concept originates with Marvin Wolfgang and Franco Ferracuti (1967).

9. There seems to be no end to the contradictory applications of this Freudian notion of sexual ambivalence and mother domination. Deviancy theories about youth provide an illustration. Sexual ambivalence and its origin in so-called mother-dominated families is used by Walter Miller (1958) to explain working-class delinquency based on concerns that boys have for achieving a "macho" identity (that is, being a tough and powerful male). But Miller does not use these notions to explain middle-class delinquency. Albert Cohen (1955), on the other hand, claims that middle-class and not working-class delinquents are created by mother-dominated households. Still another theorist, Talcott Parsons (1954), attributes a deviant youth culture that develops among both working-class and middle-class youth to sexual ambivalence and latent homosexuality created by the increased status of women in nuclear families.

10. The racist applications of these psychoanalytic ideas are also striking. Psychoanalytic theory is used by some to explain away the connection between racism and economic problems. The lack of job mobility for black men in American ghettos has been attributed to the prevalence of the so-called mother-dominated family. Rather than "mother-dominated," however, these families are actually fatherless because of long-term instabilities in employment for black males. Also, incredible as it may seem, it has been argued that the actual economic conditions in ghettos are due to mother-dominated families; therefore, family counselors and social work agencies should receive greater priority in congressional deliberations than full employment and antipoverty legislation (see Moynihan, 1969). For reasons that Freudian ideas have been useful for justifying conservative policies, see Schwendinger and Schwendinger (1974: 335-363).

11. Freda Adler's (1975) *Sisters in Crime* claims that "women's liberation" accounts for the rise in female crime, but every attempt to confirm her hypothesis has failed. See, for example, Joseph Weis (1976). In an unpublished study of women prisoners, Julia Schwendinger found no subscription by these prisoners to the ideology of "women's liberation."

CHAPTER 5

RADICAL FEMINIST THEORIES

The feminist movement contains many writers who differ on the causes of sexual inequality and rape. Excellent analyses often appear in shorter works and articles where the larger issues are discussed. In an article about battered wives, for example, Susan Schechter (1979) examines male domination within the context of the economic and social organization of capitalism. Black and Third World women, although less involved in the antirape movement, have started to address the special problems of racism and the rape of black women.[1] But most of the widely circulated and book-length explanations of rape identified with the women's movement assume that men subjugate women simply to serve their own interests. In the most extreme expressions of this feminist standpoint, words like "capitalism," "socialism," "imperialism," "racism," "family," and "state" merely signify *male* domination. All of these social relationships are reportedly created to further male privilege.

Though such views are certainly novel, the writers who take this "radical feminist" standpoint have not created a truly original theory of rape. For instance, even though she regards the rapist from this point of view, Diana Russell (1975: 109) explains rape psychoanalytically. In addition to "genital orientations" and "orgasm fixations," rapists, in her writings, are seen to be driven by severe psychological problems. Assaultive behavior is related to insecurity regarding maleness (the "masculine mystique"), psychic displacement of blocked economic opportunity for blacks, and the psychic frustrations between

women and men caused by socialized differences in male and
female sexuality.

Opportunity Structure Theory

On the other hand, we shall see that Lorenne Clark and
Debra Lewis (1977: 128-129) rely on an "opportunity structure
theory" to interpret sexual relations that lead to rape. Their
proposal is that men regard women as owners of salable sexual
properties: "From the male point of view female sexuality is a
commodity in the possession of women, even if it is something
men will come to own and control under the appropriate circumstances. Women are seen as hoarders and miserly dispen-
sers of a much desired commodity, and men must constantly
wheedle, bargain, and pay a price for what they want. And if
anything lies at the root of misogyny, this does. Men naturally
come to resent and dislike women because they see them as
having something which they want and have a perfect right to,
but which women are unwilling to give them freely. The right to
female sexuality must be purchased."

Female sexuality is allegedly bought and sold in an open
market. However, the market is dominated by male conceptions of property and therefore the best bargain a woman can
achieve is still restrictive. Furthermore, when bargaining for
sex, men reportedly use various forms of coercion. They may
make promises they cannot or will not really fulfill. They may
harass women or threaten them with physical harm.

Clark and Lewis (1977: 129) note: "The tactic of coercion
which a man uses will depend on the personal assets which he
has at hand." Men who have money and other resources can
drive a bargain in their own interests easily. Other men — who
are ugly, perhaps, but certainly if they are poor — will take
sexuality from women by force, because they have no other
means of driving a bargain.

"Nor is it surprising," the authors (1977: 130) contend, "that
rapists from low socio-economic backgrounds should frequently choose middle-class women as their victims. In a society which allots women different price tags, it is inevitable that

some women will be too expensive for some men, but that those men will nonetheless desire what they cannot afford. Some of these men will take what they want; they literally *steal* the female sexuality they desire because they lack the necessary social and economic means of acquiring it legitimately."

Thus, Clark and Lewis's theory suggests that sexual relations are based partly on coercion, partly on a competitive market. Working-class men rape middle-class women because the sexual market is similar to so-called free markets: "It operates to the disadvantage of those who are least favored to begin with, who do not begin from a position of equality in the bargaining relationship" (1977: 130). In fact, the authors conclude, "Within the technical [that is, legal] limits of the term, rape will always be an inevitable consequence of the fact that some men do not have the means to achieve sexual relations with women, except through physical violence" (1977: 131).

How well does Clark and Lewis's theory stand up under close analysis? To begin with, in criminology, "opportunity structure" theories maintain that crime is committed by individuals who lack the economic means legitimately to achieve what they want.[2] The logic of Clark and Lewis's theory is identical, even though the sexual market and rape are at issue here rather than the labor market and economic crime.

Rather than reviewing the deficiencies in opportunity theories, let us simply ask: If the lack of opportunity, money, or other resources is causally important, then why do men of wealth, good looks, or charm commit crimes, including rape? White-collar and corporate crime such as tax evasion, consumer fraud, and price-fixing are committed by middle-and upper-class persons. Furthermore, poor men may rape women more frequently; however, there is no evidence that they "frequently choose middle-class women" because of envious feelings. In fact, as we note in Chapter 14, research suggests that the majority of rape victims belong to poorer working-class families and that these women are usually victimized by men from their own class.

Sometimes opportunity theories of crime base their claims on the deprivation of vital needs, such as the needs for food, clothing, and shelter, which are absolutely necessary for survival. Crime, in this view, is seen as a means of survival when legitimate means are not available. Do Clark and Lewis conform with the deprivation of needs approach?

Sex can certainly be considered a vital need too. However, since lower-class women also need sexual gratification, lower-class men should have no more trouble than others ˀnding sexual partners. Why, then, should lower-class men, more frequently than middle-class men, rape women because of sexual deprivation?

This question leads to the observation that Clark and Lewis's theory implicitly expresses a middle-class view of working-class people. Sexual relations in our society are often debased and fraught with conflict. But can it be said that sexual relations are determined soley by coercion and commodity exchange? As a rule, they are not. In every country, millions of working-class men and women, despite enormous hardships, sacrifice themselves for each other and their children in their social relationships. Every working-class person knows of acts of selfless devotion by men and women that belie the universality of Clark and Lewis's view of social reality. Therefore, their assumption that the relations between men and women generally give rise to misogyny and hence are everywhere based on hatred and mistrust is simply not true.

Other assumptions underlying Clark and Lewis's theory are equally unwarranted. Take the assumption that sex is a commodity, for example. Sexual relations, to a degree, are affected by commodity relations, but the latter relations do not exist simply because they are imposed, as suggested, by the will of men. Commodity markets emerged worldwide centuries ago within the development of capitalism. Today, all the people in capitalist societies, including men, are subject to impersonal market forces. These forces exist because of the objective nature of the capitalist mode of production and not because they are imposed by the will of individuals.

Furthermore, the exchange relations described by Clark and Lewis in their references to sexual commodity markets and "sexual and reproductive capacity" are based largely on barter relations; they do not really involve commodities that are sold in a competitive market. First of all, only prostitutes and mistresses might qualify as sellers of so-called sexual commodities, since competitive markets involve at the very least a universal medium of exchange such as money. But even in these cases, one can hardly speak of a *competitive* market in the same sense that this term is used in economic theory. Few men choose a specific mistress because she represents the "best bargain" available. Because of legal prohibitions, maneuvering for competitive advantage between buyers of a prostitute's services usually does not occur.

Second, while some men may treat their wives and children as if they were slaves, they do not sell them as slaves to other men. Only if women were sold as slaves because they could bear more slaves would their reproductive as well as sexual capacity actually be important to their status as so-called commodities. Their sexual and reproductive capacities are therefore clearly not commodities.

The notion of a commodity market in the sexual exchange of women is unwarranted for still another reason. Granted, the selection of marriage partners for some women, especially women of property, may involve calculating and cynical assessments of private advantage. But the overwhelming majority of women in our society today are propertyless, and they choose their working-class husbands for romantic love and other reasons, most of which are not economic. They are concerned about their husbands' economic status, but, because this factor is usually far from decisive, their selection of a marriage partner cannot be explained on the basis of free market relationships. Indeed, the restrictions on free market choices in marriage selection are even more obvious once the effects of social pressures due to racial, class, religious, and nationality relationships are taken into account. The basic problem with Clark and Lewis's opportunity theory, therefore, is their reliance on the definition of women's sexuality as property.

Finally, what can be said about Clark and Lewis's proposals for preventing rape? According to these authors, "rape would cease to be a problem if all persons were sexually and reproductively autonomous, both legally and practically speaking. The law must reflect the perspective of free, autonomous women and not solely that of property-owning men" (1977: 182-183). Here, unfortunately, the authors place too much stock in legal autonomy as a preventative measure. For example, the law, in capitalist societies, does regard *men* as legally autonomous persons, but that same body of law supports a system in which "legally autonomous" men are afflicted with racism, unemployment and exploitation. Why, then, should complete legal autonomy for women accomplish more than it does for men? Even though women's rights are supported by legal autonomy, this autonomy will not fundamentally change the political and economic system in which women live.

In addition, why should full legal autonomy prevent rape? These theorists claim that "changes in the law and in social attitudes must remove the necessity of any forms of coercion. And that means removing all traces of legal and social structures which accord women status other than that of full legal persons, with complete autonomy over all aspects of their lives" (Clark and Lewis, 1977: 183). But, again, men have legal autonomy, and it is validated by schools, church, and family as well as government. Despite this autonomy and its institutional support, men are assaulted, robbed, murdered, and even raped.

Legal autonomy and its principle of equality before the law are greatly desirable, but not enough. Alone, legal autonomy will hardly prevent women from being assaulted, robbed, or raped in peacetime or in war.

Male Bestiality and Rape

An old perspective in criminology equates certain criminals with the wild denizens of the jungle and attributes crime and other social evils to the bestial instincts smouldering in men. When applied to sexual relationships, this perspective predicates the forcible subjugation of women on the savage nature of born criminals — on their lust for aggression, sex, and power.[3]

A similar view of men, women, and society is held by those radical feminist writers who are rewriting history as a universal progression of woman-hating and avaricious events. They claim that the predatory nature of man and his desire for property are the fundamental causes of sexual inequality and rape. They even believe that the "world-historic" origin of human society is based on the subjugation of women, especially through the institutions of marriage and family life.

Such a portrayal is made by Susan Brownmiller (1975) in *Against Our Will*. She further proposes that sexual inequality and rape are due to simple biological facts. She declares, "By anatomical fiat — the inescapable construction of their genital organs — the human male was a *natural* predator and the human female served as his *natural* prey" (1975: 16; our emphasis).

These ideas logically assume that all men are born rapists and that their urge to rape women into submission can be found everywhere. To prove this point, Brownmiller summons up a seemingly endless list of rapes throughout history. Reportedly, there is rape and sexual inequality almost without variation in the most ancient societies, in the Middle Ages, through the period of American slavery, during World War II, the Vietnam War, and so on.[4]

Brownmiller's thesis is not backed by scientific evidence. Countless crimes have accumulated throughout history, but this fact does not by one iota prove that crime is caused by man's animalistic nature. Neither Ceasare Lombroso nor Sigmund Freud, its chief proponents in criminology, nor anyone else has ever demonstrated the theory that biological or instinctual characteristics determine crime. The same statement of denial can be made about Brownmiller's view of male supremacy. In Chapter 8, on sexism and history, we describe anthropological evidence that denies the universality of sexual inequality.

If Brownmiller's theories are not based in social reality, then where do they come from? The answer to this question points to old-fashioned beliefs in the nature of man. Brownmiller's theory, despite its feminist themes, relies heavily for its credibility on traditional sex stereotyping. Paradoxically, such stereotyping originates in sexist ideologies, propounded by late-nineteenth-century male psychologists, sociologists, and anthropologists, who caricatured both sexes. In these ideologies, men are depicted as natural predators, and all women, by nature and at heart, are either dangerous creatures or willing subjects.

In Brownmiller's work, however, this carryover from sexist cultural types is obscured because she rejects the sexist stereotyping of women and accepts only the stereotype of men. She wrests the typification of men from its original ideological context, which justifies female submission as well as the dominant role of men. She then uses only the typification of men as natural predators to rationalize a radical feminist view of social reality. Sexual inequality and rape, in this view, cannot be attributed to any cause other than male human nature: Man is oppressive by nature and rape maintains his supremacy and privilege.

The degree to which Brownmiller is a prisoner of a traditional sexist framework can be illustrated by comparing her theory to the writings that once dominated academic scholarship. To explain the historical origins of the subjugation of women, rape, and monogamy, for instance, Brownmiller revives theories that were proposed in the formative years of North American academic sociology.

For example, in 1883, Lester Ward, a founder of American sociology, attributed the origins of private property and the enslavement of women to male egoism. According to Ward, male domination and monogamy were originally invented because they were advantageous to women as well as men. Each woman subjugated herself willingly to a man for his protection in the war *among men* over the ownership of women. Men were paid off in different coin: in exchange for their protection, they were given a monopoly over access to women's bodies, receiving regular sexual satisfaction on demand.[5]

Notice how Brownmiller's theory depends on identical assumptions and makes the same historical leaps, except that she posits two prehistoric battles. First, she writes: "The concepts of hierarchy, slavery and private property flow from, and could only be predicated upon, the initial subjugation of women"

(1975: 17-18). The source of this subjugation, she finds, at bottom is due to the predatory nature of man; hence she comments on the threat to women posed by the struggle among men. "The historic price of women's protection by *man against man* was the imposition of chastity and monogamy," she concludes, (1975: 17; our emphasis), in the same vein as Ward. In a nutshell, this "grandfather's tale" is at the center of Brownmiller's theory regarding the origins of the subjugation of women and monogamy.

Brownmiller makes further contributions to the misconceptions about male-female relationships. She conjures up the mythical war that reportedly always occurs *between the sexes*. She claims that rape is in the interests of all men, regardless of their differences. Rape, she states, "is nothing more or less than a conscious process of intimidation by which all men keep all women in a state of fear" (1975: 15). Tactically, rapists are simply the "shock troops" that do the dirty work for all men "in the longest sustained battle that the world has ever known" (1975: 209).[6]

On the face of it, such an argument seems incredible, since the interests of many men, for instance, most fathers, brothers, husbands and lovers, are hardly served by the rape of their wives, daughters, or loved ones. But this inconsistency is explained away by Brownmiller. To reconcile these cases that contradict her primary functionalist scheme, we must step back for a moment to the other "universal" struggle mentioned a moment ago: the war of man against man.

Relying on this Hobbesian imagery, Brownmiller notes that individual men war against each other by seizing, abusing, and even destroying each other's property. Since women are considered mere chattel, rape is an expression of the naturally selfish desire for property or the vengeful reaction (among blacks and other persecuted groups) to oppressive circumstances engendered by universal selfishness.

Thus, in Brownmiller's scheme, rape serves contradictory aims. Rape has always been advantageous to all men, but rapists also act for ulterior motives that defy the community of all men. They rape to obtain power over other men or to take revenge on other men. They seize and abuse females who are property of husbands, fathers, and brothers or who belong to men of intensely hated racial, national, or religious groups.

Men, in Brownmiller's mythology, are obviously so bestial, by nature so aggressive, that they sexually molest innocent women simply because they can live nowhere in peace with themselves or anyone else.

Law-and-Order

What are Brownmiller's proposals for preventing rape? The illusion that men are savage animals at heart has always served advocates of so-called law-and-order policies, who say that human beings behave themselves only when they are in great fear of being punished. Furthermore, law-and-order conservatives usually reject policies correcting discrimination in the criminal justice system or dealing with the social causes of crime. They simply recommend forcible repression as the only practical way to deal with the animals who threaten people and property.

Brownmiller is a feminist advocate of such law-and-order policies. She calls for the harsh repression of rapists and pornographers yet recommends virtually nothing concrete for eliminating the socioeconomic causes of crime or discrimination in the justice system. Aiming her sights primarily at policies that will forcibly repress the animals who threaten women, Brownmiller recommends changes that put women in control of the state apparatus of violence in order to force men to behave themselves: " I am not one to throw the word 'revolutionary' around lightly, but full integration of our cities' police departments, and by full I mean fifty-fifty as many women as men, no less, is a revolutionary goal of the utmost importance in women's rights." She calls for the integration of the sheriffs' offices, armed forces, and the police — "the entire lawful power structure" — to strip our society of "male dominance and control" and forcibly repress man's animalistic instincts (1975: 380).

We are certainly in favor of sexual integration in every branch of industry and government. However, desirable as these policies may be in themselves, what evidence is there for a transformation in "power structures," even if women were given such an opportunity forcibly to repress men? Female custodians in correctional institutions can and do buy into the system and become just as repressive as their male counterparts. Forceful women monarchs have played important roles in the development of repressive power structures. Queen Elizabeth I, for example, engaged in numerous wars and encouraged outright piracy and plunder to consolidate England's imperial power. Women royalist cadets shot down Russian workers who stormed the czar's winter palace during the 1917 Revolution. And, finally, Ilse Koch created lampshades from the skin of Jewish prisoners in the Buchenwald concentration camp.

Rapists deserve to be punished and, since some rapists do repeat their crime, long sentences combined with treatment are certainly appropriate for recidivists. However, prison experience often teaches men convicted of other crimes to become rapists. Also, harsh punishments frequently do not prevent offenses by criminals at large. The United States is among the nations with the most people per capita in jail, and it has more severe punishments than most other highly industrialized countries. But its law-and-order policies have hardly stemmed the tide of crime. Moreover, since Brownmiller emphasizes that men are in control of property as well as "the lawful power structure," how can we square her logic with the fact that most larcenies, robberies, burglaries, and auto thefts are never solved? In fact, the percentage of cases that are cleared by police for these property crimes are lower than those cleared for rape, homicide, and assault.[7] If the men in power, using law-and-order policies, cannot effectively control the men who steal their property, how can women accomplish this end using similar methods? Very simply, they cannot.

Allison Edwards (1976: 26), author of *Rape, Racism and the White Women's Movement: An Answer to Susan Brownmiller,* makes a pithy response to this question: "Law and order solutions won't stop rape. Law and order solutions won't liberate women. Law and order solutions will just create a police state in which nobody will be free."

The feminist movement has broken sharply with the androcentric tradition in theories of rape by emphasizing the connections between this crime and sexual inequality. However, more influential feminist writings have not fully exploited the implications of these connections, because they view rape laws merely as property laws and they adopt psychoanalytic, opportunity structure, or naturalistic premises. The following chapters provide alternative legal and causal interpretations. Even though they also reflect the impact of modern feminism, these chapters rely on very different theoretical assumptions.

Notes

1.   These problems are discussed in a report by I. Nkenge Toure (1981) on the Black Focus Group Workshop from a Special Population Conference, which was published in the Feminist Alliance Against Rape newsletter.

2.   For a general "opportunity structure" theory of crime, see Robert Merton (1938).

3.   A century ago, Ceasare Lombroso and Sigmund Freud contributed theories that located the origins of criminality partly in atavistic biological characteristics or aggressive instincts acquired from birth. There is no proof for either of these causal variables.

4.   However, since there are societies and circumstances in which rape is virtually absent, Brownmiller must account for these exceptions. She does so by appealing to the common belief that individuals will do anything (including giving up rape) to survive. Men, in this cynical view, will refrain from rape when they are afraid for their lives. For instance, according to Brownmiller, the Vietcong refrained from rape *only* because of their interest in *survival.* (They did not want to alienate the peasants who gave them essential food, vital information, and secure places to hide from enemy patrols.) The Arapesh are also recognized as exceptions; they do not rape, according to Brownmiller, because of their unusual belief system, which defines sex as *extremely dangerous,* especially outside of marriage.

5.   For a discussion of Lester Ward's writings on women, see Schwendinger and Schwendinger (1974: 313-315).

6.   In such a mythology, as is shown in Chapter 13, the category of *gender* is the prime reification of the social determinants of violence in general, as well as sexual violence in particular. The mythology collapses social facts into natural ones and thereby creates a sexual fetishism of violence wherein male characteristics are substituted as the source of all violence.

7.   For instance, the FBI's Uniform Crime Reports indicate that for 1976, 79 percent of the homicides, 63 percent of aggravated assaults, and 52 percent of forcible rapes founded by the police resulted in the arrest of a suspected offender. However, only 27 percent of the robberies, 17 percent of the burglaries, 19 percent of the larceny-thefts, and 14 percent of the motor vehicle thefts were cleared by the police.

PART II

RAPE LAWS AND PRIVATE PROPERTY

CHAPTER 6

CUSTOM, LAW, AND RAPE

Some American social scientists, lawyers, and journalists submit that the rape laws are simply an extension of property laws that protect the interests of men. Brownmiller (1975: 16-17) argues that legal safeguards for women emanate solely from laws designed to protect man's female property.[1] Clark and Lewis (1977: 159) take this a step further with the notion that the law *continues* to protect male property rights: "Our legal system defines and treats rape as an offense against property, and not as an offense against the person."

These statements are provocative and their implications lead us to ask: Is rape really a property crime today? Also, if rape laws in the past have actually been related to property relations, are these relations based on complex social relationships such as modes of production and social class relationships, or do these laws simply refer to women as things and merely reflect the interests of men? We answer these questions in this chapter and the next. Our answers lay the groundwork for a radically different method of analyzing rape and rape laws.[2]

Modes of Production, Property Relations, and Control of Women

Before we journey into time in search of the answers to these questions, a particular kind of historical framework is needed. Since laws and customs are better understood within a particular socioeconomic context, our discussion of historical changes will refer to such contexts repeatedly. The socio-economic formations appearing in our references are identified by their modes of production, which were based on *primitive communism* in ancient hunting and gathering societies, on *slavery* in ancient Rome, on *feudal servitude* in medieval England, and on *independent* peasantry and artisanry in a number of societies.[3] Later, the Western European and North American nations signify the *capitalist* mode of production. We shall see that modes of production are certainly not the only factors that determine laws and customs, but they are among the more important ones.

At this point, a brief synopsis of terms will be sufficient, since the history of socioeconomic formations is not our main focus. The phrase *mode of production* is the general method of obtaining and distributing the means of life, such as food, clothing, shelter, tools, and factories, that are necessary for people and the development of society.

One side of the mode of production consists of the *productive forces,* such as ploughs, tools, farms, workshops, factories, and the skills, energies, and division of labor among people who work. These forces reflect the relationship of people to the objects and forces of nature that must be utilized to create the material necessities of life. Some of these productive forces, such as ploughs, land, tools and factories, are also called *means of production* because they are the means by which workers produce what people need.

Another side of the mode of production, the *relations of production,* refers to certain interrelationships among people themselves while they are involved in producing and distributing things. In antagonistic socioeconomic formations, these relations of production are social class relationships. Some, but not all, of these class relationships are supported by private property laws that state the basis on which the means of production are owned.

Finally, the mode of production also refers to economic and political processes that are called "objective laws of social development." These laws govern the development of the relations and forces of production and vary greatly from one type of socioeconomic formation to another. For instance, certain laws affect the ways in which joint-family relations in a hunting and gathering society are organized to cope with seasonal changes in food supplies. Others force capitalist firms to exploit colonial labor abroad in order to offset a falling rate of profit at home.[4]

The analysis that follows refers to changing modes of production. First, we show some of the interesting connections between the slowly evolving rape laws and the transformations in modes of production and social institutions, such as the family, church, and state, which secure these modes. The legal changes occur because the fundamental laws of a society safeguard both its dominant mode of production and the social relations based on that mode. When the dominant mode of production changes, so do the laws.

Second, we refer to private property. The connections between the rape law and the basic structure of a society seem to be simple and taken for granted when people like Brownmiller speak about rape law and private property. However, if we are to understand these connections, we must know about the forces and relations of production that underlie a specific form of private property. Unfortunately, the plain phrase "private property" as used by Brownmiller and others does not by itself say anything about these underlying relationships.[5] For example, private property relations exist under the simple commodity production of small farmers and artisans whose farms and workshops may belong to them; nevertheless, these property owners earn their living by their own sweat. Such "self-earned" property relations (of small farmers and artisans) exist in slave, feudal, and capitalist societies, but they do not characterize the dominant mode of production. In each of these societies, the *dominant* mode of production is based on the exploitation of entire social classes and therefore involves quite different "private property" relationships. Since property relations that support a dominant mode of production often affect society as a whole, the term private property" cannot be meaningfully connected with the laws that prohibit rape unless we are familiar with how specific modes of production in a society are articulated with one another.[6]

Furthermore, even when men control women to ensure their property, this control may be legally instituted to support interests that transcend sexual distinctions. For thousands of years, for instance, the control over wives and daughters by men of property ensured the hereditary continuity of the families that owned and controlled the strategic resources of society. Such control reflected property relations based on specific types of class relationships and particular modes of production but not the interests of all men as individuals.

Finally, the control over women has functioned quite differently from the control of property. Control over women might be more fruitfully compared with social control over murder or socially destructive activities. The loss of women means losing the source of life-giving activities. Anthropology shows that all societies are concerned with reproduction of the human producers who ensure the continuity of both family and tribal relationships. Women extend the lives of kinfolk and produce children whose labor in later years will provide security for the elders; and women's activities toward these ends are prescribed by custom whether or not family life is governed by patriarchal authority.

The important issue is whether women, as responsible members of family and tribe, also exercise control of their reproductive activities as well as other activities that affect the welfare of their society. In egalitarian societies women have such control; but, as these societies are transformed by material conditions and internal stratification, lineages actively compete with each other over who will have the children and other tribal resources. (High-status women as well as high-placed men energetically engage in this competition.) As the status distinctions between lineages develop into class distinctions, the control of women's reproductive activities (and women in general) becomes organized around standards established by high-placed males, even though women comprise the majority of the population.[7]

The control of women and matrimonial policies often generate social interrelationships associated with the circulation of economic values within and between communities. For example, arrangements for marriage are frequently accompanied by exchanges of items of value through complex forms of reciprocity, gift-giving, dowry, and the simple exchange of goods and wealth. But it is important to note that these values are qualitatively *different* from "property values," which, in our society, are represented by "impersonal" systems of commodity prices that equate the value of "merchandise" or "capital" in commodity markets (Meillassoux, 1980: 196). Also, in our society, legal prescriptions for childbearing and socialization of children are quite different from those directly pertaining to property values. Consequently, although personal control and ownership of property are frequently equated, the application of this simple equation to the relationships between men and women is open to serious question.

Rape Laws Under Roman Slavery and English Feudalism

With these observations in mind, we can now turn to the development of early rape laws. A history of rape law that is directly relevant to modern Western codes begins with the class society of ancient Rome, where both law and private property relations were highly developed. Direct ties between law, property, and rape are to be found in the Roman law of *raptus* (Brundage, 1978: 63). *Raptus* was a form of violent theft that could apply to both property and persons. Because it referred to abduction and not necessarily to rape, it was not a sexual crime by definition. If a woman was abducted violently and sexually molested, the crime was merely defined as theft of a woman without the consent of those who had legal power over her. Legally, the harm was committed against her father, guardian, or husband.

But this Roman conception of rape, as a property theft rather than a sexual violation, is not a historical surprise. The Roman law concerning rape was organized around the concept of people as property because the structure of this slave society directly reflected such property relationships. Many women in Rome suffered the same fate as Greek women; they had become possessions of propertied men to ensure the production of wealth or the hereditary continuity of a ruling class (Engels, 1975). Furthermore, and most important, this change in women's status corresponded with the Roman society's dominant mode of production. Classical Rome was not simply the most highly developed system of commodity exchange in antiquity. Its mode of production was based on the labor and sale of human commodities — *slaves*.[8] Great numbers of men as well as women were denied autonomy or rights over their own bodies; often if slaves even ate of their free will, they were punished. They were merely property.

In Europe, at least, the next mode of production, feudalism, was primarily organized around caste-based agricultural societies. The rights to the means of production, chiefly land, were shared by nobility, church, and peasantry, although the agricultural surplus was taken by the ruling classes reportedly in exchange for military protection. This type of social organization pivoted on various forms of servitude and personal dependence of the peasants on their landlords, the noblemen. However, although nobility and serfs represented the main social classes, clergy, artisans, other commoners, and even slaves were incorporated into a feudal hierarchy that had elaborate distinctions in social rank.

As feudal societies evolved, the changing sex laws were a barometer of the changing status of women. Feudal Anglo-Saxon laws concerning rape, gradual and slow as they were in their evolution, typify the changes. The earliest feudal laws were written in the seventh century, during the reign of King Aethelbert in Kent (Attenborough, 1963).[9] Part of Aethelbert's law paralleled the Roman law of *raptus* which made abduction illegal. Like its Roman predecessor, Aethelbert's law had no concept pertaining directly to the crime of rape or sexual assault. A Kentish shilling was worth a Roman ounce of silver, and, according to the law, compensation of 50 shillings was to be paid "to her owner [guardian]" if a man "carrie[d] off a maiden" (1963: 15; all bracketed additions are Attenborough's).

By the ninth century, in the reign of Alfred the Great of Wessex, a variety of terms for sexual assault finally made an appearance. However, the law was still murky; sometimes no distinction was made between adultery and rape. The *idea* of attempted rape was introduced in the following section of the law: "If [anyone] throws [a young women belonging to the commons] down but does not lie with her, he shall pay [her] 10 shillings compensation." In the next section rape became more explicit saying: "If he lies with her he shall pay [her] 60 shillings compensation" (1963: 63).[10] But notice a markedly significant change here: the payment of compensation to the offended woman.

Since the social ranks mentioned a moment ago (nobility, serfs, commoners) included women, there were also status distinctions specified in the feudal laws of rape. Rape victims were by no means considered fully autonomous persons, but all of them were not lumped together as chattel either. Instead they were classified by their position in the feudal class structure or by their relations as wards, servants, or property of men who were likewise identified by their feudal rankings. In this way, a freeborn woman would belong to the commons while a ward of the king would have higher rank.

Compensation for an act of violence was differentiated by the rank of the victim. King Alfred's law stated, "If anyone seizes by the breast a young woman belonging to the commons, he shall pay her 5 shillings compensation." The compensation was small because the woman was of the lower class. But what if the breast belonged to a higher-class woman? According to these laws, if a "woman of higher birth" was "outraged" then "the compensation to be paid shall increase according to the wergeld." The wergeld stood for the value of a particular person's *life,* and it specified the amount of compensation paid by the family of a killer to the family of the person slain. Payment was made to atone for the killing and to avoid a blood feud.

Even the position of a nun was recognized by the law governing sexual assault. In the ninth century, the "lustful seizure" of a nun in Wessex required compensation twice the sum fixed in the case of a woman belonging to the laity.

The effects of feudal ranks on law can be seen if we notice the differences in punishments for rape. King Alfred's law stipulated that if a rape victim was a female belonging to the king, the punishment was greater than if she belonged to a commoner. If the rapist was a slave, his punishment was worse than that of a freeman. "If anyone rapes the slave of a commoner," the law stated, "he shall pay 5 shillings to the commoner and a fine of 60 shillings [to the King.] If a slave rapes a slave, castration shall be required as compensation."

Thus, each victim's position in feudal society was roughly equated with a monetary value. Although the specific laws varied, this general principle also applied under Aethelbert in the seventh century. Remember, rape was not stated in the law, but if a man had intercourse with a king's maiden, he was required to pay 50 shillings. The same man would pay half as much if the woman was a grinding slave. "Lying" with a nobleman's serving maid cost 12 shillings; but the amount was halved to 6, if the woman was a commoner's serving maid.

Just how serious rape and other sex crimes were considered during the seventh and the ninth centuries is not at all certain. We have no way of knowing exactly what these fines meant — 6 shillings' compensation for lying with a commoner's serving maid or 50 shillings for having sex with a king's maiden, under Aethelbert — so let us compare them with the punishments for certain crimes against men that would seem to have been quite serious. When the punishments for sex crimes are compared with punishments for crimes against men during the same reign, an educated guess becomes possible.

Under Aethelbert, anyone engaged in knife- or swordplay who pierced right through another man's penis paid 6 shillings. Causing a man to lose a foot or an eye, and thereby endangering his ability to earn a livelihood, cost the offender 50 shillings. Therefore, penetrating a commoner's serving maid's vagina was just as costly as piercing a man's penis. But sleeping with a king's maiden could have been as costly as the price of some men's lives.

All of these crimes, then, appeared to have been serious enough on all levels of society. As we have seen, sex crimes were also quite serious for the lowest caste. Even if a slave was raped by another slave under Alfred's law, the punishment was castration.

Communal Custom Versus
Law and the State

Although Anglo-Saxon law was dominated by the feudal system of social estates, it was affected by some of the traditional ways of rectifying wrongs that were preserved by still-existent family-kinship groups. Furthermore, some interventions by feudal kings in the sixth century were a way of supplementing (not replacing) customary modes of settling grievances among the kinship groups (Goebel, 1976: xi).[11] Consequently, the practice of compensating victims (and kin) and paying a fine to the king illustrates the coexistence of custom and law.

By contrast, if we turn the historical clock further back, we see that in some instances (such as in Athelbert's law paralleling *raptus*) the law broke with communal custom regarding the status of women. Some of the family-kinship groups had modes of production based on primitive communism. Such societies never conceived of sexual molestation in terms of private property infringement because women's status in these societies was that of kin, not property.

In kinship groups, as we shall see, certain transgressions were considered social harms rather than simply individual harms, and the taboo against these forms of conduct worked accordingly. For example, a rape victim's relatives and her entire joint-family group, in addition to the woman, were harmed by her rape. If violations of sexual taboos took place, they offended the entire group and, as determined by custom, were dealt with by the two extended families involved — the victim's and the rapist's. To rectify the harm, the punishment was extraction of some form of compensation, paid by the family of the wrongdoer to the victim and her family.[12]

Another unique factor shaping the law of rape in early English society was related to the developing power of the feudal state. Often, as indicated, a fine was levied in addition to the compensation. This was new. King Alfred's law, as we have seen, fined a man 60 shillings for raping the slave of a commoner while the compensation to the commoner was only 5 shillings. The slave-owning commoner was compensated because his human property was assaulted; but what was the purpose of the fine? Further, why was the fine so large—twelve times as high as the commoner's compensation?

Initially fines served as payment for the king's intervention and not as a penalty for the offense. However, in some cases, large fines were administered because government officials used the criminal law to enrich themselves and increase their political influence. Julius Goebel (1976: 132) provides an example in his work on the relations between English legal history and continental, particularly Frankish, law. By the tenth century, the objective of feudal criminal prosecution, in general, was no longer peace and order, for which it stood before the invasion and destruction of the West Frankish Kingdom. With the feudalization of government, criminal law enforcement was administered arbitrarily by selfish feudatory courtkeepers whose main interests were filling their private coffers and enhancing their personal power.

Still another reason for a large fine lies in the transition from one mode of production to another and the cost of expanding the state. The money for fines increased the King's treasury and was used to strengthen his power to extend feudalism — an exploitative mode of production — while at the same time further undermining the already deteriorating communal kin relations.

Another opportunistic use of rape law to obtain state resources is illustrated by Stanley Diamond (1971), whose study of the Kingdom of Dahomey finds that rape is extremely rare in Dahomey's traditional joint-family groups. However, despite the rarity of rape and the effectiveness of traditional controls, Diamond notes, the king of Dahomey invented rape as a civil crime punishable by the state. After making the law, the king ordered women under his control to go to the local villages and seduce men into having intercourse. The entrapped men were subjected to summary trials under the new rape law and punished with conscription into the army.

Although traditional scholars claim that law is invented to preserve order and tranquility in society, the rape law in Dahomey was not needed to preserve order among the people. "Such instances as this," Diamond (1971: 41) observes, "only sharpen the point that in early states crimes seem to have been invented in the service and profit of the state, not the protection of persons, not the *healing* of the breach" between families. In surveying anthropological literature, Diamond finds further examples of the invention of laws to serve the state rather than the population. Obviously, then, laws can define certain acts as crimes, although these acts may not cause genuine personal or public harm.

Diamond (1971: 37) uses these crimes to generalize about the fascinating effect of a changing social structure on law in societies like Dahomey: Laws "arise in opposition to the customary order of the antecedent kin or kin-equivalent groups; [these laws] represent a new set of social goals pursued by a new and unanticipated power in society."

Thus, the Dahomean rape law reflected neither the mere whim of a capricious sovereign nor a social problem. It was devised during a transition between the declining political control by kinship groups and the rising power of a social class headed by king and state. The goal of the king was to undermine the customary order of the kindred organization and to consolidate and extend the territorial boundaries of his class society by military force.[13] Although the social conditions were different, one can see certain parallels between the Dahomey rape law and King Alfred's rape law, both of which bridged the kinship and feudal orders.

Precapitalism and Rape Law

As class societies evolved, rape laws underwent changes that heralded the modern rape law in two ways: They explicitly defined rape as a crime against the person rather than against property, and they based this crime on the forcible denial of the victim's will.

In this process, according to James A. Brundage, a historian, ecclesiastic lawmakers as well as secular legislators were involved in gradually changing legal conceptions. The medieval Catholic Church, for instance, had its own juridical system which tried rapists and punished them.[14] Moreover, as early as the twelfth century, the ecclessiastic lawmakers were among the first to call for the recognition of the victim as an independent person without reference to social rank or to any guardian, owner, or employer.

In the twelfth century, in a revision of the ancient laws of Rome, rape as a crime against the person also became explicitly separated from property crimes. This change occurred when a set of revised laws was compiled, in a collection of canon law (known as the Decretum) by Gratian, a Benedictine monk of Bologna. Gratian's legal consultants, in advising him to distinguish rape as a violent crime against the person, pointed out that *raptus,* according to the ancient law, referred to both property and persons. It was suggested that *raptus* be used solely when referring to crimes against persons and that *rapina* could apply to crimes against property. Gradually during the Middle Ages, "raptus," then "rape," became a crime against the person and was defined partly in terms of its modern elements. To be defined as a rape, in the revised medieval canon law, an assault had to involve abduction, coitus, violence, and lack of *free consent* on the part of the woman. Writing about these trends in rape law from the end of the medieval period, Brundage (1978: 75) suggests that as the law evolved, it tended to legitimate a greater personal autonomy for women in late medieval society.

The new definitions of rape may have reflected the larger changes in legal ideas that focused on the individual as a bearer of rights without regard to social positions. Eventually, the *written* law, for instance, no longer imposed varying punishments when victims came from different social ranks. (On the other hand, it is well known that, in practice, some such distinctions are still made.)

Such ideas are taken for granted today when people speak about individual rights and responsibilities, but they required centuries of precapitalist legal developments to become firmly incorporated in the criminal codes. From the twelfth to the fourteenth centuries, feudalism remained dominant; however, in the flourishing mercantile centers (for example, in Italy prior to the Renaissance), individuals increasingly appeared as bearers of rights to salable things called commodities. These commodity relationships eventually spread throughout the world and influenced laws of contract and criminal responsibility that laid the basis for modern law.

Notes

1. For the theoretical models underlying Brownmiller's work, see Schwendinger and Schwendinger (1976: 79-85). Brownmiller (1975: 16-17) proposes that women have always needed to turn to a man for protection of themselves and their children. Consequently, a woman's fear of rape was especially important. In return for male protection, women sacrificed their autonomy and ownership of their bodies. Furthermore, "Once the male took title to a specific female body . . . he had to assume the burden of fighting off all other potential attackers, or scare them off by the retaliatory threat of raping their women." Rape laws were enlisted for the protection of male property rights; therefore, when the laws finally developed, their focus was on property, not persons.

2. This chapter does not pretend to present a complete history of rape law. Earlier examples of rape laws can be found in the Babylonian and Mosaic laws. For examples, see Smith (1974) and Brownmiller (1975: 18-19).

3. For the concept of mode of production, see Marx (1959). Importantly, this chapter is primarily concerned with clarifying the issue about rape law and private property, and we have opted for a simple classification and treatment of the category of modes of production to keep the main goal clearly in sight. We do not pretend to deal with the research and arguments about gender and modes of production which have modified the concept of mode of production and which have appeared in recent years. See, for example, Kohl and Wright (1977) on Neolithic stateless cities, and Rapp (1977) on the theory of the relationships among gender, class, and state. Other references are cited in the coming chapters.

4. For a discussion of the relation between these laws and the extended concept of mode of production, see Wolpe (1980: 1-44).

5. Brownmiller's notion of property simply intimates that women were things, like spears and flint axes, that were owned by individual men.

6. Wolpe (1980: 7) defines the concept of articulation as "the reproduction of the capitalist economy on the one hand and the reproduction of productive units organized according to pre-capitalist relations and forces of production on the other."

7. We are grateful to Eleanor Leacock for pointing out these relationships.

8. Weidmann (1981: 6) notes: "Slavery was universal in Greece and Rome, even if its role cannot be quantified."

9. It was not until the end of the thirteenth century that rape was first elevated to the position of a true felony in England. Prior to the Statute of Westminster of 1285, this crime was an illegal attack on a person punishable by castration. However, as Hanawalt (1979: 104) notes, "In practice, few rape cases were tried and those that were, ended in acquittal or some concord with the victim such as a fine or marriage." According to the new law, in addition to an appeal made by the victim herself (where she bore the burden of proof), a rape indictment could be initiated by presentment jurors, thus lessening the burden on the victim. Furthermore, the penalty for rape was the same as for other felonies. On the other hand, the social position of the woman was considered before the indictment was made. An indictment was more likely if a victim was young, a virgin, or of noble or high birth than if she were of low status or "questionable" character.

10. The remaining quotations of King Alfred's laws are cited in Attenborough (1963: 63-93).

11. For example, kingly intervention first occurred when the appearance of unknown malefactors, in an urbanized context, made customary ("private") redress ineffective.

12. Again, though feudal law secured the dominant (feudal) mode of production, it recognized other modes. Consequently, these laws may have demanded mutilation (such as castration) or payments of fines to the state; but they also required compensation for the victim and her relatives, as required under traditional authority. Further examples of the coexistence of such customary and legal punishments, which spanned traditional and feudal practice, were blood feuding and other acts of revenge involving whole clans. Blood feuds, prefeudal in origin, were recognized by feudal courts. For further information, see Bloch (1966: 126-127).

13. This political process as it occurred in antiquity is analyzed by Engels (1975: 172-173), who points out: "The first attempt at forming a state consists in breaking up the gentes by dividing their members into those with privileges and those with none, and by further separating the latter into two productive classes and thus setting them one against the other." From Engels's perspective, the new powers mentioned by Diamond extend beyond civil bureaucrats and the king's family estate. They are embodied in the class of wealthy persons who have seized political power for themselves and their families. Since the state is essential to the consolidation of class societies, most of these families control state power directly rather than operate through intermediaries.

14. The civil courts, which also claimed jurisdiction over rape cases, often followed Roman law. Whereas ecclesiastical courts imposed harsh penalties, they were somewhat more humane in that they avoided sentences of death or mutilation. The civil courts frequently imposed death sentences, confiscation of property, or bodily mutilation such as castration.

CHAPTER 7

CAPITALISM, LAW, AND WOMEN'S RIGHTS IN THE NEW WORLD

Modern capitalism, with its now familiar mode of production, expressed as wage labor and capital and structured by giant industries and multinational corporations, did not emerge full-blown or pure. Especially in its early, mercantile stages, capitalism was supported by different kinds of productive relationships. Articulated with the capitalist mode of production were precapitalist units of production in the feudal principalities of India and the slave plantations of North America. Therefore, besides wage labor, the primitive accumulation of capital in the United States depended on the world wide exploitation of indentured labor, convict labor, peasant labor, and slave labor.

Moreover, slavery in the new world was not a mere survival of the past. It was largely driven by the growth of a world capitalist system. It was introduced and consolidated by mercantile capitalists and landowners who could not maintain agrarian production for international markets without absolute control over a major part of the labor force. "With the limited population of Europe in the sixteenth century," Eric Williams (1944: 67) writes, "the free laborers necessary to cultivate the stable crops of sugar, tobacco and cotton in the New World could not have been supplied in quantities adequate to permit large-scale production." The massive enslavement of African people eventually provided the labor force required for this scale of commodity production.

Prior to the great expansion of the African slave trade, European immigrants were also being encouraged to work on the plantations. However, capitalists found that most immigrants preferred to work for themselves instead of wages. Immigrants dispersed rapidly into the vast wilderness, established their own farms, and founded communities composed chiefly of smallholders. Left without enough recruits for the all-important surplus labor force (those who perform the "dirty work" of the capitalist epoch, the drudgery of domestic service, field labor, and unskilled factory work), capitalists turned to indentured labor and forced labor to make up the difference.

Consequently, seventeenth- and eighteenth-century European capitalists, who profited from large-scale production of agrarian commodities in the New World, relied for almost a century on the massive exportation of indentured servants, felons, people in debt, religious heretics, and men, women, and children who were kidnapped by the thousands in cities like London and Bristol. The profits and experience of the white indentured servant trade proved especially valuable: "Bristol, the center of the [indentured] servant trade, became one of the centers of the slave trade. Capital accumulated from one financed the other. White servitude was the historic base upon which Negro slavery was constructed. The felon-drivers in the plantations became without effort slave-drivers," says Williams (1944: 19).

An already developed system for supplying forced labor to the plantation economy reached out to millions in Africa, whose enslavement was even more profitable than indentured service. The money that bought a white man's labor for ten years purchased a slave for life.

As the primitive accumulation of capital proceeded on the basis of African slavery, racist customs and ideology exploded rapidly to justify and consolidate the slave system in the South; and the growing numbers of blacks in the North were being absorbed as slaves or as free but unskilled laborers.

Rape, Racism and American Slavery

These economic and racist developments strongly affected the legal codes. From the seventeenth through the nineteenth centuries, state legislatures, courts, and everyday citizens grappled with the questions: Are blacks people or are they property like horses and land? If they are people, are they a species apart from whites, requiring separate and different treatment in law? Such questions and the answers provided by racist legislators still support racism today.

The racial discrimination legislated and adjudicated in the North American colonies was sometimes influenced by religious and moral beliefs; nevertheless, economic interests dominated criminal procedures regarding slaves as well as other legal procedures (Higginbotham, 1978: 11). A. Leon Higginbotham, Jr., a black jurist, writes about these concerns in 6 states. Regarding Pennsylvania, for example, he says: "Previous attempts to punish slaves had led to frequent petitions by masters for the commutations of their slaves' sentences in recognition of the masters' economic investment in these slaves" (1978: 281).

Furthermore, economic concerns led to the establishment of special courts to deal with serious crimes, such as rape, by blacks, and special sanctions were imposed against the judges and freeholders who comprised these courts when they did not expedite a speedy trial. During the slave's incarceration, work time was lost and therefore imprisonment, before and after trial, cost the slave owner money. Consequently, as early as 1725, when a slave was found guilty of a capital crime, the court immediately assessed the slave's value and paid that sum to the owner for loss of property. Such reimbursment, rather than commutation or reduction of a slave's punishment, also applied in Virginia, South Carolina, and Georgia.

Capital punishment was made part of the rape law during this period. It did not exist in the American colonies before the expansion of slavery. Allison Edwards (1976: 21), notes that "death was first made a penalty for the crime of rape as part of the Southern slave codes before the Civil War. The Mississippi slave code had a mandatory death penalty for a slave found guilty of raping a white woman." While slave masters and other white men raped black women freely, death was the punishment for a black man convicted of raping a white woman. But capital punishment was not limited to the South.

In Pennsylvania's 1700 law on the trial of Negroes, various special crimes and punishments were established for blacks (Edwards, 1976: 282). For example, in order to satisfy both the victim's and the owner's interests, rather than imprisonment, attempted rape against a white woman or maiden was punishable by castration for all blacks — both "free" and enslaved. In 1706, this was amended, and blacks convicted of attempted rape were given thirty-nine lashes, branded on the forehead, and deported from the province. For all blacks, completed rape of a white woman or maid, murder, buggery, and burglary were punishable by death. Except for murder, these were not capital crimes for whites until eighteen years later. Control of blacks was a greater legal priority.

Not surprisingly, the rape law, where there was slave labor, was restricted in scope. If the victim of rape or attempted rape was a black woman, the law was silent, whether the attacker was black or white (Higginbotham, 1978: 282). Winthrop Jordan (1968: 160), author of *White Over Black: American Attitudes Toward the Negro, 1550-1812*, quotes a Maryland lawyer who lived in a slave state. The lawyer stated: "Slaves are bound by our criminal laws generally, yet we do not consider them as objects of such laws as relate to the commerce between the sexes. A slave *has never maintained* an action against the violator of his [sic] bed" (our emphasis).

Other authors note that the law claimed in principle to protect women yet did not actually include slave women.[1] Ulrich Phillips writes: "Although the wilful killing of slaves was generally held to be murder, the violation of their women was without criminal penalty."[2] Legally, the rape of another man's slave was a "trespass" on his property, whereas the rape of a slave by another slave had no official status — it merely produced additional exploitable children. (If any punishment occurred, it was meted out by the master of the accused.) Slave owners, by themselves, could do as they would with their property; and, as the records of the South show, raping slave women was common practice among owners, overseers, neighbors, and other men (Phillips, 1929: 273-274, 500).[3]

Although these rapes themselves were not matters of record, the slave retaliation, and therefore the rape as well, was sometimes recorded. James H. Johnston (1970: 306-307), author of *Race Relations in Virginia and Miscegenation in the South, 1776-1860,* cites a number of murder trials involving black men and black women killing masters and overseers for sexually assaulting slave women. In one instance, in 1859, a male Negro slave was tried for the murder of a white man. During the trial the slave's lawyer attempted to introduce the testimony of a slave woman, named Charlotte, who was the wife of the prisoner. The lawyer proposed to prove with this testimony that in the morning of the day on which the killing took place, Coleman, the overseer, had raped her. When her slave husband was told about the rape, he killed the overseer. However, since slaves had no access to criminal courts for redressing injuries and since they could not give evidence against whites, objections were raised and sustained against Charlotte's giving testimony in defense of her husband.

The end of slavery did not mark an end of the use of capital punishment for blacks who raped white women. It was maintained after slavery was abolished. The legal conditions established by the Ku Klux Klan and the southern ruling class encouraged capital convictions of black men for rape; moreover, based on flimsy evidence, black men were frequently hanged or burned alive by white supremacist lynch mobs taking the law into their own hands. On the other hand, whites who were in favor of racial equality were also terrorized and lynched. According to Eugene Genovese (1974), although lynching was a mark of the pre-Civil War South, white "nigger lovers" were more often its victims before the war than blacks.

Nor has the enlightened capitalism of the twentieth century meant an enlightened penal system. Capital punishment still epitomizes racist justice. Marvin Wolfgang and Eric Riedel

(1975: 667), sociologists, analyzed the convictions for rape in Georgia from 1945 to 1965. They conclude, "Our current analysis suggests that racial combinations of defendant and victim form the most important discriminating variable: black defendants who rape white victims are most likely to receive the death penalty."[4]

Racism and the rape laws are unquestionably inseparable. Furthermore, the rape laws of a repressive mode of production are likely to be one strand in a whole web of repressive legislation. Blacks, whether freed or enslaved, were forbidden by law to have interracial sex in southern states from the earliest colonial days. To protect the white race from "racial pollution," black men, black women, and white women were punished for consensual, interracial sex; but white men usually had little fear of being punished so long as they refrained from marrying black women. As recently as 1968, miscegenation laws in Virginia still paid a bounty to anyone reporting a black and white marriage.

Colonialism and Rape Law

More examples of rape laws, where the law serves purposes of racism rather than deterring and punishing rapists, are to be found in the history of modern colonialism. One illustration is the Papuan 1926 White Women's Protection Ordinance. Papua, previously British New Guinea, became an Australian colony in 1905.

Concentrated in the town of Port Moresby, the "Europeans," as the whites were called, regarded the Papuans as black, naked, dirty, betel-chewing people who did not have the decency to use lavatories. They believed that criminal codes could be employed to civilize the natives even though the latter were stereotyped as inferior, childlike, and given to lust and immorality. These codes, however, actually supported no purpose other than repression of the Papuans, who were exploited by the Europeans as extremely low-paid wage laborers and servants.

Gill Boehringer and Donna Giles, Australian legal scholars, write about the imperial domination of the Papuans. This colony was based on a plantation economy with a tiny urban sector to service and administer it. The administrators were white and the agricultural labor force was composed of indigenous laborers "coerced to work through a system of legal constraints, e. g., the Head Tax and a Labor Contract System with penal sanctions effectively applying only to the laborer," according to Boehringer and Giles (1977: 59). Native workers were hired to work under near-slave conditions. Also, under the Labor Contract System, wages, which were mainly in kind, were sufficient only to support individual workers. The families of the workers had to fend for themselves.

Racist policies were gradually introduced to repress and control the native population. In 1907, gambling by natives was forbidden, and in 1908 and 1925 curfews were passed in Port Moresby and in the native villages. The Papuans were further prohibited from laughing at, threatening, or insulting a European. They had to use separate entrances, exits, and seating areas in places of public entertainment, and they were also served in separate sections when they shopped in the town stores.

Thus, the White Women's Protection Ordinance, passed in 1926, followed a series of racist policies introduced by the Europeans. However, the legislation itself was precipitated by a *moral panic* engineered by a law-and-order faction of whites that wanted Sir Hubert Murray, the Lieutenant Governor, to be removed from office because they felt his policies toward the natives were not repressive enough.[5] To embarrass Murray, the faction began to publicize "a series of [native] crimes and insults" against the white population in the virulently anti-Murray newspaper. They petitioned the governor to take action and accused him of refusing to protect white women (Inglis, 1975: 62).

To justify the ordinance, their petition to Murray reported three attacks against whites. In the first attack, a white woman was allegedly assaulted by a Papuan as she walked along a busy thoroughfare. (Her assailant was frightened off by a passerby.) Another situation involved a child and a 14-year-old native houseboy who "it was said" placed "his person" against her leg. The third case consisted of an assault on a white man, a case that had no bearing on the rape ordinance.

The clamor over the "black peril" escalated with two more attacks on white women. In one case, a merchant's wife was awakened at night by a man who was touching her, as she quaintly put it, "in the fork" (Inglis, 1975: 58). White women became frightened if a black man peeped at them or touched them. White men condemned peeping and touching as "infamy against white womanhood and an outrage against the prestige of the white race."

Eventually, to protect his position and authority among the white population, Murray knuckled under and issued the ordinance — a colonial version of rape law — imposing a death penalty for both rape and attempted rape of white women. After the ordinance was passed, additional policemen were hired and searches of native quarters without warrants were allowed. Finally, Murray agreed, in principle, to build a fence across the entire town to keep natives out of Port Moresby altogether unless they were shopping, working for whites, or charged by whites with a specific duty.

The central fact about the White Women's Protection Ordinance is that while black women, who were not protected by the ordinance, had been raped by white men, no white woman had been raped by a Papuan. The Lieutenant Governor, writing to the Prime Minister in Australia in 1930, four years after passage of the ordinance, said, "It is well to remember that there has never been a case of rape of a white woman in Papua" (Inglis, 1975: 117).

Rape Law, Property Rights, and Married Women

The change in a woman's status from single to married affects rape law, and this should also be placed in a specific historical context. Following the late feudal and pre-capitalist developments in rape law, Western societies, from the seventeenth century onward, consolidated the definition of rape as a crime against an individual woman but only so long as the rapist was not the husband.

This restriction on the married woman's rights bears special consideration because it reflected a larger code, established chiefly by the English common law, known as the doctrine of coverture, which maintained the husband's supreme authority in family life. Under this doctrine, patriarchal authority was safeguarded economically through chattel ownership codes: The corporal punishment provisions of the codes allowed husbands to enforce their authority through violence.

English common law adopted the feudal doctrine of coverture to secure the economic base for patriarchal authority. According to this doctrine, both money and landed property, *after marriage,* ranked in law as chattel interests over which the husband gained dominion. Upon marriage a woman turned over all her property to her husband. She lost her power to engage in contracts with either her husband or third parties. Interest and profits from the property she had owned were also transferred to her husband, and he could spend this money as he wished. Her children too were assigned legally to her husband, whose authority in these matters was supreme.

The ethical basis for the coverture doctrine traces back to patriarchal biblical injunctions about a husband and wife belonging to "one body," which in reality always resolved itself as the body of the husband. Nevertheless, the mere survival of biblical injunctions could not have been the sole reason the married woman's rights were restricted so sharply. Single women were also severely restricted by biblical injunctions; yet, they were not consistently discriminated against in the areas of contract and property, even though they were denied the rights to vote and serve on juries. Except for the period when the system of primogeniture prevailed, *propertied single women* enjoyed almost equal legal status with males in certain economic exchanges.[6] Under English common law, "If they were not under age, they could contract with other persons, sue and be sued, manage and control their lands and chattels, and appropriate for themselves earnings accruing from their property" (Kanowitz, 1971: 35-36).

The denial of married women's rights was grounded in a number of interrelated social conditions. During early capitalism most economic ventures were family enterprises, and therefore the legal restrictions on married women encouraged a consolidation of property that favored ever greater capital accumulation. Furthermore, by concentrating family wealth in male hands, the laws ensured the hereditary continuation of private property, in a manner that dated back to the origins of social classes, private property and sexual inequality.

Common law itself was produced largely by the rising class of bourgeois landowners and manufacturers. Because of the influence of this class on the law, similar legal standards were established for other social classes. Consequently, the legal restrictions on the wife's possession of her earnings — or her right to seek employment independent of her husband's will — were also applied to working-class families. The law required employed married women to transfer their earnings to their husbands.

This extension to the working class, however, was also favored by the economic and political forces that externalized the social costs for the reproduction of capital. These costs were shunted from business to the individual household. In Chapter 12 we describe how the household economy became organized chiefly around production for use, not exchange.[7] By restricting married women's productive activities to the family, women were engaged primarily in the massive production of simple use values. Such values were consumed by wage earners to reproduce themselves, to replenish their capacity to work for capital. However, even though housewives helped reproduce the labor force for capital, their labor was expended without monetary remuneration. The household labor of women — and married women in particular — provided services that cost capital relatively little and thereby supported higher rates of capital accumulation.[8]

Simultaneously, the prevailing ethos of commodity-producing societies downgraded the importance of the household worker. On one hand, that ethos strongly supported the granting of moral and juridical autonomy to commodity holders, to those who were in a position to earn money. All others — who seemed to be dependent for their economic existence on another person's earnings — were defined as personal dependents. Consequently, the married woman was regarded as a dependent despite her vital contributions to her husband's welfare. Even though he was equally dependent on her labor for his personal well-being, only the husband was regarded juridically as an autonomous person because of his status as a commodity holder, a seller of labor power or property.

The unprecedented establishment of this singular set of family relationships is masked today by political movements that eulogize the so-called traditional family and that ignore the fact that this family came into existence on a widespread basis only with the rise of capitalism. The creation of the "traditional family" required the coercive power of the church and state as well as the sexist restrictions of economic life.[9] In previous centuries, for example, whether they were employed or not, whether they turned over their wages or produced use values in the home, or even if they inherited property from their families, married women in the United States were forced by law to remain personally dependent on their husbands.

The Struggle for Legal Autonomy

However, during the second half of the nineteenth century, mature capitalist developments rapidly generalized commodity relationships throughout the United States. At the same time, structural conditions and contradictions that could undermine the common-law marriage precepts regarding property ownership were established.

These social and economic developments encouraged political processes which showed that the relations between a mode of production and legal institutions were much more complicated than has been suggested previously. Usually, for instance, the effects of a mode can be detected in the formulations of fundamental laws. Thus, in the United States, one finds laws defining economic rights that directly reflect the primacy of private property relationships because they are supported by the Constitution. But, these rights were expressed in law because of the efforts of political movements engaged in a protracted revolutionary struggle for national independence. Everywhere, in the struggle for individual rights, numerous political movements have intervened between changes in modes of production and modern legal systems.

Militant movements for sexual equality certainly played an important role in the dismantling of sexist restrictions on married women; moreover, these movements drew strength from the broad social outcry against slavery in the South and from worker's struggles for better working conditions in the North.

Leaders of the early women's movement woke to their lack of equality and the need to fight for their freedom when some of them submerged themselves in the abolitionist movement. The slave mode of production eventually became a living contradiction within the developing capitalist mode, and it was in the 1830s, during an upsurge against slavery, that early feminists, who were also abolitionists, learned to organize and tied their struggle to the antislavery movement. Attacked by the church for their public activism, feminists, Eleanor Flexner (1970: 47) notes, began to "answer their critics, linking the two issues of slavery and the position of women."

Furthermore, with the vast accumulations of capital by landowners, the women found some ready supporters among men in their struggles for economic and property rights. Although the rich had already established a legal right to protect their daughters' property through marriage contracts and trusts, many wealthy fathers were pleased at the prospect of a less expensive and cumbersome way of assuring that their daughters' inherited money and property would not be squandered by profligate husbands. Babcock, Freedman, Norton, and Ross (1975: 599), authors of *Sex Discrimination and the Law,* point out: "This motive for reform was widely held amongst the wealthy Dutch farmers of the Hudson valley."

Other forces, such as early socialist ideas about equal rights for women, came into play. In 1836, the same year that New York's revised property law for married women was introduced into the legislature, Ernestine Rose, a 26-year-old Polish socialist of the Robert Owen school, emigrated to the United States. She had successfully defended her own right to her deceased mother's estate against the claims of a spurned fiance when she was younger, and now, a strong supporter of women's rights, she embarked on a twelve-year campaign, soon supported by other feminists, in favor of the new property bill (Schneir, 1972: 125-27).

Yet another historical development, the influx of women into the paid labor force, encouraged women to organize against legal enforcement of sexual discrimination. With the employment of women in factories and offices (there were over four million employed women according to the 1890 census), women began to have self-earned incomes which under common law belonged to their husbands. The first married women's property law gave women the right to property they brought with them into marriage, but it required further struggle to achieve the later laws that gave a working woman the right to wages she earned.

Thus, the feudal doctrine of coverture was progressively whittled away. In the United States, a patchwork of married woman's property acts developed during the second half of the nineteenth century by all the states, beginning with New York, finally enabled married women to make contracts, sue and be sued without their husbands' consent, manage and control the property they brought to the marriage, engage in wage-earning employment without their husbands' permission, and keep the earnings gained by this employment.

Similar kinds of developments also dismantled the legal justifications for using corporal punishment to keep married women in their place. The state's direct enforcement of married women's subordination was buttressed by legal support for the customary use of corporal punishment. Old English common law, as previously mentioned, also justified the husband's use of corporal punishment to maintain his supremacy in family life. Cultural reinforcement of family violence is exemplified by a vintage American rhyme:

> A woman, a dog, and a walnut tree,
> The more you beat, the better they be.

However, toward the end of the nineteenth century, the right of husbands to chastize disobedient wives forcibly was progressively narrowed and then repudiated. At least as far as legal principles are concerned, American courts finally decided that "the moral sense of the community revolts at the idea that the husband may inflict personal chastisement upon his wife, even for the most outrageous conduct" (Eisenberg and Micklow, 1977: 146).

On the other hand, such decisions have not *completely* eliminated the legal supports for "wife beating," because the "unity doctrine," the biblical injunction about husband and wife being of one body, still has an independent affect on how domestic relations laws are written (regarding domicile restrictions on married women, for example) and on how they are interpreted (especially as they relate to assaults on wives [Eisenberg and Micklow, 1977: 45]).[10] Also, it must be kept in mind that, with the exception of women's suffrage, legal changes affecting married women's rights have been passed individually by the different states; consequently, the rights conferred on women have been much greater in some states than in others. The lingering legal inequities due to this variation are graphically seen in the recent state-by-state struggle for the enactment of laws similar to the Equal Rights Amendment (ERA). The passage of equal rights legislation within a number of states has eliminated some of the remaining laws that until passage had placed all household goods in the husband's hands. In non-ERA states such as Georgia, a couple's home belongs to the husband even if the wife paid for it; in several states like Louisiana, a wife can be sued for her husband's gambling debts; and in New Mexico, before the state ERA was adopted, a wife could not advertise for the sale of the family dishwasher without her husband's consent (Conway, 1979: 15). In many states a housewife still cannot obtain credit apart from her husband. The legal changes that remove such inequities have been uneven, and they have by no means guaranteed independence for women.

Nevertheless, when taken as a whole, legal changes over the last century sharply contradict any claim that the rape law or even the marriage law today is totally or predominantly organized around male property relationships.[11] The massive entrance of married women into the labor force (which is now establishing the ground for new fundamental changes in family relationships) also contradicts such claims. But women in the United States need not consider these recent changes or look back at their own history to remind themselves of the nature of women's status at an earlier stage of the struggle. The condition of Irish women today, even though the Irish Constitution promises equality to all, duplicates the status of their now luckier sisters a century ago.

Mary Kenny (1973: 7), a writer for *Agenor,* which is published in Brussels, says: "To begin with, the legal situation of Irishwomen must be one of the worst in Europe." Women do not sit on juries, and it is only since 1957 that a married woman in Ireland has been allowed to hold and dispose of property. Nevertheless, "she must have her husband's permission for almost every legal or contractual commitment: opening a charge account at the store; a bank account; a mortgage," says Kenny.

The law also safeguards patriarchal authority over the Irishwoman's reproductive capacity and her children. She must ask her husband's permission for most gynecological operations. "*The children are his;* he is their legal and moral guardian," Kenny adds. "She may not put her children on her passport or take them out of the country without his permission — a situation which does not obtain for him."

Divorces are prohibited. If she deserts her husband, she forfeits further access to the marital home or the children; yet this is not true for men. The wife is defined as legally dependent, and the law is predominantly guided by the feudal doctrine of coverture. Nevertheless, there is no doubt that, as economic and political conditions in Ireland change, movements for sexual equality will ultimately put an end to these restrictions.

We have pointed out that the historical development of rape laws has been influenced directly or indirectly by modes of production. Consequently, rape laws are also affected by property relationships since such relationships legally regulate particular kinds of production (such as commodity production) and certain relations of production (such as social class relations in capitalist societies).

But this chapter has also continued to argue that rape laws cannot be adequately understood by reducing the relationships between men and women to property relationships based simply on the possession of women by men. Certainly, while this restricted use of the term "property" may be somewhat meaningful when referring to legal and economic relationships in certain slave societies, it is not very useful and may even be misleading when dealing with the nature of kinship societies like those in Dahomey, newly emerging feudal distinctions in ninth-century England, colonial relationships in Papua, or personal dependency relations in the modern American home.

Americans who support legal reforms for greater equality for women should also recognize that, for the most part, our laws have broken decisively with the feudal doctrine of coverture. It would be an insult to the accomplishments of the women's rights advocates over the last century and a half to overlook this qualitative change. At the same time, legal developments are taking place in a *class* society. Under these conditions, women who become wage workers can, at best, only replace personal dependency relations in the family with a double burden and a dependence on exploitation by capital. Moreover, in this mode of production, labor market exploitation continues to be sustained by sexual, racial, and economic discrimination.

Finally, some of the legal gains made in recent decades can be reversed temporarily and are now, in the 1980s, being threatened by the massive conservative backlash lead by the so-called moral majority (of which they are neither). In the name of preserving life and the family, these defenders of the "traditional family" would even go so far as to rescind a woman's right to decide whether or not to terminate a pregnancy when she is raped. Consequently, the desire to combat violence against American women must still confront social inequities that shape the way laws are written and implemented. At the same time, women should take heart, because the historical changes in law that have been accelerating in this country point to one conclusion: Whatever the setbacks in the struggle for legal change, they will be only temporary. They will be overcome by militant movements which recognize that the historical time for the complete recognition of women's rights has finally arrived.

Notes

1. An 1851 Louisiana Supreme Court said, regarding the use of slave concubines, "The slave is undoubtedly subject to the power of his master; but that means a lawful power, such as is consistent with good morals. The laws do not subject the female slave to an involuntary and illicit connexion with her master, but would protect her against that misfortune" (Catterall, 1932: 316). However, only naive persons can believe that courts controlled by slave owners ever protected slave women. Also, it can be argued that such judicial decisions came about only because of late developments in the history of southern slavery, such as the embargo on the slave trade and the rise of the abolitionist movement.

2. See, for example, Paxton (1833: 189-197).

3. We are aware that Fogel and Engerman's (1974) study contradicts our statements about how black women were treated in slavery. While pointing out that black women were not adequately protected by law, they insist that such conditions as Victorian morality and sentiments, the promotion of the black family in plantations for economic reasons, an aversion to interracial sex, and the need to maintain "an air of mystery and distinction" between the races inhibited the sexual exploitation of black women. Such assertions are not merely highly speculative, they are also chauvinistic and reactionary.

Furthermore, contrary to the authors' opinion, the factual support for these claims is in doubt and often devoid of historical context. Immanuel Wallerstein (1976) indicates that the slave owners' concern for developing black families (to reproduce new slaves) was especially apparent only toward the end of the slave period prior to the Civil War, when the blockade prevented the importation of slaves. In another argument, Fogel and Engerman (1974) assert that prostituting slaves was not lucrative to owners, because half of Nashville's prostitutes were totally illiterate and therefore capable of earning wages only by unskilled labor. This argument is absurd. Even the census data on mulattoes used by the authors to disprove sexual exploitation is suspect. Traditionally, census data are not reliable for oppressed racial groups especially regarding such personal matters as sexual relationships that identify paternity.

Finally, Fogel and Engerman's opinions apologize for sexism as well as slavery. The dual legal system whereby slaves' lives are controlled by plantation codes is excused because such a duality existed in medieval Europe. When granting sexual exploitation of black women, these authors minimize it, insisting that "sexual exploitation by white men was not limited to black women" nor limited to the South.

4. A newer study of homicide in Florida also shows racist justice. Here the *victim's* race is the key variable. It was found that there is little difference if the murderer is black or white, but men who kill white victims are more likely to receive a death penalty than those who kill black victims. Radelet (1981: 926) notes: "Racial differences in the processing of those indicted for nonprimary homicides in Florida appears to place a lower value on the lives of blacks than on the lives of whites."

5. For the dynamics of "moral panics," see Hall et al. (1978).

6. Primogeniture is the right of the eldest son to inherit his father's estate.

7. For a further discussion of this issue, see Schwendinger and Schwendinger (1980: 11-13).

8. According to Holstrom (1981: 194), "Domestic labor allows a higher rate of surplus value because this socially necessary labor is either free or very cheap."

9. George (1973) indicates that although there was some improvement initially, women's status declined in England as capitalism evolved from the sixteenth to the eighteenth century.

10. With regard to domicile restrictions, Kanowitz (1971: 47) notes: "Though exceptions have been carved out in recent years, the general rule persists that a wife's domicile follows that of her husband." Domicile is important since many rights and privileges, such as the rights to vote, run for office, receive welfare assistance or qualify for tuition assistance in state-operated schools, are dependent on one's domicile. In addition, feminist literature (Eisenberg and Micklow, 1977: Russell, 1982: 305-308) is replete with examples of assaults on wives that were treated as domestic matters or social problems but not as crimes by the criminal justice system. Also, see Kanowitz (1971: 76) regarding the rule, based on the unity doctrine, that neither husband nor wife can bring a civil suit against the other for willful personal injury caused by the other. Since husbands more often assault or batter wives, a greater number of wives than husbands are deprived of redress for injuries inflicted by their spouses.

11. Even the exemption of rape by husbands has been stricken down in Sweden, Denmark, South Australia, the USSR, Poland, and some individual American states. Furthermore, in a study of the Swedish situation, Geis (1978: 302) found that after more than twelve years of the revised law, the cases arising as a result have been very small.

PART III

AN EXPLANATION OF RAPE

CHAPTER 8

SEXISM IS NOT UNIVERSAL

The history of rape still remains to be written. Will that history expose man as a born criminal? Does he come into this world with a primordial obsession for power that cannot be satisfied unless he rapes women into submission? Are all preexisting societies characterized by a battle of the sexes because of this male desire for power? We have seen these claims made by Susan Brownmiller, who imagines sexual assault in virtually all societies, including the prehistoric ones.

Brownmiller's writings make an additional point, which we have not emphasized previously: "From prehistoric times to the present, I believe, rape . . . is nothing more or less than a conscious process of intimidation by which *all men keep all* women in a state of fear." Rape became "man's *basic weapon* of force against women, the principal agent of his will and her fear"(1975: 14-15). Sexual violence, in this now popular view, was an astoundingly effective tool for achieving male *control* over women.

Three decisive objections can be made against Brownmiller's conception of these social control relationships. First, while rape has been used consciously to support male supremacy in some societies and under certain political conditions, it is, in fact, censured in most societies. Therefore, to claim it as a universal form of social control defies all reason. It is simply impossible to have one-half of all humankind control the other half by rape when it is outlawed in most societies.

Rape is not only a legal crime in all modern European and American countries, but it is also banned overwhelmingly in the precapitalist societies for which there are research data available. Julia Brown (1952: 146), an anthropologist, conducted a comprehensive study by examining the sexual mores and taboos in 110 societies, 84 of which had documented information regarding rape. Brown writes: "Incest, abduction and rape are the forms of behavior most frequently tabooed and most severely punished." Rape was proscribed for married women in 99 percent and for unmarried women in 95 percent of the societies in the sample she studied.

Moreover, in these societies the rapist's own family might even move against him to rectify his wrong. Stanley Diamond (1971: 41), an authority on custom and law, examined punishments for rape in Dahomey. He notes that "if rape had, in fact, occurred in the joint-family villages — and such an occurrence would have been rare . . . — the wrong could have been dealt with by composition (the ritualized giving of goods to the injured party), ritual purification, ridicule, and perhaps, for repeated transgression, banishment; the customary machinery would have gone into effect automatically, probably on the initiative of the family of the aggressor."

Second, custom and law aside, the socioeconomic organization of some groups encourages nonexploitative sexual relations. Compared with fictionalized claims about the universality of rape and male violence, anthropological research by Margaret Mead and others could not be more contradictory in its findings. Besides Diamond's illustration, which shows the rarity of rape in Dahomey, an examination of the Arapesh also points up these contradictions.

Societies like that of the Arapesh have economies based on hunting and gathering food or on horticulture and husbandry, which are pursued chiefly for collective use and not for commercial exchange. The Arapesh economy, for instance, depends on hunting game, gathering breadfruit, growing taro, banana, and tobacco plants, and raising pigs. The gardening, hunting, house building, and other activities are chiefly communal enterprises, and Arapesh trade is a form of informal gift exchange. Cooperation and sharing are strongly emphasized in work and ideology.

Such societies tend to be characterized by little or no sexual violence because, under these socioeconomic conditions, male-female relations are cooperative and compassionate. Margaret Mead (1963: 34), writing about the Arapesh, regards theirs as "a social order that substitutes responsiveness to the concern of others and attentiveness to the needs of others for aggressiveness, initiative, competitiveness and possessiveness."

This cooperation and compassion applies equally to sexual activity. Mead (1963: 111) reports that rather than violence toward women, the male "must approach his wife gently . . . to be sure that she is well prepared to receive his advances. . . . There is no emphasis on satisfaction in sex-relations; the whole emphasis for both men and women is the degree of preparedness. Either man or wife may make the tentative advance that crystallizes a latent consciousness of the other into the sex act." To the Arapesh the ideal of a sexual relationship is "essentially a domestic one, not a romantic one" (1963: 106).

The recently discovered Tasaday, a Stone Age people living in a Philippine rain forest, have a still more archaic economy than the Arapesh. John Nance (1975), author of *The Gentle Tasaday*, tells about his first visit among the people of this band. The Tasaday informed him about their methods for making stones into scrapers and pounders, and they showed how they used their Stone Age tools. The band does not garden or build houses. It survives on hunting and gathering food, and its members dwell in caves. Their economy is also based on the production of use values, and their only exchange is informal gift-trading with the single native outsider who visits them occasionally.

Nance (1975: 25) comments on the social and political relations observed among the Tasaday: "Younger children were constantly carried, held, nuzzled, caressed; older Tasaday spoke together warmly, touched gently, shared food and shelter with no trace of friction." He adds that they demonstrated "no greed, no selfishness. They share everything" (1975: 75). They also had little hierarchical structure; decision making was "based on discussions in which men and women expressed views equally, with age and experience determining degrees of influence" (1975: 24).

For the Tasaday, sexual relations are not romantic affairs. Marriages are usually arranged with the most suitable available woman from another tribe or group. A Tasaday gave his interviewers an example: "Tekaf's wife, Ginun, had been brought from Tasafeng because she was a deaf mute like Tekaf." By way of explanation, the informant added: "Sambal, his uncle and Bilangan's father, had heard of Ginun and arranged the marriage" (1975: 184).

Tasaday people marry when they are mature sexually, stay married to the same partner for life, and, although there is a very serious shortage of women, wife sharing does not occur. Intercourse is called "playing together" and is practiced only by married couples. The play nature of sex carries over into verbal joking and pantomimes. All their interactions seem rooted in love. "Their love was everywhere — for each other, for their forest, for us — for life," writes Nance.

A third objection to Brownmiller's views is that they are based on the myth of an omnipresent male supremacy which in prehistory instigated a battle of the sexes. One set of antagonists was composed of strong men and, in the other set, there were weak, powerless, and isolated women who were overcome by a nagging fear of sexual violation. The Arapesh and Tasaday alone could suffice to demonstrate that these ideas are woefully inaccurate but more evidence presented here in later parts of this chapter, clinches the argument.

According to Eleanor Leacock (1975), there have been numerous other agricultural or nomadic people whose households were communal. Here sexual equality predominated and the division of labor between the sexes was reciprocal. Among such tribes, women restricted their own activities if their mobility was limited by pregnancy, infirmity, or the nursing of infants. Understandably, others who were handicapped, physically or by age, male or female, had similar restrictions. Otherwise, although there was a sexual division of labor, large collective hunts including men and women were quite common. Also, women took small game alone and men likewise did some food gathering. It is believed that women's autonomy and their close supportive relations with men were cardinal features of prehistoric societies.

Speaking about economic relations in these societies, Leacock (1975: 33) emphasizes the independence and mobility of wives: "[Their] economy did not involve the dependence of the wife and children on the husband." She adds, "Women did not have to put up with personal injuries from men in outbursts of violent anger for fear of economic privation for themselves or their children." Unlike women today, some of whom are bound (without protection from relatives and friends) to brutal husbands, a woman in these societies at the very least could call on her relatives for redress. If amends were not made, she could leave freely and return to her own family.

Rise and Expansion of
Sexual Inequality

Yet Brownmiller's thesis seems real enough in light of the male-female antagonism in modern societies. If this antagonism did not exist forever, what explanation can be offered for its original appearance? Also, why did it expand historically? Why has it spread in recent centuries?

Answers to these questions must leave behind the fiction of an endless battle of the sexes and turn to the modern "anthropology of women." This anthropology is being developed by feminist and nonfeminist scholars who usually regard Frederick Engels's theory of sexual equality as an important theoretical contribution. Engels generally proposed that the status and power of women deteriorated with the rise of *class societies* and their colonial systems.

Engels theorized that within ancient communal societies the accumulation of wealth in private hands was stimulated by production for exchange and the creation of economic surpluses. Further developments involving war, population growth, and patrilineality increased private accumulation and

channeled it along male lines for posterity. Eventually, powerful wealthy families appeared and contested ancient egalitarian
customs. The families finally coalesced into ruthless
aristocratic classes.

In early Greece, the exploitation of slaves was employed to
generate more wealth in the new exchange economies. Slavery,
limited first to prisoners of war, soon branched out into the
enslavement of local people. This historically important expansion of slavery was spurred by commercial crises and the
inability of peasants to pay their debts. "The debtor, in order to
meet his creditor's claims, had to sell his children into slavery
abroad. . . . And if the bloodsucker was still not satisfied, he
could sell the debtor himself as a slave," Engels (1975: 173-74)
writes.

One thing was missing to guarantee the consolidation of
class developments: an institution that could safeguard the
newly acquired property of private individuals against the
communal traditions of ancient societies. This institution, the
political state, playing its role to the hilt, secured exploitative
modes of production by force. It perpetuated the growing
cleavage into classes of slavers and slaves, exploiters and
exploited, within politically established territorial regions.

The state crushed prehistoric communal relationships
whenever they stood in the way of the ruling classes. Individual
members of these classes dismembered and appropriated
communal property. Within the class society, sexual equality,
matrilineality and the communal joint-family group were replaced by male supremacy and the patriarchal family.

These changes produced the "Athenian family", which became, according to Engels, a model for family relationships in
Western class societies. The origin of monogamy — a marital
relation reportedly debased with pecuniary values was to be
found in that family. Engels (1975: 65) noted that this family
"was not in any way the fruit of individual sex love, with which
it had absolutely nothing in common, for the marriages remained marriages of convenience, as before. It was the first
form of the family based not on natural but on economic condi-

tions, namely, on the victory of private property over original, naturally developed, common ownership."

Thus, as the ancient societies were overwhelmed by vast social forces, male supremacy was imposed within a framework of social class developments. Wherever this happened, ancient kinship traditions were swept away and women's status underwent drastic change. Among the newly emerging kinship units, according to Engels, "Household management lost its public character. It no longer concerned society. It became a *private service;* the wife became the head servant excluded from all participation in social production" (1975: 137). The household economy operated within patriarchal family relations and women who were not slaves were usually restricted to domestic labor only.

To underscore this interpretation, Engels (1975: 58) observed that the Roman word *familia* — from which the modern term "family" is derived — did not at first signify a married couple and their children, but only *the totality of slaves belonging to one man.*

Now Engels's theory was written one hundred years ago, when anthropological research was in its infancy, and it would be miraculous to find his work free of erroneous information. For example, his depiction of the *world historic defeat of the female sex,* the loss of female equality, is based essentially on the history of Greece and Rome but does not touch on the causes of sexual inequality in nonclass societies and in other parts of the world. Also, although subjugated to men, women's status varied more in Greece and Rome than Engels suggests (Lacey, 1968). Furthermore, there were class differences among women and, even though they were strictly subject to male authority, many women were not equated with slaves, by custom or law. Slaves were subject also to the will of the wives and daughters of slave owners, because the differences between slaves and the rest of the population transcended the differences between the sexes (Weidemann, 1981).

Despite the limitations in his work, as indicated, a number of feminist anthropologists believe that Engels's theory is important because certain major ideas appear to be accurate. Such ideas relate sexual inequality to the evolution of social classes, private property, the family, and the state.

Equality in the Neolithic Period

Feminist anthropologists are also convinced that for tens of thousands of years men and women lived in equality. Reportedly, in very ancient societies, as we have seen, the relations between the sexes were generally cooperative and peaceful. The patterns of sexual oppression and violence, so familiar today, were unknown. By comparison with the millenniums of social evolution, male supremacy may therefore have existed for only a small fraction of social history.

The fairly recent archeological discover of Çatal Hüyük, a neolithic city of 5,000 or 6,000 thousand people, which flourished more than 8,000 years ago, totally belies the notion that men subjugated women at the dawn of civilization.[1] This cradle of civilization was found in the western Tigris-Euphrates region — on the ancient Anatolian peninsula of southern Turkey — at about 3,000 feet above sea level. Archeological excavations reveal that women of the city were seen as rulers, farmers, healers, mothers, and educators. "Women were buried with their hoes and adzes, as well as jewelry, and children were buried either with the women under the large platforms or under smaller platforms, but never with the men — suggesting that the society was matrilineal and matrilocal," says anthropologist Ruby Rohrlich (1980: 78). Religious artifacts show women in the roles of ritual leaders and deities.[2] In fact, "the principle deity was a goddess," writes James Mellaart (1967), the archeologist who directed the excavation of Çatal Hüyük.

Early modes of production influenced women's status but did not create a social class system. Excavations of fourteen successive building levels at Çatal Hüyük reveal that as hunting declined, women's status became even greater between 6250 B.C. and 5400 B.C., when people of the city derived a living from irrigation agriculture and cattle breeding, supplemented by gathering, hunting, and fishing (Rohrlich, 1980: 7). During this time there still was no evidence of social stratification beyond that of the ritual leaders. Significant differentiation in grave wealth, a prime indicator of economic stratification, was found almost entirely absent.

Finally, evidence suggests that this advanced ancient Stone Age culture was peaceful even though urbanization occurred as such Neolithic towns and villages drew together into cities, walled as a defense against periodic raids by nomadic pastoralists (Rohrlich, 1980: 80-81).

But, as the neolithic period came to an end, Sumer, the *earliest* known state society, evolved out of Çatal Hüyük and other cities in the region. Evidence indicates that classes emerged from 5000 to 2500 B.C. as the Sumerian civilization gradually evolved. Rohrlich speculates that this change first included a theocratic elite who also functioned as city managers. Because of their traditional high status and role as ritual leaders, the status of women continued to be important despite the existence of classes. On the other hand, she also suggests that chronic warfare over vital resources between city-states generated a large military force, and the power among ruling elites shifted from the hands of a priesthood to the military commanded largely by men.

Class developments were held back by the egalitarian clan structures. To destroy these structures, the high status of women had to be undermined and the patriarchal family institutionalized. Legal codes that subordinated women to men subverted democratic clan relationships and consolidated the political power of patriarchal ruling families. "Analysis of the archeological data, and of the religious, literary, and economic documents shows that the subordination of women was integral to the emergence of a rigidly stratified, militaristic society," reports Rohrlich (1980: 76,84).

Military and economic developments expanded the class system greatly by increasing the numbers of slaves and slave prostitutes. Slaves were obtained from prisoners of war, but the larger number were people unable to pay their debts. Moreover, male and female slavery did not emerge simultaneously: Women slaves appeared earlier. It was also common to sell one's wives and children when debts could not be paid in Sumer. The female slave was "used as a concubine, for breeding purposes, for her labor, and for the profits her master acquired by prostituting her." Both slavery and prostitution "made all women vulnerable." (Rohrlich, 1980: 92).

Rohrlich (1980: 84) concludes that the devalued role of women "occurred in the context of chronic warfare, which became a male occupation and a significant factor in the emergence of male supremacy." She further notes: 1980: 84) that warfare was significant "in the development of private property and its generational transmission, secured in the male line by law. The changeover to a patrilineal, patrilocal system led to the creation of the patriarchal family, probably the most important element in the creation of male supremacy. This type of family reflected and confirmed the divisions throughout the society."

Rohrlich's thesis differs from that of Engels, although there certainly are similarities. Social classes, in her theory, are sufficient but not necessary for the development of sexual inequality. Also, the catalytic importance of a male military caste introduces specific conditions that Engels may not have considered. On the other hand, the basic elements of her thesis (such as social classes, private property, the patriarchal family, the clans, and the state) are similar to elements of Engels's theory.

Moreover, although there are undoubtedly a number of accurate models of precapitalist societies and the development of sexual inequality, the differences between Rohrlich's and Engels's explanations might be narrowed if certain conditions are taken into account. Momentous societal developments were far more gradual thousands of years ago than they are today. Sexual equality and classlessness endured for a long time in Çatal Hüyük even though its inhabitants carried on long-distance trade. (The excavations at Çatal Hüyük and the surrounding region provide evidence of trade centering on obsidian [a brittle but hard volcanic rock used in making cutting tools] and perhaps leather goods.) Also, compared to later developments, Çatal Hüyük remained fairly peaceful because chronic warfare over tribute, land, mineral resources, slaves, and so on primarily accompanies the expansion of trade by class societies. However, later developments did produce social classes and they conceivably laid the groundwork for the emergence of the city-states and chronic warfare, as well as the military castes and their patriarchal characteristics. Consequently, in these very ancient times, the full development of sexual inequality may have resulted from the gradual reorganization of economic and political institutions created by an earlier, extended development of class relationships.

Equality in the Fairly Recent Past

It is difficult to prove conclusively the general assumption that sexual equality existed in prehistoric societies. Furthermore, we cannot verify equality beyond the Neolithic period by sending a time machine into the past. Nor has archeological examination of the ashes of campfires or the tools and drawings of Paleolithic and Mesolithic cave dwellers uncovered artifacts indicating the quality of the relationships between the sexes. But it is still possible to judge whether women have always been subjugated to men by examining evidence from the fairly recent past.

Although conventional anthropologists have largely ignored women's independence in societies existing in the recent past, a feminist trend in anthropology is now calling for the reexamination of ethnographic data about women's status. Ruby Rohrlich-Leavitt, Barbara Sykes, and Elizabeth Weatherford (1975) suggest that women in some societies should now be considered far more independent than they have been made out to be. They insist that traditional studies of these women were based on culturally biased observations made especially but not exclusively by male anthropologists. The studies have projected androcentric biases onto observations of tribal relations and, as a result, they discount and distort the role of women. Women's dignity, independent thinking, rituals, and associations are ignored. In these traditional studies, evidence of egalitarian relations is minimized while the spheres of male domination are exaggerated.

Efforts by less conventional anthropologists to discover existent egalitarian societies have begun to pay off. A study in 1978 of the Agta, a Negrito people of the Philippines, by Agnes Estioko-Griffin and P. Bion Griffin, discovered continuing egalitarian relations. After a well-specified definition of equality, the authors (1981: 140) concluded: "The case must be rested that Agta women are equal to men. They do have authority, and they do regularly contribute a significant portion of the subsistence resources. Their freedom of choice in sex and marriage seems to support the hypothesis of an egalitarian society."

Colin Turnbull (1981: 219) presents another exception to androcentric anthropology, finding, among the Mbuti, no sense of "superordination or subordination" between the sexes but rather an emphasis on interdependence. He says: "Plainly then, 'Womanhood', for the Mbuti, is associated with motherhood, and indeed both men and women see themselves as equal in all respects except the supremely vital one that, whereas the woman can (and on occasion does) do everything the male does, she can do one thing no male can do: give birth to life" (1981: 206).

Another important point ignored by androcentric anthropologists is the degree to which male supremacy did not really originate within tribal life itself. This supremacy has often been imposed on archaic societies violently by outsiders. Over the centuries, thousands of bands and tribes have been forced to adopt social standards that actively discriminate against women. In recent years, most of the remaining egalitarian societies have been undergoing similar transformations because of their contact with class societies. The association between sexual equality and commodity relations is largely based on the impact of metropolitan class societies on pre-capitalist formations.

Aboriginal societies, such as the Warrabri of Central Australia, existed for tens of thousands of years before white settlers invaded their homelands. As Diane Bell (1981: 316) notes, these societies were egalitarian. "Under the Warrabri's laws, established in the dreamtime [when mythical ancestors wandered across the land] men and women had distinctive roles to play but each had recourse to certain checks and balances which ensured that neither sex could enjoy unrivaled supremacy over the others." However, since 1788, mining and farming industries have taken over some of the best Warrabri lands, and today "many descendants of the original owners of Australia live as paupers." With the settlement of the whites, new laws that are "male oriented, controlled and delivered" were imposed on the aborigines. Also, the division of labor between the sexes is evaluated differently. Now, in the towns, missions, settlements, and cattle stations, women are valued as "feeders and breeders" and the men are given greater authority and even groomed as politicians by whites. When they lived in small bands, female solidarity was possible, but now male solidarity as well as authority is enforced by outside economic and political agencies. The old balance between the sexes has been undermined.

Such outside contacts have, also, more or less changed the highly egalitarian horticultural people of North America, including the Iroquois and Huron of the American Northwest, the Cherokee of the Southeast, and the Hopi and Zuni of the Southwest, according to Eleanor Leacock. She asserts this claim after examining documentary evidence about the prior status of women in these societies.

This evidence, too, contradicts the notion of universal inequality. The power of American Indian women, for instance, has been well documented in chronicles. In 1724, Father Joseph Lafitau of the Society of Jesus described the position of matrons of the Iroquois and/or Huron tribes: "It is of them that the nation really consists. . . . All real authority is vested in them. The land, the fields and their harvest all belong to them. They are the souls of the Councils, the arbiters of peace and of war. They have charge of the public treasury" (cited in Brown, 1975: 238).

Others have been struck by the independence of Indian women prior to colonization by the white man. The autonomy of Indian women can be seen when we look at the freedom of women to marry. John Phillip Reid (1970: 69), a professor of law, observes, "We must not think of 'contract.' Cherokee marriage was not binding on either the kindred or wife, and to imagine that a girl could be impelled to wed ignores the fact that no relative — neither her mother, her uncles, nor her brothers — exercised compulsory authority over her."

Leacock (1977: 33) writes, "Among the Iroquois, as is well known, the matrons nominated the sachems of the intervillage councils and could depose them." Wyandot women participated equally with men in tribal councils. The Cherokee women were absolutely equal on all levels of the social structure, from tribal affairs to their personal lives. Cherokee women who became prominent as military figures were known as "Beloved Woman," "Pretty Woman," or "War Woman." In 1781, a woman with such a title negotiated a peace treaty with the American settlers' invading army.

A story about these negotiations, reported by Reid, shows that Cherokee men expected women to play such roles. Reid (1970: 69) mentions the woman who negotiated the peace treaty and adds, "Earlier, her uncle, Little Carpenter, attended a council meeting in Charlestown and startled Carolineans when he asked them why they were all males. 'It was the custom among Indians to admit women to their councils,' he told Governor Lyttleton. 'White men as well as the Red were born of women,' he pointed out and 'desired to know if that was not the custom of the White People also.' It took Lyttleton two or three days to come up with the rather lame excuse that 'the White Men do place a confidence in their Women and share their Counsels with them when they know their hearts to be good.' "

Dramatic examples of outsiders imposing male supremacy can be found among the Montagnais-Naskapi bands. Jesuit priests, during the seventeenth century, came among these bands, backed up by military support. Arrogant about the rightness of their own convictions, they attempted to impose European patriarchal relations on both men and women.

The Superior of the Jesuit Mission at Quebec, Paul Le Jeune, for instance, spent the full winter of 1633-1634 traveling in the interior with a Montagnais band. He wrote chronicles of this period, recording in them his contempt for the independence enjoyed by all band members.

Eleanor Leacock and Jacqueline Goodman (1976) analyze the chronicles and emphasize their significance for the anthropology of women. Quotations from the chronicles can be used to illustrate Le Jeune's responses to the freedom enjoyed by all members of the band — male and female.

For instance, Le Jeune, reacting sharply to the political independence of band members, expresses his derision: "[The band members] imagine that they ought by right of birth, to enjoy the liberty of wild ass colts, rendering no homage to anyone whatsoever, except when they like. They have reproached me a hundred times because we fear our Captains, while they laugh at and make sport of theirs."

Despite his displeasure at their disdain for authority, Le Jeune seemed envious of the absence of violence and materialistic values: "As they have neither political organization, nor offices, nor dignitaries, nor any authority, for they only obey their Chief through good will toward him, therefore they never kill each other to acquire these honors. Also, as they are contented with a mere living, not one of them gives himself to the Devil to acquire wealth." Le Jeune felt that the establishment of political authority based on a system of permanent chiefs was essential to civilizing aboriginal peoples.

Further, Le Jeune believed that formal punishment would have to replace the customary forms of compensation for wrongs committed by band members. With regard to the family, male and female attitudes had to be changed through religious training in which a man, for instance, was instructed "that he was the master and that in France women do not rule their husbands."

The sexual autonomy of the Montagnais was especially shocking to Le Jeune, who bemoaned the absence of patriarchal relationships. He tells this anecdote about a discussion with a male band member: " I told him that it was not honorable for a woman to love anyone else except for her husband, and that this evil being among them, he himself was not sure that his son, who was there present, was his son. He [the Montagnais] replied, 'Thou hast no sense. You French people love only your own children; but we all love all the children of our tribe.' I began to laugh, seeing that he philosophized in horse and mule fashion."

Supporting such essential transformations in the Montagnais society was the evolution of commodity relationships based on the fur trade and other commodity markets. Communal and egalitarian customs were soon undermined by a system of private property relations with its economic individualism and competition. Eventually, individual control over hunting and furbearing territories along with monogamy, female fidelity, and the principle of male supremacy were consolidated among the Montagnais.

Such changes did not completely eradicate egalitarian traditions among the band members, but they drove the final spikes that nailed the Montagnais to the European cross.

Notes

1. Çatal Hüyük is not the only Neolithic nonmale-supremacist city discovered. Mellaart (1967) implies that women may have dominated men in Hacilar, a somewhat later culture also located in Anatolia.

2. Based on archeological and historical evidence for the Near and Middle East, Merlin Stone suggests that the earliest religions worshipped a goddess, who created all life. Later religions, Judaism, Christianity, and Islam destroyed most of the female idols and the literature of goddess worship as pagan or heathen, subsituting a male god. With this transformation, woman the farmer, hunter, ruler, and deity was dispossessed, and, in her place, stereotypes of women in the image of the mythical Eve, the dangerous temptress and sex symbol, were foisted upon future generations of women. Addressing herself to women, Stone (1978: xxvi) notes: "The image of Eve is not *our* image of woman."

CHAPTER 9

SEXUAL INEQUALITY AND MODES OF PRODUCTION

Bring a group of knowledgeable anthropologists into one room for a serious discussion of violence against women and the interchange begins with the realization that sexual inequality is entirely rooted in historical conditions. In light of the historical variations in sexual equality, the so-called perpetual battle between the sexes becomes a myth without substance (Caulfield, 1977; 1981).[1]

Women were not subjugated or violated by men in the dawn of time. In previous chapters we described anthropological studies of societies in which the status of women was autonomous or equal to that of men. On the other hand, the use of rape as a mode of subjugating or controlling women, in addition to other violent measures, has also been reported by anthropological studies. In some societies, for example, rape is institutionalized to keep a woman in her place after other measures fail to restrict her sexual activities. In Mundugamor, says Margaret Mead (1963: 219), "A woman of equal violence [to the excessively violent man] who continuously tries to attach new lovers and is insatiable in her demands, may in the end be handed over to another community to be communally raped."

The Iatmul headhunters also call in their age-mates to rape their wives into submission (Mead, 1969: 76). Anthropologist Gayle Rubin (1975: 163) generalizes: "In the Amazon valley and New Guinea Highlands, women are frequently kept in their place by gang rape when the ordinary mechanisms of masculine intimidation prove insufficient; 'We tame our women with the banana,' said one Mundurucù man."

We notice, however, that this form of rape exists in societies that are violent in other respects. Among the Mundugamor, according to Mead(1963: 219), the punishment for a *man* who exceeds the norms of violence is death; he may be killed treacherously during an intertribal battle or a member of his tribe may kill him directly (Mead, 1963: 219). The Mundurucù and Iatmul provide further evidence that institutionalized rape is usually embedded historically in supremacist warlike cultures (Mead, 1969: 77, 115, 117; Bateson, 1958: 59-72, 138-141). Consequently, it is possible that the adoption of rape is partly determined by the general level of violence in these societies.

The economies of such male supremacist tribes figure importantly though not universally in creating the level of violence. While, allegedly, tribes like the headhunting Mundurucù were extremely violent traditionally (Murphy, 1960), in other tribes, violence may be a function of production for exchange which, in some cases, includes production for capitalist markets. Furthermore, while some of these tribes may not be internally divided by social classes or characterized by private property ownership, their relations with neighboring groups may be antagonistic. They engage in raids and military campaigns; at times, their violence is aimed at capturing wealth, tribute, natural resources, children, or the abduction of slaves, especially women. In this context, wars are, at least in part, economic policy. Further, some societies with sexual inequality are based on "lineage systems" that concentrate economic resources and surplus goods in the hands of male elders. Often the tribes are distinguished by patrilineal estates or individual male property ownership. Even though they are not yet class societies, exploitative developments move them in this direction (Dupre and Rey, 1980; Meillassoux, 1980).

The appreciation of the effects of socioeconomic relations on sexual inequality directs our attention, in this chapter, to a comparative study by Karen Sacks (1975), an anthropologist. Sacks contends that sexual inequality varies greatly depending on socioeconomic relationships. Her thesis will be extended to suggest that within the context of modes of production and their articulation, both private property relations and a woman's participation in social production affect her status to different degrees.[2] Furthermore, we will hypothesize, in Chapter 11, that the *general level of violence* in the societies studied is also associated with their modes of production and degree of sexual inequality, although this association is not necessarily invariant.[3] We provide a preliminary test of our hypothesis by examining evidence of violence in the same four African societies studied by Sacks.

The Four Tribes:
Modes of Production and Autonomy

As indicated, sexual inequality varies depending on the dominant mode of production within a society. Sacks prepared a fascinating account of changes in sexual relations ranging from enviable equality to the subjugation of women in four African societies. She selected the four from anthropological writings on East and Southern Africa, ensuring that the sexual, economic, and political data were adequate and comparable. The societies ranged from the highly egalitarian Mbuti of Zaire to the inegalitarian class society of the Baganda in Uganda. She included the Lovedu and Mpondo of South Africa because their egalitarianism falls between the others. Sacks analyzed each of these societies, modifying but keeping in mind Engels's theory of sexual inequality and class relations. (Engels [1975], it will be recalled, attributed the emergence of sexual inequality to the rise of social classes and their institutions, the family, private property, and the state.)

The *Mbuti* are a simple forest people who, like prehistoric societies, survive chiefly by hunting and gathering the necessities of life. They live communally in family households, but both sexes collect and process necessities for direct use by the entire band. Thus, they have an "economy of use," according to Sacks (1975: 221).

The Mbuti sexual relations are completely egalitarian. There are no sexist standards, and the Mbuti marriage, for instance, does not restrict a woman's authority over her work, her children, or her socializing. Woman's labor is "public labor"; it is not confined to the immediate family household but contributes to the entire band's survival.

The traditional *Lovedu* mode of production is organized around communal production for use within the family estate and the reciprocal exchange of these use values with kinship groups. This mode is being threatened by a growing money economy and the absorption, chiefly of the men, into agrarian commodity production. Nevertheless, the traditional mode of production was still dominant in the tribal communities when E. Jensen Krige and J. D. Krige(1943) wrote *The Realm of the Rain Queen*. The Lovedu mode of production is also articulated with the capitalist economy maintained by the South African government. The Lovedu operate within the framework of a racist state apparatus which ruthlessly represses activities that threaten the total supremacy of the white population. The white government also thwarts any and all developments that threaten such prerequisites for capital accumulation as labor, land, orderly commerce, and political conformity.

Among the Lovedu, egalitarian relations in the public and domestic spheres are somewhat contradictory. Because of their patrilineal organization, women are discriminated against in domestic life, especially in relation to property ownership and transfer of family resources. Also, women are subject to some restrictions based on their reproductive capacity, menstruation, pregnancy, and adultery. However, women are not wards of men, and even within the household they enjoy some degree of independence.

The relationships outside the home deny extensive patrilineal discrimination. Lovedu women are powerful in tribal political life. They hold political office, officiate at certain religious rituals, and participate in political decisions and the settlement of disputes. Like the Mbuti, both sexes among the Lovedu give and receive food, an activity that is the material basis for exercising political power.

Lovedu women have personal autonomy outside domestic life. One measure of their freedom and independence is that women and men regularly participate in most of the same social activities. Women exercise independent choice with regard to marital and extramarital sex and divorce. Regarding extramarital affairs, the Lovedu, like the Mbuti, have a single, not a double, standard.

Significantly, unlike the Mbuti, the Lovedu society is organized around patrilineal family estates and male ownership of property. On the other hand, like the Mbuti, the Lovedu have an economy of use. Furthermore, the existing sexual and social restrictions on women's activities are weakly enforced or limited. Despite their patrilineal restrictions, the Lovedu, Sacks (1975: 222-223) concludes, are predominantly egalitarian.

On the other hand, for the *Mpondo,* commodity production centered on the individual ownership of cattle; and wage labor in European owned mines and plantations was rapidly becoming dominant when this tribe was studied by anthropologist Monica Hunter (1961), author of *Reaction to Conquest.* Although the Mpondo economy is based on hoe agriculture and cattle exchange, Hunter reports that now more and more people in Mpondoland are using money for exchange and have adopted ploughs in their fields. In fact, the Mpondo raise cattle for cash and speak of money as cattle.

The Mpondo is a male supremacist society with deep antagonisms. For example, Mpondo men view their own extramarital affairs as right and proper, yet they define the women's affairs as immoral. The women have an adult status outside the home, although their domestic status is that of a ward. Thus, with regard to domestic authority and inheritance of the marital estate, the Mpondo men actively discriminate against women in domestic life. But it should be noted that this discrimination is limited. It does not extend to divorce, socializing by women, or a woman's right to represent herself in legal proceedings.

Notably, the Mpondo *women* work in a use economy. Their labor is social because they produce food and so forth for persons outside their immediate family group. The *men,* on the other hand, while working in the agricultural use economy, also raise cattle, make war, and raid other communities for livestock. Most of their violence and warlike activity are based on conflicts over cattle and grazing land. Like the Lovedu, patrilineal estates are characteristic of the Mpondo but, unlike the

Lovedu, as indicated, Mpondo men are partly engaged in an early form of production for commodity exchange centered on cattle, according to Sacks.

Now, let us turn to the fourth tribe. Compared with the Mpondo, commodity relationships among the *Baganda* are far more developed. Organized as a patrilineal *class* society in which both men and women are exploited, the Baganda subsist on hoe agriculture but they primarily produce their crops to sell — that is, for exchange (Roscoe, 1965). Economic individualism is also very important, because a man's economic interests are less subordinated to family obligations than they are in the other tribes.

Sexism among the Baganda prevails everywhere. The Baganda woman's status is strictly that of wife and ward. Women are unequivocally subordinated to husbands in marital and extramarital relations. In fact, a violent man can kill his wife for adultery, whereas she has little recourse if the situation is reversed. Nor can women represent themselves in legal proceedings. A male guardian brings a woman's case to court; moreover, since he is held responsible for her conduct, he receives compensation for wrongs done to her.

With the Baganda, moreover, "women's work" is individual production for household use. Women do not engage in social labor that extends outside the immediate household. Also, women are excluded from a major portion of social activities given by patrons or state officials.

When Roscoe's observations were made, the Baganda tribe was organized as a kingdom in which the king's wives, sisters, and daughters had privileges such as economic power and freedom from work. This distinguished them from peasant women, but even they were subordinated to the men of their station. Peasant women, of course, were exposed to class as well as sexual oppression and they had no access to political positions that were available to their husbands.

At the opposite end of the scale from the Mbuti, the Baganda have individual male ownership of private property, domestication of women's labor, an economy based on production for exchange, social class relations, and sexual discrimination, including violence toward their wives.

Social Labor, Private Property, and Mode of Production

With this capsule portrait of the four tribes, we can return to Sacks's analysis. Her study seeks the causes of sexual inequality in the different types of socioeconomic formations. Her work is extremely valuable, because it clearly demonstrates that sexual discrimination cannot be understood simply as a monolithic and universal phenomenon. Sexual discrimination may be nonexistent, it may be restricted to certain spheres of life, or it may permeate every aspect of a society.

Analyzing this variation, Sacks focuses sharply on discrete socioeconomic conditions. In this research, she finds that sexual discrimination is correlated with commodity exchange. The Baganda's economy is based chiefly on *commodity exchange;* as a result, women are restricted everywhere in life. The Mpondo men engage mostly in commodity relations and to a lesser extent in production for use. While they actively discriminate in domestic affairs, there is less discrimination outside the home. The Mbuti and Lovedu, however, whose economic lives focus for the most part on *production for use,* are predominantly egalitarian.

Sacks emphasizes another discrete relationship, social labor. Participation in production for use *by a social unit larger than the immediate members of the family* seems especially significant to women's autonomy. The Mbuti and Lovedu women engage in this extended form of social production, and they have an independent adult status. This production among Mpondo women also supports some degree of independence outside the domestic sphere. Among the Baganda, however, women's labor is totally restricted to the private household, and their status reflects this. They do not have autonomy; rather, they are only wards of the men.

Private property is relatively unimportant to Sacks's analysis. Although she agrees with Engels that, in general, women in nonclass societies stand in a more equal relationship to men, she stresses the exclusion of women from social production beyond the immediate family as more important than private property for determining their independence: "It follows that a society would have to exclude women from public labor or in some way denigrate women's performance of such labor in order to deny them social adulthood for any length of time" (Sacks, 1975: 229).

In a later work, *Sisters and Wives; The Past and Future of Sexual Equality,* Sacks (1979) modifies and extends her analysis. First, she states that "mode of production [is] a central analytic concept for understanding women's places" (1979: 103). Sacks differentiates two nonclass modes of production: communal and kin corporate. The former are the foraging societies or bands, and the latter are the tribes and chiefdoms. She then observes that wives and sisters each have different relations to production. "Sister," in corporate lineage circumstances, means one who "is an owner, a decision maker among others of the corporation, and a person who controls her own sexuality. By contrast, a wife is a subordinate in much the way Engels asserted for the family based on private property" (Sacks, 1979: 110). In other words, "sisters," who share in the ownership and control of the means of production, have greater power than "wives," who do not. Sacks (1979: 123) suggests that "class societies, to the extent that they develop from patricorporations, transformed women from sister and wife to daughter and wife, making them perennial subordinates."

We would add that another aspect of the private property issue, exploitation, is involved. Certainly, when considering the economic supports for women's status and power, a mode of production cannot be completely defined by such concepts as "production for use" or "exchange," because these concepts refer to social relations affecting the circulation and consumption of economic goods and do not directly denote the social aspects of production relationships. The questions of how goods are produced in addition to who actually owns and controls the means of production must also be addressed: Are goods produced cooperatively or is exploitation involved?

For instance, in later English feudalism, an "independent mode of production" was expanded among small farmers and artisans and involved both production for household use and petty commodity exchange. This mode was supported by private property relationships because small farmers and artisans owned their farms, tools, and workshops. Nevertheless, since its social production relations were organized primarily around the cooperative labor of household members, this mode of production was not necessarily exploitative. On the other hand, more than one mode of production may exist in a socioeconomic formation, and one of them is often dominant. In addition to the independent mode, the dominant "feudal mode of production" in Western Europe entailed the extraction of the agricultural surplus (in the form of labor or rent) directly from peasant producers by landlords. Moreover, the extraction of surplus did not occur through commodity exchange but rather as a result of the political, ideological, and legal authority the ruling class was able to exercise over its subject class. Political authority was backed by a military caste, ideological authority emphasized the serf's oath of fealty, and legal authority was founded in the private ownership of land. Moreover, this legal authority was backed by patriarchal laws and doctrines about property that affected the organization of family life because they influenced ownership and control of the means of production among serfs and nobles alike.

We suggest that private property relations, under certain circumstances, may actually outweigh women's role in social production. However, first we note that the concept of private property cannot stand alone in our analysis because the effects of property relations on women depend on the mode of production. A comparison of property relations within the four tribes will make this clear. For instance, the Mpondo and Baganda but not the Mbuti and Lovedu have private property relations linked either to exploitative modes of production or methods of appropriating property. The Baganda engage in wars for property and have exploitative class relationships; and even though the Mpondo may not now be internally divided by social classes, their raiding and warring over cattle are extensions of economic life that represent one of the earliest methods of appropriating goods by force or stealth.[3] Such relationships are associated with differences in degree of sexual equality between the former and latter tribes.

By comparison, where the mode of production is nonexploitative, private property relations may be limited and have little effect on women's status. Lovedu production, for example, is not exploitative. The Lovedu breed cattle, but uses of this property are not what one might expect. Cattle are not raised for trade but for such family use as dowry. Moreover, women as well as men own the cattle that bind the family groups into a network of reciprocal relationships through marriage.

E. J. Krige and J. D. Krige (1943; 42), the husband-and-wife team that spent more than a decade studying the Lovedu, note: "Cattle are individually owned by both men and women, but the kind of ownership, except in the case of some fifteen per cent, is entirely different from what we understand by the word. For the vast majority of cattle are linked to the chain of *munywalo* (bride-price) exchanges and as such the individual's rights over them are subject to many restrictions. The primary value to the Natives of cattle is not economic, but social."[4] It is not surprising, therefore, that the Lovedu property relations are not strictly governed by patrilineal norms and that certain aspects of these property relations as well as the dominant mode of production support women's authority in most spheres of life.[5]

The economic relationship between private property, mode of production, and social production should also be emphasized. We believe that the differences in modes of production must be considered in evaluating women's participation in labor for people beyond the immediate family (that is, social labor). A "use economy," as in the case of the Mbuti, is based on the collective as a whole (the band) as well as individual families. In that instance, there is a direct relation between women's social labor and their autonomy. However, under other modes of production social labor hardly affects women's status. For instance, in slave modes of production, enslaved women labor in the fields alongside men, but this labor does not make them independent. They remain the slave owner's property, and their participation in social production is itself a condition of their servitude. Consequently, if property relations refer to who owns the means of production, the products of labor, labor power, or even who owns the laborer, then private property relations enter into the determination of women's status despite their participation in productive activities extending beyond the family.

Furthermore, in precapitalist and capitalist societies, property relations need not affect women's status negatively. In fact, where individual women are able to own the means of production, in addition to the products of their labor, their status is usually increased. The same applies to ownership or control over the distribution of goods. For example, wherever precapitalist forms of commodity production prevail, women's independence is heightened by their ability to own and sell as well as produce cash crops, by their owning, selling, and processing foodstuffs, and by their merchandising other commodities that they have not produced at all.[6] Also, under capitalism, the independence that employed working-class women achieve from employment may be due more to their status as private *owners* of labor power (a commodity salable for cash) and the earnings from the exchange of this power than to their *participation* in commodity production per se.[7]

When we compare some of the characteristics of the two variables, ownership of commodities and participation in production, we can see why one contributes more to status than the other. The sale of commodities results in money income, a readily observable value contributing to autonomy, while the underlying values of social production activities are hidden from view due to the complicated and indirect social relationships on which they are based. These indirect relationships are experienced by people only as relationships between people, on one hand, and salable things, on the other.[8] Since status appears to be based merely on commodity ownership and money, a worker's contribution to production cannot usually be observed in terms other than money earnings. Therefore, the fact of participation in social production alone does not have the same social psychological effect that property relations have.

In other words, depending on the mode of production or its articulation with other modes, both property relations and a woman's participation in social production affect her status in society, to different degrees. They may support either sexual equality or inequality, depending on the concrete modes of production within which they operate. Usually it is the mode of production that informs us about who owns or controls women's ability to labor. It determines both the products of their labor and the means of production that are used to create these products. And it is the mode of production that informs us how independence is dynamically related to the nature of property relationships as well as woman's participation in social production outside her immediate family.

Let us speculate for a moment on how these factors, private property and mode of production, might increase the small degree of sexual inequality among the Lovedu. First, inequality might be extended if two new factors were to evolve in the patrilineal estates: (1) a mode of production based mainly on the exploitation of individual Lovedu or neighboring people, and (2) the kind of private property relations that safeguard this mode of production. (As evidence that inequality might increase, we note that among the Mpondo males, where the economy was partly based on these relationships, the amount of sexual discrimination was greater.[9]) Second, if these economic changes were to occur, the emergence of a state based on exploitative class relations would then also be possible; moreover, it would be controlled by the wealthier estates, as the Baganda situation implies. Under such conditions, male supremacy would become generalized to the remaining spheres of Lovedu life.[10]

Furthermore, such speculation is not unrelated to evolving socioeconomic realities. Originally, the traditional Lovedu sexual division of labor was balanced. The Kriges (1943: 40) note, "Both men and women hoed, weeded and reaped. Only men cleared the forest but against this only women cultivated certain crops, such as groundnuts. The old pattern is still more or less maintained at least in principle." But the Kriges also observed that economic life among the Lovedu was beginning to change. The men were becoming engaged in plough agriculture for cash crops and in work as laborers in nearby settlements while the women were maintaining the agrarian production for use based on hoe agriculture.

The Kriges (1943: 37-38) point to the results of these departures from tradition: "Crops specially planted by women tend to fall behind in the race. Women do most of the hoeing today, and their labour, valuable as it is on the steep slopes and among the stones, cannot keep pace with the plough. Moreover, men make the modern gardens by the sides of streams where furrows can be irrigated and the plow can cut more easily, and the mung beans, groundnuts, and native potatoes, which the women planted, disappear before the advance of European vegetables. This is as yet not a great change, because there are very few of these gardens, and it is far beyond present resources to construct irrigation furrows." The pace of economic change among the Lovedu, therefore, depends on numerous factors: the availability of forces of production — of animals, implements, and wage labor — and the development of markets for the new European crops.

If these changes should increase, the division of labor between the sexes would grow more uneven (with women performing a greater share of the traditional labor), especially with the decline of other male work activities, such as hunting, because of South African government restrictions. In addition, the women were still subject to monotonous labor, but the younger men were beginning to feel that hoeing was women's work and that the men pulled their weight if they went out periodically to earn wages, ploughed the field, and built the huts.

Finally, an important change is that some of the Lovedu have converted to Christianity and have migrated to the towns. The Kriges (1943: 58) say: "The Christians are notable . . . because . . . they have eagerly accepted whatever differentiates them from their heathen brothers. They are competitive, money conscious; they exploit their brothers." The Christians are squarely integrated into the South African — capitalist — mode of production.

In short, numerous factors are changing because of the articulation between a capitalist mode of production and the precapitalist mode that traditionally characterized Lovedu society. The Lovedu mode appears to have been somewhat preserved, yet it is undergoing very gradual decay in the face of South African economic developments.[11] Eventually the traditional mode of production among the Lovedu may disappear entirely. Consequently, one can conclude from the direction of these developments that the effects of property relations cannot be evaluated without reference to the differences and changes in precapitalist modes of production and how they are articulated with capitalist relationships.

Notes

1. In another article, Caulfield (1981: 217) concludes: "The myth of universal sex oppresion, which acts to isolate women's devaluation from the process of change in modes of production, tends to negate [women's] historic role and to restrict the goals of the women's movement to a *struggle for 'equality' of women under capitalist relations.*"

2. The phrase "social production" or "social labor" in this context refers to a woman's participation in work (done singly or in a group) for use or appropriation by people who are outside of her immediate household.

3. The level of violence can be affected independently of socioeconomic characteristics by repeated aggression against a society from external sources.

4. The Kriges (1943: 42), in this case, are equating the word "economic" with the value of the cattle in a competitive market, while the word "social" refers to the value of cattle for integrating joint-family groups into a network of reciprocal relationships. Both cases, however, actually involve socioeconomic relationships but of different types.

5. For instance, "a well marked characteristic of Lovedu society, one that clearly distinguishes it from the strictly patrilineal Zulu, Xhosa, and Mpondo, is the importance of the mother's side of the family," say the Kriges (1943: 77).

6. Material conditions such as these provide the material basis for women's organizations that maintain or extend the status of women. In "Down to Gentility: Women in Tanzania," the anthropologist James Brain (1978) suggests that, during the precolonial period, the favorable position of the Igbo women in Nigeria was based on their economic success and trading and on their tightly organized women's groups. In addition, Brain describes how a "money economy" and Victorian bourgeois ethics contributed to the deterioration of women's status in a Tanzanian resettlement program.

7. This discussion does not deal with the issue of the long-term effects due to participation in social production under capitalism. This participation provides a material base for the economic and political organization of women, or men and women, which affects women's position in society.

8. In the opening chapters of *Capital,* Volume 1, Karl Marx indicates that because of commodity fetishism, the appearances of these relationships mask their essential characteristics.

9. According to Monica Hunter (1961: 135, 379-386), cattle raiding afforded an opportunity for enterprising men to get rich quickly. Mpondo men also acquired wealth by serving a chief, or wealthy man, and receiving in return the loan or gift of cattle. Wages could be acquired through work in gold mines and sugar plantations owned by European corporations or settlers. Further, it is important to note that though Sacks classifies only the Baganda as a class society, we are not sure about the absence of class relations among the Mpondo. Hunter indicates that prior to annexation with the Union of South Africa, the Mpondo chiefs had more cattle, land, and grain than other members of the society and were more wealthy than others. Her description of traditional economic life suggests a stratification system based on wealth and political power which is partly sustained by the labor of commoners. Such relationships may be confined; nevertheless, they do appear to represent incipient class developments.

10. The logic of this argument is derived from Engels.

11. Meillassoux (1980: 198) provides insights into the articulated relations that conserve precapitalist formations and lead to their gradual rather than rapid decay. For an excellent collection of articles on articulation relations, see Wolpe (1980).

CHAPTER 10

LEVELS OF VIOLENCE AND SOCIOECONOMIC FORMATIONS

Male supremacy, sexual inequality, and violence — we suggested in Chapter 9 that these three seem to be correlated in certain socioeconomic formations.[1] Following this observation, we asked: Do exploitative modes of production, culminating in precapitalist class societies, produce or intensify sexual inequality and male violence? In the next chapter, we offer a preliminary test of these hypotheses; but first there are some important theoretical and empirical issues to be considered. These issues emerge because the evolutionary theories stimulated by Engels's work bear on our hypotheses. While they do not invariably unlock the secrets of sexual inequality, we will see that these issues are important because they deal with factors affecting rape as well as other forms of violence.

Violence and Inequality

Sexual inequality and rape appear to be interrelated with the general level of violence in a society. The connections between (1) rape and other forms of violence against women and (2) evolutionary theories of sexual inequality are complex because the development of this inequality itself changes from one society to another depending on historical circumstances. There are at work, for instance, various "autonomous" historical processes involving political, economic, and social factors. Discussing these factors, Simi Afonja (1981: 299) asserts that modernization and a capitalist mode of production alone cannot explain sexual inequality in a number of instances. Traditional customs may lend themselves, under changing conditions, to inegalitarian developments. For example, even in subsistence economies, such as the Yoruba, landownership may be limited to men and men may control women's labor and reproduction. In discussing cash crop developments and their effects on "the egalitarianism of such a precapitalist society," Afonja (1981: 306) remarks: (1981:310) "the entire enterprise was initiated by Africans" adapting local customs to new products. She emphasizes, (1981: 306) "The salient point to be considered in understanding the subsequent transformation to an inegalitarian structure is that men, particularly in patrilineal households, exploited their position as guardians of family and lineage values, status, and resources".

Regarding violence against women, such autonomous factors are also associated with the general level of violence as well as sexual inequality within precapitalist societies. Such linkages are evident in a number of state societies, including Sumer, the earliest state society so far discovered. Recall that the Sumerian civilization emerged from sexually egalitarian societies such as Çatal Hüyük. Moreover, in Sumer, according to Rohrlich (1980), the subjugation of women was related to militarism and the political consolidation of a patriarchal class society. Besides engaging in chronic warfare aimed at the capture of tribute, slaves, and land, the Sumerian state destroyed sexual equality and democratic clan institutions wherever necessary, by violence.

This development is shown by the epics and myths associated with the political history of the Sumerian civilization. Initially, the ancient epics tell about democratic assemblies of men and women that give way to male assemblies. At a later stage, kingship is institutionalized and men no longer have the right to elect leaders; finally assemblies become mere token bodies (Rohrlich, 1980: 94). Moreover, administrative documents of the time suggest that one important turning point in the position of women rulers possibly took place when a powerful priest, Urukagina, took control of the extensive property of the female ruler, Shagshag, of whom he was probably a consort. (It is suggested by the documents that Urukagina also made himself king and reduced Shagshag to the status of consort.) The legal system then was employed to destroy customs that supported women's status. Rohrlich (1980: 85) writes: "This event [the reversal of Urukagina's and Shagshag's roles] probably took place after Urukagina issued a series of edicts (the earliest law code so far discovered . . .) that contained a regulation imposing monogamy on women only . . . and institutionalized patrilineality." The new laws included violent punishments. Polyandry, which had been customary, was converted into the crime of adultery, punishable by death. Urukagina's laws, passed around 2415 B.C., also ordered mutilation of women and legalized woman beating for women resisting their loss of autonomy. Further restrictions on women priestesses and businesswomen were later written into the Code of Hammurabi (Rohrlich: 88,90).

Changes in perspective on mythical accounts of rape are associated with Urukagina's violent repression. Rohrlich (1980: 95) notes a change in attitude from rejection to relative acceptance of raping women: "When women had relative autonomy, rape was considered a heinous crime, punishable by exile even for the king. When Enlil rapes the goddess Ninlil, the assembly of fifty male and female deities is 'dismayed by this immoral deed,' and despite the fact that Enlil heads the pantheon, he is seized and arrested as a sex criminal and banished from his own city of Nippur to the nether world." However, during the time of Gilgamesh, and even earlier, probably before 2700 B.C., "the ruler had established the right of first sexual access to all the women in his realm, thereby demonstrating his power over the men as well" (Rohrlich, 1980: 95). Gilgamesh also engaged in sexual extortion. Herbert Mason (1970: 15) reports: "As king, Gilgamesh was a tyrant to his people. He demanded, from an old birthright, the privilege of sleeping with their brides before the husbands were permitted."[2]

Theoretical and Empirical Issues

Thus, the Sumer state society suggests that the development of violence against women was synchronized with other forms of violence as well as sexual inequality. However, the analysis of such relationships for twentieth-century societies, on the basis of evolutionary theory, is confronted with more complex lines of social development. There are also problems with obtaining representative data for this analysis, because egalitarian societies deteriorated much more rapidly than inegalitarian societies under the destructive impact of colonialism. After contact with the world economic systems created by class societies, few social systems with a high degree of sexual equality remain. Therefore, since male domination is the rule today, tribal societies that contradict evolutionary theories are easy to find, while positive examples are, by now, relatively rare.[3]

Moreover, there are sexually inegalitarian tribes and bands (with a history of violence) that seem to have none of the characteristics that Engels felt were necessary to its original development. The Mundurucù tribespeople are relevant in this context. They lived in the savannahs of the Amazon basin, where they engaged in horticulture and hunting during the contact period. They had no private property in the means of production and no social classes or state apparatus. The Mundurucù relations of production were organized communally, and food was distributed to each according to need. Finally, while Mundurucù women participated in production beyond their immediate households, contemporary anthropology implies that they were still dominated by men. Reports about the traditional culture of the Mundurucù men suggest that they were male supremacists, despite the apparent absence of virtually every economic relationship important to evolutionary interpretations of sexual inequality.

How do critics of theories of prior egalitarianism interpret and support such contradictions? One critic is Maurice Godelier, who uses the Mundurucù and other tribes to discount the theoretical relevance of Leacock's societies in which women have autonomy. In a nutshell, Godelier (1981: 10) assumes that sexual inequality is universal. He states that "men have so far dominated power in the last analysis" and their dominant position is due to several causes. First, according to his thesis, men were more mobile than women in hunting and gathering societies, and this difference encouraged men to become hunters.[4] The sexual division of labor led men to adopt a "differential value system" that set "a higher value on men's activity insofar as it involved greater risks of losing one's life and greater glory in taking life." Cooking, by comparison, was not valued so highly, since "both sexes can perform it" (1981: 12).

Second, men assumed a dominating position in order to force women to "reproduce the life that maintains the group," that is, by bearing and raising children who become productive social beings. They also required dominance to force women to marry into and live with the husband's group (patrilocality), thereby establishing reciprocal relations among families (1981: 12-14). Godelier also claims that the ban on incest exists because it is a survival mechanism. It maximizes the number of families that establish reciprocal relationships. Finally, he suggests that the ideology of male supremacy is based partly on ego defense mechanisms. Men compensate for their inability to bear children by elevating their roles as hunters and warriors and by denigrating the roles of women.

In sum, Godelier's theory is functionalist, regarding male domination as a means for optimizing the chances of social survival when natural resources are scarce.[5] Presumably, also, women are unable or indisposed to engage in the reproduction of producers and kinship relationships without male domination. Besides having to force women to reproduce and raise children, men must exercise violence against women, in this context, because women resist being controlled. Furthermore, violence arises when solidary kinship relations disintegrate. Out of this social disorganization "raiding, rape, war and expropriation" emerge (1981: 15).

But is this an adequate theory? Even though Godelier considers himself a Marxist, his theory appears to be composed of a melange of Durkheimian and Freudian ideas which, besides having factual shortcomings, are susceptible to the same kinds of criticism that plague other structural-functional theories. First, this criticism presents "equifunctional alternatives" that would be egalitarian and that would enable a given "society" to survive equally well. Second, the existence of these alternatives undermines the facile structural-functional assumptions that certain relationships, such as male supremacy, monogamy, prostitution, and even social classes or the state, are necessary for the survival of society (see Davis and Moore, 1945). Inquiring into equifunctional alternatives, one would ask: Do Mundurucù women really need to be dominated by men to reproduce tribal existence? Why couldn't the women easily achieve the same results by ensuring cooperation among their own sex? After all, most women are just as intelligent, capable, and interested as most men in recognizing the need to establish mutual aid among families and ensure the survival of their tribe, children and kin.

Third, why should any violence, male or female, be pitted against women to achieve this purpose? Intratribal violence is exceptional among tribes like the Mbuti or Lovedu. Couldn't female persuasion, ridicule, shame, and even banishment perform the same social control function? These are accepted methods of social control in nonviolent bands and tribes. Another theory of Mundurucù violence will be presented shortly, and by contrast it will make Godelier's theory seem extremely unconvincing and hopelessly androcentric.

Godelier, for all practical purposes, virtually ignores the extent to which the world economic system, introduced by early mercantile and capitalist developments, transformed tribal societies. True, he mentions that colonialism affected egalitarian societies adversely, but this awareness plays no role in his theory of sexual inequality. Certainly, with regard to the Mundurucù, one should inquire whether it was perhaps the European penetration of the Amazon valley that produced inequality rather than any general necessity to control the fertility of women. Were autonomous factors also at work here, or were sexual inequality and violence imposed by invading class societies?

To help us answer these questions, we must look at the colonial penetration of the Amazon valley. As indicated, conventional accounts of the Mundurucù suggest that they have always been warlike; yet this impression seems to have originated mainly from their furious attacks, in 1770, against Portuguese settlements along the shores of the Amazon. (More on this point in a moment.) Robert Murphy (1960: 29) writes that this period also witnessed an epic attack by the Mundurucù into the State of Maranhao, an amazing 500 miles away. We suggest that these attacks may have reflected some extraordinary events that provoked the Mundurucù by either offending their sense of justice or threatening their survival in the face of an invasion rather than adverse conditions of nature. Although Murphy, unfortunately, does not explore these possibilities, we shall hypothesize such an event shortly.

The Mundurucù may have both become warlike and been later pacified as a result of the colonizing invaders and the trading advantages that accompanied them. We are informed that a mere twenty-five years later, in 1795, the governor of Para, using superior weapons, directed a successful military counterexpedition against the Mundurucù, thus establishing colonial supremacy by force. This was followed by contact with Jesuit missionaries. Murphy also notes that the Mundurucù continued, for a time, to engage in warfare with other tribes as they migrated closer to "civilized settlements" for *trade*.

During the nineteenth century, the area was pacified and the Amazon valley became progressively assimilated into a more developed, capitalist, colonial economy. By 1852, as this assimilation proceeded, the Mundurucù in the lower Tapajos River region lost their cohesiveness and became fragmented. The upper-river Mundurucù were also assimilated from the last half of the nineteenth century into the twentieth through trade in farinha and through the penetration of capitalist rubber-gathering enterprises. Rubber companies, expanding rapidly, as early as 1860, in the lower parts of the Tapajos River, eventually overcame all resistance to their domination of the regional economy. By the twentieth century the Mundurucù in the upper river region had become integrated into plantation networks headed by "patrones" who were part of the economic system established by Brazilian descendants of the Portuguese ruling class.

Sexual relationships were strongly affected by these economic and political changes. It was during this active colonizing period that traditional kinship relations disintegrated and that matrilocality gained importance to facilitate the women's work of farihna production as it became an important trading commodity. While women's status, according to Yolanda Murphy and Robert Murphy (1974), was temporarily somewhat improved by these developments, this improvement in status may have ended with the nuclear family relationships brought about by the rise of rubber plantations.

The argument concerning the increase in violence and male dominance can be buttressed by scrutinizing the scant information on other Indian tribes in the Amazon basin *before* the Mundurucù attacked the Portuguese settlements. In this context, Leacock touches on early European contacts in an observation on a group of Yanömamö, who lived on the borders of the Amazon basin. This observation may be extremely significant, because the Yanömamö seem to bear certain similarities to the Mundurucù. Marvin Harris (1975: 279), in his widely read anthropology textbook, characterizes the Yanömamö as coping with overpopulation in the Amazon Valley by developing a culture entirely dominated by incessant quarreling, raiding, beating, and killing. According to Harris, this culture is "regarded as among the world's fiercest and most male-centered cultures."

Leacock (1981: 198) challenges Harris's neo-Malthusian explanation of the extreme degree to which the Yanömamö practice male supremacy. She points out that "in a study of another Yanömamö group . . . one reads that these people may have first gained their reputation for fierceness when they fought off a Spanish exploring party in 1758. In that period, Spanish and Portuguese adventurers were ranging *throughout the Amazon area searching for slaves*. The author [Smole, 1976] of the account worked with a relatively peaceful highland group, and he suggested that the exaggerated fierceness of the lowland Yanömamö is not typical, but may have been developed for *self-protection*" (our emphasis). Regarding male-female relations, Leacock (1981: 198-199) says: "In the village he studied, elder women, like elder men, are highly respected. When collective decisions are made, mature women 'often speak up, loudly, to express their views.' Younger men, like younger women, 'have little influence.' "

Now, it is quite possible, as suggested, that the Mundurucù gained their reputation as fierce warriors after attacking Portuguese settlements. It may also be that their attack was a response to prior contact with European slavers who are known to have been in the area at that time. In support of this thesis there are numerous accounts of European contacts with North American Indian tribes that similarly justify tribal attacks against white settlers. Almost everywhere, from the fifteenth to eighteenth century, tribal societies were waging fierce struggles against enslavement and colonialism.

Furthermore, the number of Indians in the Amazon basin does not at all suggest that population density was a critical factor for the development of warfare or sexual inequality. Only 1,500,000 lived in the vast river valley, and this figure dropped drastically to 75,000 after the conquest and assimilationist periods ended. True, the Mundurucù were among the most ferocious headhunters in the Amazon Valley and they were noted for attacking neighboring tribes, killing the adults, and incorporating the children into their own families. But their warlike culture may have been due primarily to Portuguese influence, and the Mundurucù may have captured children because of the drastic diminution of their own population resulting from both warfare and disease. Their actions may have had nothing whatsoever to do with high population density or scarce resources.

On the other hand, the effects of such changes alone cannot tell us anything about their relation to male domination unless war, Jesuit missionaries, and other colonial-induced factors influenced the social organization of male activities so that they encouraged sexual inequality. That the Jesuits steadfastly encouraged male domination is a certainty. Also, considering that men are its primary participants, warfare in this context may have led to the male control of organized violence, the glorification of male warriors, and dominance relations headed by men. If the earliest engagements in warfare against the colonial settlements did not encourage male domination, then later engagements at the behest of the Brazilian authorities, who used the Mundurucù as mercenaries, may have done so.

Another historical example suggests that the effects of war on the status of women also depend on whether other aspects of a dominating imperial culture are being assimilated. This example involves the struggle by the Bari (commonly referred to as the "Motilones") of Colombia against invasions by Spanish, Colombian, and Venezuelan colonizers in the sixteenth century.

The Bari are described as a fully egalitarian, gentle, classless society (Buenaventura-Posso and Brown, 1980). However, in the face of the European invasion, they reacted like the Mundurucù. Furthermore, while other indigenous neighboring groups were being enslaved, absorbed as workers and mercenaries, or simply decimated, the Bari continually fought back, attacking colonial landholders and successfully resisting organized military expeditions.

In spite of their show of fierceness, however, Sebastian Joseph Guillan, a colonial envoy, noted in 1772, that this much-feared group remained internally peaceable. In the first written description of the Bari, Guillan wrote: "Between themselves one does not see fights or even heated discussions" (Buenaventura-Posso and Brown, 1980: 121). Regarding this paradoxical situation, being at once aggressive to outsiders and harmonious within, anthropologists Elisa Buenaventura-Posso and Susan Brown (1980: 68) state: "Two points, then, should be made clear: (1) the aggressive and hostile behavior exhibited by the Bari towards the surrounding colonizing societies was a successful self-defense reaction to threats of usurpation and extinction and (2) the harmonious, classless, internal social organization characteristic of the Bari was not altered by their fierce struggle for self-preservation." The authors continue, "The first point needs little elaboration . . . the Bari have the highest regard for peace and only fight out of extreme necessity — to defend themselves from attack and to recover possessions lost at the hands of outsiders. The second point deserves fuller attention for, while the classless nature of Amazon horticultural societies has been frequently reported, such groups are not generally described as harmonious and peace-loving. In fact, studies of South American groups that have been *more extensively exposed* to Western imperialism, such as the Yanömamö, the Mundurucù, and the Jivaro, indicate quite the opposite. In such societies we find reported not only hostile relations with neighbors, but also a high degree of intragroup antagonism between the sexes, including such behaviors as verbal combat, the gang rape of women and woman beating" (1980: 114-115; our emphasis). For the Bari, external forces were directly accountable for the increased general level of violence toward outsiders; but will this group, like the Yanömamö and the Mundurucù, also develop sexual inequality and intragroup forms of violence?

In 1964, after three centuries of efforts to "civilize" them, the Bari defenses were finally broken by a young North American missionary who originated the Motilon Development Plan. Under this plan, male chiefs are being cultivated and given education and Colombian citizenship; patriarchal nuclear family units are replacing collective living units; male wage labor and cash cropping are being introduced; women's work is shifting from production of fabrics, baskets and food to services such as washing clothes, and their role as healers is being usurped (Buenaventura-Posso and Brown, 1980: 125). While the older generation of Bari still resists, a slight tendency toward cultural change is now becoming apparent among the younger Bari. According to Buenaventura-Posso and Brown (1980: 131), "The future of those Bari groups or individuals who continue to be exposed extensively to the Western culture and economic system seems decided. Slowly, they will be absorbed into industrial society, mainly as peasants, while a few Bari males will enter into slightly more privileged positions. Today, this process is well under way and the sexual equality and individual autonomy characteristic of the Bari are already in the process of disintegration." It appears that, so long as the Bari were able to resist the imperial Western culture, their military engagements did not destroy their sexual equality. Accomplishing this end required a deep penetration of the so-called civilized institutions into the structure and culture of the Bari society.

Certainly, if the mode of production is not itself conducive to violence, then this violence has to emerge from external sources. And if the mode of production is not conducive to sexual inequality, then there have to be mechanisms based on the assimilation of external relationships that engender inequality.

In the preface to her book of collected articles, Leacock (1981: 4-5) comments on how egalitarian social relations are undermined. She notes that in societies that are otherwise egalitarian, "indications of male dominance turn out to be due to either: (1) the effects of colonization and/or involvement in market relations . . . ; (2) the concomitant of developing inequality in a society, commonly referred to in anthropological writings as 'ranking,' when trade is encouraging specialization of labor and production for exchange is accompanying production for use . . . ; or (3) problems arising from interpretations of data in terms of western concepts or assumptions."

Furthermore, it is possible to posit that in relation to sexual inequality, modes of production that establish such rankings, and warfare that encourages the male monopoly of organized violence, though independent, have additive effects, and that these effects *converge* in class societies. We entertained such a possibility when we hypothesized that the general level of violence — including violence against women — would correlate with socioeconomic formations that have greater sexual inequality. Data to test this hypothesis for the four African societies were obtained from the Human[5] Relations Area Files, which index primary anthropological research on precapitalist formations.[6] By classifying economic, kinship, ecological, and other relationships, the Files isolate information for comparative research. In light of such information, were our expectations substantiated or were they unfounded? In Chapter 11, we discover the answer.

Notes

1. Rather than changes within or among similar social formations, our concern here is with the variation between different formations.

2. Cited in Rohrlich (1980: 95); original source is Herbert Mason (1970: 15). Other interpretations can be made of this sexual custom (for example, ruling nobles wanted to have sons in other families with divided kinship loyalties).

3. These considerations are in addition to those associated with levels of generalization. Since they are highly general explanations of sexual inequality, these evolutionary theories are conceived abstractly and independently of numerous countervailing influences. They can shed light only on general social changes and are not meant to cover every historical instance. Consequently, although these theories seem to deal well with global changes, contradictory instances still remain.

4. For factual objections, see Leacock's (1981: 141) criticism of the notion that women did not engage in hunting: "The association of hunting, war, and masculine assertiveness is not found among hunter-gatherers except, in a limited way, in Australia. Instead, it characterizes horticultural societies in certain areas, notably Melanesia and the Amazon lowlands." (The Mundurucù belong to the latter group.) Leacock (1981: 142) also properly criticizes the idea that these male activities were, in the past, more prestigious than the creation of new human beings. Finally, the old "active-passive" sexual distinction is implicated by Godelier's assumptions; and Leacock also refutes this distinction. For the use of this antiquated distinction of early sociologists, see our discussion entitled, "W. I. Thomas: Women are Stationary — Men are Mobile 'Look! Jane, See Dick Run! Look! Dick, See Jane Hide!' " (Schwendinger and Schwendinger, 1974: 314).

5. The form of Godelier's theory, in our opinion, is identical to structural functionalism. For descriptions and criticisms of structural-functional justifications of inequality (which use optimization functions of inegalitarianism for "society"), see Schwendinger and Schwendinger (1974).

6. The Files generally contain qualitative material, but since they are usually based on works resulting from lengthy observation, they are not simple random impressions. We limited our pilot study to the four tribes studied previously by Sacks because our resources were severely restricted and the closest available Files were 90 miles from our residence.

CHAPTER 11

VIOLENCE IN THE FOUR SOCIETIES

Before describing our empirical findings about the relationship between modes of production, sexual inequality, and levels of violence, we should note that violence can be expressed in several ways. For example, it can be expressed by the state itself whenever legal codes are enforced by corporal punishment instead of persuasion. Military activities and the treatment of prisoners or slaves are other indicators of violence. Finally, we learn much about the level of violence of a society from its child-rearing practices and from other interpersonal relations. By scrutinizing observations in the Area Files, which are indexed by topics pertaining to war, social sanctions, child rearing, sexual relations, and so forth, we were able to evaluate the variations in violence among the four precapitalist societies discussed in Chapter 10.

Mbuti

Examination of the hunting and gathering people, the Mbuti, along these lines suggests that their violence is minimal compared to the other three tribes. The Mbuti have no police force, court, army, or permanent council that dispenses violence. On the other hand, they make reprisal raids against plantations of villagers who have treated a Mbuti tribe member violently. Intertribal conflicts over territorial claims may evoke threats of war, but they are usually settled peaceably since the Mbuti are not a warlike people.

Authority among the Mbuti is dispersed throughout the society; each area of band activity has its own leader. Furthermore, the Mbuti discourage individuals from aggressively assuming authority; when leadership is assumed, its exercise is restricted to persuasion alone. Colin Turnbull (1965: 181), who studied the Mbuti in their forest environment, says: "Such adults as have respect in any particular field at any particular moment do not even have any authority; they can merely claim to be heard."

What happens when a member offends another person? If there is a dispute regarding food, sex, territory or anything else, it is usually settled quickly and quite painlessly. Retributive sanctions against an offending member are infrequent and even then sanctions are expressed by ridicule or criticism rather than a show of violence. Turnbull finds no evidence of blood payment of any kind for serious offenses. For even the most serious offenses, such as incest, Turnbull's field observations indicate the use of ostracism and ridicule rather than torture, imprisonment, or execution

Interpersonal violence is restricted to fighting between two or three people at most. Disputes over reciprocal duties and personal jealousies occasionally lead to fights; consequently, the daily routine of life is punctuated at times by squabbles and beatings involving a couple of youngsters, an unmarried couple, or a husband and wife. These conflicts, however, do not last long and may be reconciled by gift giving or compensation. Moreover, intervention by other tribal members usually prevents these conflicts from becoming magnified. Importantly, Turnbull (1965: 121) could find no incidence of rape, even among the youth. He reports much sexual activity when youth are on the trail together and he mentions the fact that it sometimes degenerates into orgies. However, he says, " A boy may rip off a girl's outer bark cloth, if he can catch her, but he may never have intercourse with her without her permission. I know of no case of rape, though boys often talk about their intentions of forcing reluctant maidens to their will."[1]

Turnbull (1965: 201) describes the sources of common disputes and the quick and equal method of arbitration: " A number of disputes arising over food indicate trivial domestic disagreements, and seldom reach major proportions. A wife is late in cooking her husband's food, or cooks it badly; he spills some precious oil or fails to catch any game on the hunt. Such disagreements are confined almost entirely to the younger married couples, and they usually settle them by beating each other. If the beating gets too severe then the older women intervene, slapping both boys and girls soundly."

Marital disputes not forced on the attention of the band are ignored but they may evoke ridicule and complaints if they become noisy and keep people awake. Turnbull (1965: 206) writes: "Certainly a fight going on between husband and wife inside the hut is followed with zest by all the youths and some of the younger married couples. These may even stand around watching the hut shake, ready to catch whoever comes flying out first and prevent further damage." Sometimes such a squabble is followed by the couple making up loudly so everyone will hear; then they will walk hand in hand about the camp in ostentatious amity. Turnbull (1965: 207) notes: "This is considered a good thing."

The Mbuti child is treated with much attention and affection, and a woman, if she is childless, is considered unfortunate. A birth, according to Turnbull (1965: 129) is looked upon as a happy event: "After a few days, when the child is brought freely into the open, the hunters and elders will fondle it and compliment the parents. The father is as proud as the mother, and just as likely to carry the child around to show it off".

Socialization of the child is shared by the entire band. Infants crawl everywhere, are fondled by anyone, are soundly slapped and brought back to the mother's hut if they get in the way or crawl into the fire. If they are too noisy in the children's play area, they are criticized.

The parents are responsible for the child only until it is 3 or 4 years old, and then it is cared for and educated by its age peers, the band's youths, and the oldest of the elders. Children learn the ways of the band and forest through playing games with each other and with the youths. In these activities, the controls applied to them are mainly ridicule and ostracism.

Turnbull (1965: 125) describes a typical learning situation and the form of discipline used: An "important imitative game is the hunt, in which a youth or an elder pretends to be an antelope. . . . any child who fails to react properly is laughed out of the game."

When little boys and girls play house, they hunt, fish, and gather and thus contribute in a small way to the food economy of the band. Important behavior and personality patterns develop and carry over into the future. Highlighting the value of these children's activities, Turnbull (1965: 125) notes: "They also learn not only to rely on their fellow age mates for help in food-gathering activities, but to share with them. The sharing is largely left to the girl's decision."

Lovedu

Engaging in sedentary agriculture, the Lovedu have developed a much more complicated mode of production and social structure than the Mbuti. However, the Lovedu are nonaggressive, even though they have experienced centuries of war with invading tribes and Europeans, who finally pressed them into a mountainous region in South Africa.

Although the Lovedu are not a class society, authority relations among the Lovedu are partly consolidated in a royal family and district heads. Since the beginning of the nineteenth century, the royal family has been headed by a queen. The Kriges (1948: 285) report: "Nowhere else are so many women heads of districts or in so many important political positions."

Disputed claims or injuries are judged by male judges who sit in the *khoro,* which is like a court, although it does not enforce legal statutes or dispense corporal punishment. A parallel system of authority over family disputes and the allocation of compensation for various wrongs center on older women, especially "the cattle-linked sisters," who also present the dowries for their daughters.

Furthermore, the Kriges (1943: 197) point out that the older sister is "the legal 'builder' of most houses in the country. [It is] she who 'cuts' cases arising within the house and regulates the inheritance of goods and of widows." The role of the older sister is fully recognized in *khoro* proceedings. In fact, in complicated cases the male judges often postpone their decision again and again until she appears, and they rely on her to suggest a solution and to guarantee its being put into effect.

Not just the older sister but women generally have high status in Lovedu society. The Kriges (1943: 198) observe: "Women are the strongest pillars of the social structure and without their support there can be no guarantee that the adjustments in the superstructure will be lasting or effective; and in a society that relies on compromise and not on coercion, this role becomes even more important."

It is notable, too, that the men who sit in judgment in the *khoro* rely completely on voluntary compliance. The enforcement of their decisions is left to the disputing parties because the court cannot enforce its edicts violently. Therefore, the proceedings are aimed at compromise and conciliation (Krige and Krige, 1943: 200-201).

Clearly then, the principal mechanism of conflict resolution is compensation rather than violence. Gifts and compensatory fines reduce the strains in social life. For instance, in one case noted by the Kriges (1943: 202), a father intervened in a squabble between his son and his son's wife, and the son, in anger, stabbed the father. The incident was reconciled when the son provided his father with a goat and begged pardon.

Other examples suggest a remarkable consistency in their nonviolent means of settling offenses. If an adulterer is discovered, he asks pardon by giving a goat or cattle as a gift to the offended husband. Even homicide is reconciled through compensation, although sometimes restitution is also made by converting the criminal into a kinsman. When this mechanism is invoked, the slayer makes restitution by assuming some of the obligations of the person he killed.

Accounts of child-rearing patterns indicate that discipline is achieved primarily through encouragement by parents and pressure from age mates. Punishment of children, is infrequent though threats are common. Parents are affectionate and gentle with their children (Krige and Krige 1943: 104, 102-125).

Since the Lovedu are not a warlike people, the foreign policy of the queen is appeasement rather than war. This policy affects child-rearing. The Kriges (1943: 284-285) observe: "There is no need to direct [initiation rites] towards hardening the youth or instilling manly courage, and military discipline and regimentation are of little or no importance." Because of these nonaggressive relationships, the Europeans feel that the Lovedu are cowardly and deceitful — lacking the manly qualities of the Shangana-Tonga, a neighboring society that is more commercially oriented and whose people have aggressive dispositions that make them favorable candidates for native South African police forces. Finally, although native courts and customs deal with violations of tribal rules, a South African criminal justice system is imposed on the Lovedu. This system appears to restrict itself to violations of South African laws, including laws containing intertribal warfare and protecting the government and the white population.

Mpondo

Monica Hunter's observations of the Mpondo, who own cattle and perform wage labor for Europeans, indicate that they are more violent than the Mbuti and the Lovedu. The Mpondo engage in cattle raiding and armed conflicts with neighboring tribes, even though these acts are suppressed by the South African government. She reports that some warfare is caused by external attacks, but cattle raiding by the Mpondo themselves is probably the most frequent of all occasions for war (Hunter, 1961: 412).

Customary authority in Mpondo society is centered on male political leaders. Each headman, or chief, with the men under him, forms a court of the first instance. From this court a person can appeal to the court of the headman's immediate superior and thence to the court of the paramount chief. The sanctions administered for wrongs are usually fines, but in some cases an offender is punished by death (Hunter: 413).

The suppression of raiding has had limited success, and it seems to have had almost no effect on traditional standards of masculine conduct. For example, young boys exhibit warrior traits at early ages. Hunter (1961: 410) observes: "Small boys begin to carry sticks at about 5 years, and from that age are constantly fighting one another with sticks." She reports herdboys fighting each other in tournaments. They continue into adolescence fighting over grazing land and girls.

Hunter (1961: 410-411) reports that "the boys of one ridge, of one subdistrict, fight those of another. Sometimes they dare not enter each other's territory. . . . Subdistricts fight over grazing, and over girls. Gatherings in the hut of a girl being initiated, weddings, and festivals are usual occasions for a fight. Fights at festivals between subdistrict and subdistrict often become serious. Older men join in, and sticks are exchanged for spears. Women give the war cry, and word goes out, *ilizwe lifile!* [The country is at war!] One such fight began at a beer drink which I attended at Ntontela. . . . As always the division was on territorial lines, each man fighting with his neighbors. Three men died of wounds received in that fight." Hunter adds that such local disputes sometimes envelop whole tribes.

The headmen, according to Hunter (1961: 427), report people involved in these violent encounters to the South African magistrates, who impose fines and imprisonment. Despite these sanctions, "Fights between young men of different districts, in which sticks and occasionally spears or guns are used and individuals killed, are not unusual."

Mpondo fathers are devoted to their children, carrying them about in their arms, fondling them, playing with them, and teaching them to dance. As children grow older, however, they are taught respect and obedience, which are particularly due their fathers because of the patriarchal traditions. These traditions also encourage the use of violence toward women. Hunter (1961: 30) reports, for instance, that one man beat his brother's wife because she had beaten only one of a group of quarreling children.

Most of the quarrels between husband and wife turn on the double standards in sexual morality, according to Hunter (1961: 42). Men can have as many wives as they can afford, but a wife is forbidden to have relations with any except her own husband. In practice, many of the married women have lovers, even though their husbands make every effort to catch and prosecute the adulterer. Sometimes the jealousies between husbands and wives over adultery lead to wife beatings (Hunter, 1961: 41-45).

As with the Lovedu, the South African criminal justice system involves itself in certain aspects of life among the Mpondo. Responding perhaps to the greater interpersonal violence, South African magistrates seem to be more active among the Mpondo than among the Lovedu. Imprisonment and execution are used as sanctions by the South African government.

The Mpondo are obviously more violent than the Lovedu or Mbuti, but for a quantum leap in violence beyond the others, we must examine the Baganda.

Baganda

The Baganda's dominant mode of production is based on the extraction of an agricultural surplus (in the form of labor, rent, or tribute through taxation) directly from peasant producers by landlords and political officials. The Baganda had their own judicial system at the time they were studied by John Roscoe, an anthropologist and missionary who spent twenty-five years in Africa.

The Baganda belong to a *class* society in which the juridical system, headed by the king's court, enforces the law and administers punishment. When fines are used as punishment, the state typically takes a lion's share and gives the rest as compensation to the injured party. In addition to levying fines, the king's court administers justice through imprisonment in stocks, agonizing torture, and execution.

Roscoe (1965: 259) notes: "The King often brought a spurious charge against a chief who was becoming rich, and fined him heavily, or sent him to prison, intimating to him that he must pay a handsome sum if he wished to be freed; failing that, he would be cast into the stocks, where he would be so much ill used, that he would be glad to pay any fine to escape the torture and the danger of being put to death."[2]

In the "lower courts", petty theft and disobedience on the part of a child are often punished by burning the child's hand or cutting off his ear. "The punishment of children was usually far in excess of the fault; and little mercy was shown when the child was a slave or an orphan. Adults often have their hands cut off for theft," says Roscoe (1965: 267).

Adultery is punished severely: "Though death was usually the punishment inflicted for adultery, an offender's life would sometimes be spared, and he be [sic] fined two women, if he were able to pay them; the culprit was, however, maimed; he lost a limb, or had an eye gouged out, and showed by his maimed condition that he had been guilty of a crime. A slave taken in adultery with one of his master's wives was invariably put to death" (Roscoe, 1965: 261).[3]

Corporal punishment could also be inflicted by any man on his wives or slaves, but this was a private affair. Punishment might consist of cutting off a person's lips, ears, or one hand, or gouging out an eye. Moreover, a husband is also allowed to torture his wife until she confesses if he suspects her of committing adultery. Roscoe (1965: 263) indicates the following procedure for the torture: "The woman was stripped and made to lie down; her legs and arms were stretched out and tied to the posts of the house; she was flogged, and then left in this position for the whole night, or until she made confession. The husband would not be punished by law, even if he killed his wife under such circumstances; her relations might have the case tried, but if it was proved that she was in the wrong, no one would condemn the husband. If the husband was proved to have unjustly tortured or killed his wife, her relations would be satisfied with fining him."

Women's roles among the Baganda are defined in terms of serving their husbands and supplying them with children. This is apparent in the differential socialization of boys and girls. Boys are allowed time for fun, while girls are put to work that is unremitting. Roscoe (1965: 77) says: "Boys had a free and happy life while the time of herding lasted; they met together daily, and while the animals browsed, they had ample time for all kinds of games." He notes further: "Girls seldom played games; they were kept busy for the whole day, and were taught to make mats and baskets to occupy their leisure time; they also drew water and brought in fire-wood. From the time that a girl arrived at puberty, she was called Mulongo, a term used of a cow when it was old enough to have calves." Girls learned their female roles early. Roscoe (1965: 79-80) observes: "Girls were taught to cook and to cultivate as soon as they could hoe."

The mother had charge of the child temporarily in its earliest years, but it would soon go to one of the father's relatives. Roscoe (1965: 61) says: that "children as they grew up had some regard for their parents; the father was at least feared and respected, while there was something approaching love shown towards the mother. . . . She might hug it, and pat it, while it was small, when it was cross or had been hurt."

In previous centuries, the ruling classes of the Baganda engaged in war and raids to capture people for the slave trade. When Roscoe made his observations, the Baganda still attacked neighboring tribes and were known for their merciless treatment of conquered people. The acquisitions from war could number hundreds of women and servants and more than a thousand cattle. Male prisoners taken in battle were speared or clubbed to death, while the women were enslaved and some of them awarded for valor to military personnel. If the army won a battle, the defeated enemy was made to suffer greatly; their wives, servants, cattle, goats, sheep, ivory, and anything else valuable they possessed were seized. All the men except the children were put to death.

It is not necessary to continue describing the Baganda to illustrate our hypothesis about the general relation between violence, sexual inequality, and socioeconomic formations. We grant that variations in violence are produced by historical conjunctures that affect the evolution of a mode of production or the class struggles and political institutions that secure a mode.[4] Nevertheless, the variation in violence that we have seen here and elsewhere on the face of the globe is not produced by the inherent nature of man. Clearly, this variation is socially determined, and different modes of production are basic to this determination. Finally, the exploitative modes of production that have culminated in the formation of class societies have either produced or intensified sexual inequality and violence.

Notes

1. Unfortunately, other anthropological sources on the four tribes provide no information specifically on rape. However, this lack of information does not negate the importance of Turnbull's observation of no Mbuti rapes or of our general hypothesis about sexual inequality, violence, and modes of production. Since Uganda has a central government (or at least a semblance of one after Idi Amin's dictatorship), statistics on rape may be available. For instance, Turnbull's field study was published in 1965, and in that year, there were 1,063 convictions in Uganda for rape, murder, and armed robbery (see Herrick et al. 1969: 385). The numbers of convictions, however, are not very useful, because they are grouped with other violent crimes and apply to the country as a whole. Also, the actual number of crimes is obviously much higher than the number of convictions; moreover, these figures are very conservative, since as Herrick et al. (1969: 382) note, police in remote rural areas do not use formal courts, nor do they report crimes to the central government. On the other hand, some comparison may ultimately be possible regarding *levels* of violence, since rape, murder, and armed robbery are far less frequent among the Mbuti.

2. Roscoe's account appears filled with moral and European bias associated with anthropologists who are also missionaries; however, even if we discount some of his observations, there remain enormous differences between the other social groups and the Baganda.

3. On the other hand, the husband's own life may be at stake if the adulterer is powerful. "If a peasant found that his chief was making love to his wife, he would pack up his goods and leave the district by night lest he should be put to death on her account; should his wife refuse to go with him, he would leave her behind," according to Roscoe (1965: 263-264).

4. Such variations include, for example, differences in violence and inequality within the capitalist mode of production during stages involving the primitive accumulation of capital and monopoly capital, or historical conjunctures involving bourgeois democracy and fascism. Other refinements would consider whether a mode of production is based on visible forms of exploitation, such as slavery, feudalism, or tributary modes, or on forms that are not immediately apprehensible, such as capitalist commodity relations. Finally, such variations should take into account the violence created by metropolitan nations within dependent, peripheral nations and not the violence within metropolitan nations alone.

PART IV

PRIORITIES FOR RAPE PREVENTION

CHAPTER 12

SEXUAL SUBJUGATION AND MECHANISMS OF VIOLENCE

Rape, as we know, repeats itself through the annals of class societies. The conquering hordes of Genghis Khan raped and plundered during their innumerable forays. European feudal mercenaries, when fighting in neighboring principalities, raped and looted towns and villages. Homecoming bands of sixteenth-century British soldiers, embittered by denial of pay and defeat abroad, raped and pillaged at will after landing on English soil. The Force Publique of the Congo, a native colonial army, adopted the ethos of their imperial Belgian masters; they too raped and plundered Congolese people.

Furthermore, early accounts of the Iroquois and other American seaboard tribes indicate that rape was not used in warfare before the Europeans arrived. Tribal societies in the New World, conquered by European settlers, learned to meet force with force, adopting the new violent tactics of the conquerers along with their more sophisticated weapons. For example, the Europeans raped Indian women, burned villages, scalped the men in punitive raids, and in some cases massacred entire tribes in order to force the Indians from the land. In retaliation, rape and other tactics were used by the Indians who sought to match the Europeans' ruthlessness and ferocity. In the Philippines today these events are being partly reenacted. Coveting the traditional territories of neighboring tribal communities, Christian settlers hire thugs and bandits to rape and terrorize the tribes.[1]

Consequently, in an endless spiral of cruelty and violent counterreactions, numerous forms of violence, including rape, were conferred on the people of the world. Rape itself became associated with violent practices organized around broader aims: the subjugation of women and the exploitation of tribes, classes, and other social groups. Violence became the focus of a seemingly endless struggle by individuals, classes, and nations for power and property. Since rape is associated with violence in other forms, it is important to discuss the mechanisms of other violent relationships that reinforce it.

We consider some mechanisms of interpersonal violence, first showing that they can include perceivable social pressures backed by military force. Then we will describe a social mechanism that is hardly discernible, because it involves circumstances in which violence seems to emerge from purely personal motives and and not society at all.

Mechanisms of Interpersonal Violence

Although some societies were violent and patriarchal before contact with Europeans, for those that did not already have these characteristics, the contact often stimulated violence as well as patriarchy. Some of these changes are illustrated in the article by Leacock and Goodman (1976) referring to the seventeenth-century chronicles of Paul Le Jeune, the Jesuit missionary mentioned earlier.

After wintering with Montagnais families, Le Jeune wrote: "They are very much attached to each other, and agree admirably. You do not see any disputes, quarrels, enmities, or reproaches among them" (Leacock and Goodman, 1976: 82). But Le Jeune's admiration was outweighed by his mission to "improve" the level of native morality. He and his countrymen systematically instigated the changes that seriously undermined this interpersonal amity. They substituted such unfamiliar mechanisms of violence as torture and corporal punishment for women and men.

Le Jeune's chronicles show that French missionaries and troops pressured or cultivated social changes that were religious, familial, and political. For example, when some of the

Montagnais converted to Christianity, they adopted the patriarchal family and accepted a "system of permanent chiefs" that
enforced religious and colonial mandates, violently when
necessary. Economic changes were also imposed: The French
encouraged fur trading with European class societies. As the
Indians warred with each other over the gains from fur trap-
ping, the Montagnais took delight in torturing their Iroquois
prisoners.

Furthermore, before the arrival of the French, the Montagnais abhorred corporal punishment. Three incidents will show
how their outlook changed.

At first, when the French introduced corporal punishment,
it was rejected even when it was administered to a French boy
who had wronged one of the Montagnais. In the chronicles, Le
Jeune tells this story: "One of [the Montagnais] was looking
very attentively at a little French boy who was beating a drum;
and, going near to see him better, the little boy struck him a
blow with one of his drumsticks and made his head bleed
badly." Immediately all the tribal onlookers took offense and
loudly demanded compensation. They cried: "Behold, one of
thy people has wounded one of ours; thou knowest our custom
well; give us presents [compensation] for this wound."[2]

Le Jeune, noting that "there is no government among the
Savages," recorded the native mode of settling accounts. He
said: "If one kills or wounds another, he is . . . released from all
punishment by making a few presents to the friends of the
deceased or the wounded one." Once again, Le Jeune had
encountered an absence of internal mechanisms of violence.

The French viewed the incident with the boy as an opportunity to teach the Montagnais an object lesson. The interpreter
turned to the Indians and said: " 'Thou knowest our custom;
when any of our number does wrong, we punish him. This child
has wounded one of your people; he shall be whipped at once in
thy presence.' As the Savages saw we were really in earnest
. . . they began to pray for his pardon, alleging he was only a
child, that he had no mind, that he did not know what he was
doing; but as our people were nevertheless going to punish him,

one of the Savages stripped himself entirely, threw his blankets over the child and cried out to him who was going to do the whipping: 'Strike me if thou wilt but thou shalt not strike him.' And thus the little one escaped" (Leacock and Goodman, 1976: 90).

After the mission priests converted some of the Indians to Christianity, further internal violence was brought about as they set these persons against the others. The Christian Indians became surrogates of religious authority and its sexual morality. European standards of punishment were then imposed on the members of the band with the aid of the converts as well as colonial troops. Le Jeune's chronicle illustrates this imposition after the authority of the Christian chiefs had been established.

Le Jeune also tells how a young Indian woman, who had separated from her husband, was chased, captured, and then threatened with imprisonment in a dungeon if she did not return to her husband's domicile. Imprisonment and other harsh measures were recommended by the Indian Christian converts, who had learned that it was the custom in France to "proceed in that manner" with recalcitrant wives.

The chronicle reads: "When the Savages returned from their great hunt, one of the Fathers called the [leaders] together, and told them that he was greatly edified because they had put a stop to the disorderly conduct that occasionally occurred among them; but that he was astonished at their permitting that a young baptized woman should live apart from her husband. The Captain, under whose jurisdiction this woman was, replied that he had tried all sorts of means to make her return to her duty and that his trouble had been in vain; that he would, nevertheless, make another effort" (Leacock and Goodman, 1976: 87). The Father asked the Captain to consult his group of converts and ask their opinion of what should be done to make the wife obey her husband. "They all decided upon harsh measures. 'Good advice,' they said, 'has not brought her to her senses; a prison will do so,' " Le Jeune writes (Leacock and Goodman, 1976: 87).

Two captains were ordered to take the disobedient woman to a dungeon in Quebec. When they arrived at her cabin, however, they found that she had seen them coming and, suspecting their errand, fled to the woods. The captains dashed into the woods after her. She was caught and dragged back to the settlement. Le Jeune continues, "As she tried to break away from them, they bound her and placed her in a canoe, to take her to Kebec [Quebec].

"Some Pagan young men, observing this violence — of which Savages have a horror, and which is more remote from their customs than Heaven is from Earth, — made use of threats, declaring that they would kill any one who laid a hand on the woman. But the Captain and his people, who were Christians, boldly replied that there was nothing they would not do or endure, in order to secure obedience to God. Such resolution silenced the infidels. The woman was taken to Kebec; but when she saw that she must enter either a dungeon or her husband's house, she humbly begged to be taken back to Saint Joseph, promising thence forward she would be more obedient. Such acts of justice cause no surprise in France, because it is usual there to proceed in that manner. But, among these peoples . . . where everyone considers himself from birth, as free as the wild animals that roam in their great forests . . . it is a marvel, or rather a miracle, to see a peremptory command obeyed, or any act of severity or justice performed."

With satisfaction at the changes in the Montagnais, Le Jeune reflects, "Some Savages, having heard that in France, malefactors are put to death, have often reproached us, saying that we were cruel, — that we killed our own countrymen; that we had no sense. They asked us whether the relatives of those who were condemned to death did not seek vengeance. The Infidels still have the same ideas; but the Christians are learning, more and more, the importance of exercising justice" (Leacock and Goodman, 1976: 88).

Men also became objects of corporal punishment, sometimes inflicting violence on themselves. Once again, religious zeal was involved. In one such account, the punishment expressed the personal guilt, sexual obsession, and self-flagellation cultivated by Christianity. One can imagine the moralistic sentiments imposed by the French for this to happen.

Le Jeune wrote: "A young savage, recently married, felt tempted to leave his wife, and the thought caused him deep sorrow. The Devil pictures to him the delight of changing a wife whom one hates for another whom one loves. . . . He remembers the word that he has plighted to God and to his wife; he wishes to be faithful, but nevertheless, he feels himself inclined toward infidelity. He goes to his Director. . . . The mere idea of changing his wife seems to him so great a crime that he entreates to be sent to prison and to be put into a dungeon or to be publicly flogged. Seeing his request refused, he slips into a room near the Chapel and, with a rope that he finds, he beats himself so hard all over the body that the noise reaches the ears of the Father, who runs in and forbids so severe a penance" (Leacock and Goodman, 1976: 84). In religious, familial, and political life, the Montagnais were adopting internal mechanisms of violence under the tutelage of their European "betters."

Spontaneous Mechanisms of Violence

While the use of violence against women by some Montagnais did not take hold until colonial domination occurred, this violence emerged within the great colonial powers such as France, England, and others under somewhat different circumstances.

Violence against women has its own basis in each socioeconomic formation. In feudalism, the status of women under the doctrine of coverture justified the violence against women in family relations. However, in early capitalism, this status was more complex than it might seem. It became intertwined with the personal dependencies based on class control of rents and income stemming from early capitalist, agrarian commodity relations rather than serfdom.

For instance, H. Perkin (1969: 37), author of *The Origins of Modern English Society,* 1780-1880, writes: "In the small communities, the villages and tiny towns, of the old society . . . the source of income itself, with the rest of the 'life chances' of the individual, was controlled by a paternal landlord, employer or patron. . . . In a world of personal dependency any breach of the 'great law of subordination,' between master and servant, squire and villager, husband and wife, father and child, was a sort of petty treason, to be ruthlessly suppressed. . . . Literally so in the case of women who murdered, or were accessory to the murder of their husbands, who were burned at the stake for their 'petty treason.' "[3]

In "Rape Victims and the False Sense of Guilt" (Schwendinger and Schwendinger, 1980) we have indicated that the dependency relations imposed on women have been grounded historically in the socioeconomic changes that have restricted most women to the continuous production of use values in the home and men, to production for commodity exchange. Such dependency makes wives vulnerable to sexual violence in the home and liable to blame themselves if they are raped. Male authority and dominance patterns are also related to these dependency relations (1980: 11-13). With the advent of the industrial revolution and the factory system, most families were forced to change from relatively self-sufficient producers in an agrarian economy to commodity consumers in an industrialized economy. This type of consumption requires the purchase of commodities produced *outside* the home and sold in the market for a profit (Zaretsky, 1976).

During this period of industrialization, families were given a new reproductive role and socialization task. The emphasis now was on reproducing, socializing, and maintaining a work force to be employed *outside* the household. Families raised new generations of wage earners, and they nourished and cared for those who went out of the home each day to perform wage labor. In a sense, reproduction was involved in the care of both generations of wage earners.

In addition to demanding that the work force be constantly reproduced and expanded at little cost to capital, the economic forces that changed family life also forced married couples apart. To maximize profits, employers demanded a fully exploitable labor force that could toil where and when the market commanded.[4]

Two developments important to understanding female dependency grew out of these economic prerequisites. New industrial firms, with some exceptions, hired a predominantly male labor force extended by a female force of largely single women, to produce commodities for sale. Simultaneously, the household economy was reorganized primarily around married women engaging in production for use, that is, producing items not for sale but for consumption by the immediate family.

The roles of working-class men and women changed as a result of these developments. There was a critical reduction in the father role as men were separated from the household and traveled to work further away from their homes. Women's role was being more and more narrowly defined as private houseworker, childbearer and child raiser. The role of many women, now restricted in its economic functions, became even more firmly circumscribed within the family, especially when they married. Among the majority of families in the industrialized West, a new economic basis was developed for defining the woman and her children as dependents.

The married woman came to be seen as an economically nonproductive person dependent on others for access to food, clothing, and shelter. On the other hand, this view of the woman as nonproductive actually refers solely to her absence from participation in commodity markets where people earn money. Within the household economy, the working-class housewife, as indicated, usually engages only in the production of use values. In addition to processing vital foodstuffs, she extends the life of the furniture, clothing, and other equipment essential for living. She prolongs the lives of family members by seeing to their medical needs and by keeping the living quarters clean. Her productive activities further include inculcating in children the habits and attitudes that are essential for reproducing the work force through the generations. In other words, her labor penetrates the lives of family members in innumerable ways, and the husband as well as the children are fully dependent on it. If the wages are especially low, the wife is driven to exhaustion trying to close the gap between income and need.

The married woman is forced to engage in this production because a substantial portion of the costs of maintaining herself and the children are not covered by her husband's wages. Despite chauvinistic claims to the contrary, working-class husbands do not really earn enough to sustain their families by themselves. Under these conditions the wife cannot obtain a "wage" because there is no money that can be exchanged for the value of her labor. Employers will never pay women for work they cannot exploit directly, and husbands do not earn enough to pay wives what their labor is worth. Who, then, is left to pay? No one. Consequently, wives engage in *unpayable* labor to make up the difference. After the husband's wage is spent on necessities including recreation, there is simply no money left.

Why then should working-class housewives be considered dependents? Once the family is established and the wage earner's reciprocal support becomes a fundamental obligation, he himself cannot endure on the job without her labor unless he can afford to pay outsiders to look after his family's requirements. He cannot work vigorously on a daily basis while eating a diet of uncooked meat and raw potatoes. Neither can he be free of vermin and disease, which result in loss of time on the job, if he lives in filthy quarters. Simple logic reveals that he is just as economically dependent on her as she is on him. Yet, even though her labor is so vital that the husband is equally dependent on her, the housewife alone is assigned a dependent status.

The nitty-gritty of these social relations and the answer to the question, "Why are wives dependents?" takes us into a more theoretical realm for a moment. The source of the wife's dependent status centers on the relationship between the economy based on *the production of use values* in the household and the economy based on *the capitalist mode of production* outside.

How do these complementary economies interact? The working-class husband engages in production for exchange, and his wage is a measure of his contribution. His wage is used by family members, but they do not control the way the capitalist or the law defines ownership of it. The wage transaction is based on the use of his labor power, and the contract is made only with the individual worker. His labor power is consumed in exchange for the wage; therefore it is his wage, not his wife's. Since the housewife only produces for family use, her labor is necessarily unpayable labor and, while her needs are partly supported by the husband's wage, she is totally dependent on that wage for access to the commodities necessary for the family's existence.

Although legally the male worker has an obligation to maintain his wife and children, the wage's status as her husband's property influences her relations with the marketplace. She is not viewed as an autonomous person. She spends *his* money when buying necessities. Despite all the hours she must work to make up the difference between the wage and the price of commodities, she cannot automatically regard the wage as collective property. She can take her husband to court if he does not give her enough money for the most basic necessities, but even this option shows that she cannot take for granted that the wage is collectively owned.

Since the wife has a highly productive role in production for use, why doesn't this contribute to her autonomy? From the beginning of capitalism, the validation of autonomy has anchored itself deeply in the ideological reflections of commodity relationships. After the bourgeoisie come into control of the state, market relationships become a central pillar of bourgeois law. This form of law codifies and extends some of the ideas of the competitive market. It conceives of people as juridical subjects (people whose social relations are defined by law) who enter into relationships with one another as formal equals, each engaging in commodity exchange. Furthermore, the things that are exchanged, such as money, land, and the products of labor are fetishized: they appear to have living power to "make money" when they are invested, rented out, or sold. In this "market economy," the validation of autonomy wells up spontaneously but only for those commodity holders whose livelihoods are based on property holdings or earnings that can renew the individual's daily existence.

Thus, the same capitalist conditions that have concentrated men in productive activities for exchange, and women in activities for use, spontaneously trigger the customary practices that define housewives as dependents. These practices vest family authority in husbands so long as the so-called unproductive housewife is dependent on her husband's wage to purchase commodities. Even though this relationship between commodity ownership, status, and authority may not be reflected in some of the newer laws about married women's rights, its influence still pervades everyday life. Also, because of these restrictions and dominant moral standards in capitalist societies, the dependency of women has been equated ideologically with inferior abilities and capacities. Such ideological equations also enter into the determination of the status relations that legitimate sexual inequality.

Similar changes in family economies, dominant-submissive relations, and violence against wives continue to occur today in developing nations. A study by Patricia Draper (1975) dealing with the impact of modern African labor markets on village family relationships illustrates these changes. Although they are taking place under different circumstances, the effects of capitalism on sexual relations and patriarchal violence, in this study, parallel the changes that occurred in Western societies. Draper's study is also significant because it contrasts aboriginal *band* sexual equality and relatively nonviolent family relations, on the one hand, with *village* inequality and greater family violence, on the other.

Draper's field experiences focus on the !Kung Bushmen aboriginal bands that forage on the edges of the great Kalahari desert. However, in addition, she details the changing patterns of life among those band members who have migrated into village settlements. In the villages the egalitarianism of the band is disappearing, yet this change does not appear to be imposed by any force from the outside. Importantly, from the standpoint of everyday life, it seems to arise *spontaneously* from the personal inclinations and the changing roles and relationships of people inside the village itself.

Draper's (1975: 87-93) observations begin with the familiar correspondence between primitive communism and sexual equality. She notes that among the people living in bands, in the economic sphere, which is based on hunting and gathering, !Kung women have personal autonomy. Also, there is no rigid sextyping for most adult activities, including domestic chores and raising children in their communal society. Finally, the !Kung nomads are gentle and actively discourage any sign of harmful competition among males and violence between the sexes. The aboriginal bands are unquestionably characterized by sexual equality.

All of this is changing, however, as the !Kung are relocating in villages where the economy is partly organized around commodity production. This commodity activity involves the private ownership of livestock on land surrounding a village and the exploitation of male wage labor in nearby Bantu or European settlements (Draper, 1975: 100-103). In the villages themselves, the authority of males is gradually increasing and the status of women is declining.

Why are these changes taking place? Partly it is because the desire for higher living standards encourages the men to leave the village, frequently for several days at a time, to work for Bantu employers. When they return, their authority is heightened by their control over goat and cattle raising and their mastery of the Bantu language and customs. These work experiences and the knowledge of Bantu also encourage male participation in political relations that are largely based on contacts with the other settlements.

Village women likewise have become enmeshed in household economies whose material inventory is much richer than that of the nomadic bands. In the village, food preparation becomes more complicated. Furthermore, Draper (1975: 101) says, "Women do the greatest part of the cooking, and they also do most of the [food] drying and storing." Household possessions also require more energy to maintain. The women, therefore, spend more time and work harder at domestic tasks.

In addition, village relations are being affected by severe economic and political constraints that operate behind the scenes. The village economy is organized around independent peasant households, and it is essentially based on a pre-capitalist mode of production in the process of being shaped by its articulation with a capitalist mode of production. However — unlike the Montagnais under seventeenth-century French colonial rule — there is no military or religious institution blatantly imposing these changes in the village itself. Instead, the allocation of men, in everyday life, to commodity production and women to household labor, outside of the economic constraints, appears to be based on spontaneous choices exercised freely by individuals.

Along with their competition for status and material wealth, the men are becoming more aggressive and contemptuous of women. In the nomadic bands, a woman finding herself with an uncongenial husband quickly leaves his company and spends a year or two in casual flirtations before marrying again. In the village, however, couples are held together in fitful marriages by economic pressures. At the same time, public censure is addressed to the wife; and slander by boastful husbands in public settings deflects social criticism of marital conflicts away from the men (Draper: 97).

Simultaneously, the organization of space and privacy in the villages isolates marital conflicts. Village men spend more of their time in economic activities away from the village or on its periphery while women are more restricted to the household economy centered on the residence. Moreover, in the bush, choice of residence is such that over time married couples live about equally — often simultaneously — with the kin of both the husband and wife. Consequently, a bushwoman who is involved in a marital dispute usually has several of her kin to support her interests nearby. Village wives, however, live only with their husbands and are more readily denied such support because the family is considered a private sphere. "In the bush," Draper (1975: 107-108) says, "people can see each other and determine, on a variety of grounds, whether it is appropriate or timely to initiate social interaction. In the . . . villages one heard such exchanges as 'So-and-so, are you at home?' and 'Shall I enter [your space]?' "

These apparently spontaneous developments are also creating new patterns of violence among the men. After experiencing the gentleness of the nomadic bands and the joyful cameradery shared by both sexes, Draper (1975: 109) was chilled when she heard a !Kung woman say: "If a [village] man is angry with his wife he could put her in their house, bolt the door and beat her. No one could get in to separate them. They could only hear her screams."

The same !Kung woman observed that this violence would not occur among the people in her nomadic band. First of all, the nomads would not even have their own houses with bolted doors and fences or customs that mark off an inviolable private space for domestic violence. Second, the band members move quickly to curb such aggression. If couples argue, people do not hesitate to intervene if either spouse loses self-control. "When we !Kung fight, other people get in between," the woman said (Draper, 1975: 109). The !Kung, then, like the Mbuti, actively intervene to control interpersonal violence so that it does not get out of hand.

Notes

1. This reference to Philippine tribes involves the Tboli. See Nance (1975: 80-83).

2. For a discussion of compensation in relation to laws and custom about rape, see Schwendinger and Schwendinger (1982).

3. However, one cannot overestimate the degree to which violence against women and women's status changed with advanced forms of capitalism. Although personal dependencies still flourish where power is tightly consolidated in the hands of single individuals, for example, in civil bureaucracies or corporations, the growth of industrial capital and working-class organizations has substantially undermined these relations outside the family. Furthermore, as capitalism continued to develop, the feudal doctrine of coverture and the legal right of husbands to administer corporal punishment in the United States has also fallen by the wayside. Today, while corporal punishment remains a serious problem in its use, only customary male-supremacist practices (not laws) justify corporal punishment for maintaining the wife's obedience to patriarchal authority.

4. The material that follows on women's position in family relations is derived partly from Clark (1968), Dixon (1978), Rapp (1979), Smith (1978), West (1978), and McIntosh (1978).

CHAPTER 13

FETISHISM OF VIOLENCE AND MOTIVES OF RAPISTS

In addition to the mechanisms of violence that support rape, as indicated, there are cultural standards that assign women less status than men. These standards operate within the context of traditional ways of thinking — or "cognitive schemata" — and they provide additional layers of symbolic meaning that support sexual inequality and violence.

Further, when we consider the attitudes of rapists, in just a moment, from the standpoints of political economy and social learning theory,[1] it is important to keep the social context of these attitudes in mind. Though the capitalist mode of production did not invent male supremacy, it provides its own foundations for this supremacy. Draper's observations in Chapter 12 provide further evidence of the degree to which sexual inequality is promoted by the articulation between the capitalist mode of production and precapitalist types of production.

As stated, capitalism did not invent violence, but it gives birth to conditions that reproduce violence anew. Capitalist conditions produce the personality developments that link the experiences and ideas of masculinity with violence and femininity with nonviolence. For instance, the allocation of women to social production for use within the family is consequential for character formation. Under these conditions, women undergo early childhood experiences that greatly restrict their engagement in violence and many other antisocial forms of conduct. Women act far less violently than men, whose character structures are more closely aligned with the exploitative requirements of the capitalist mode of production and the in-strumental norms of its competitive market. Furthermore, men retain a monopoly over weapons and training for war. With respect to crimes based on personal victimization, such as robbery, assault, burglary, and rape, female criminality can hardly be compared to criminality among men.

Also, the synchronization between masculinity and vio-lence and femininity and nonviolence is cultivated ideologi-cally. Everywhere in the United States, for instance, the mass media display the archetypal images of men whose innate vio-lence is presumably acted out in myriad situations. These media portrayals also leave a lasting impression that male ag-gression, rather than socioeconomic relationships, is the fun-damental source of violence in general.

Furthermore, in everyday life this synchronization appears to be firmly rooted in biological differences. Two sets of condi-tions create this appearance. First, the relationship between violence and gender is often perceived firsthand within one's family, while the sociohistorical determinations of this relation-ship are not experienced directly. That is, the face-to-face rela-tions are readily observable, but the *historical* relationships are understandable only by theoretical reflection; they cannot be understood by simply observing everyday life.

Second, the weight of our cultural traditions favors biologi-cal explanations of social relationships. This is true especially whenever sexual, racial, or other biological traits seem obvi-ously correlated with social relationships that are seen day after day: women and kitchens, blacks and menial jobs. Thus, the personal appearances of things are influenced by preexisting interpretations of reality. Under these conditions, it is not sur-prising that the relationship between violence and gender seems to validate natural facts of life established from birth by genetic differences between men and women.

Sexual Fetishism of Violence

Such relationships underlie what we call the *sexual fetish-ism of violence*. Fetishism is a false and illusory notion about social or natural relationships. Fetishists harbor the illusion that a person or thing, such as a guru, idol, money, or natural object, has secret properties it really does not have. At the earliest level of religious evolution, the fetish is an object of worship. Fetishism is therefore defined as the deification of various things or objects (fetishes) to which mysterious supernatural forces are then attributed.

Male idols, for instance, were attributed vast powers of destruction, and female figures were associated with fertility and the force of life. Modern-day fetishes have similar qualities, although they do not necessarily involve religious symbols. In the case of the sexual fetishism of violence, the powers for determining war, crimes of violence, dictatorships, and colonial oppression are attributed to the nature of man, often in contrast to the nature of woman.

Thus, from a theoretical point of view, human relations are "fetishized" when social facts are seen as natural ones. Fetishism is involved when complex social relations are explained as resulting from natural or supernatural laws "governing" the power of people or things. When people take for granted that nature has made men predators on women or, for that matter, made them predators on all other living things, violence is itself fetishized sexually. *Here, the category of gender substitutes for the real social determinations of violence in general, as well as sexual violence in particular.*

Finally, since people have fetishized violence sexually for thousands of years, their sexual stereotypes operate as archetypal reference points for self-identity. Today, many men actively see themselves and are emotionally conditioned by these symbolic relationships. Regulating their behavior stereotypically, they believe in ready-made axioms and other "essential truths" about sexual relationships and act on the basis of their beliefs. They feel an obligation to act benevolently toward women who submit willingly to their "innate desire" for mastery but they easily find justifications for violence when women are "ungrateful." They believe too, that when women submit willingly, it denotes a natural passivity; although, on occasion, women can be dangerous. Despite the logical contradictions, they are equally convinced that whenever women do become their enemies, the Machievellian tendencies lurking deep in their feminine hearts are revealed.

Such stereotypic notions characterize the fetishism of violence. But, again, since many forms of violence are fetishized sexually, the words "man," "masculinity," and "machismo," in everyday life, stand for more than male domination of women. In the grammar of motives, these words serve as master symbols of male violence in general. In all sorts of circumstances, these words associate masculinity with violent power and domination: thus, they glorify violent sports, glamorize war, and idealize ruthless businessmen. Violence is even separated ideologically from its myriad ends and conditions; in this context, it appears to validate masculine ideals all by itself.

This sexual fetishism helps us understand why some rapists define homosexual rape as an affirmation of "manhood." Alan J. Davis (1968: 15-16), who studied homosexual rape in Philadelphia jails and prisons, says, "A primary goal of the sexual aggressor, it is clear, is the conquest and degradation of his victim. We repeatedly found that aggressors used such language as 'Fight or fuck,' 'We're going to take your manhood,' 'You'll have to give up some face,' and 'We're gonna make a girl out of you.' Some of the assaults were reminiscent of the custom in some ancient societies of castrating or buggering a defeated enemy."

Davis (1968: 15-16) suggests that these sexual assaults are not primarily caused by sexual deprivation. He concludes: "They are expressions of anger and aggression prompted by the same basic frustrations . . . [which] can be summarized as an inability to achieve masculine identification through avenues other than sex". Denied other avenues for expressing their "manhood," male prisoners displace their frustration in rape.

Davis's observations, in our opinion, are valid, yet his psychoanalytic causal explanation is not. Whatever its form, rape is mediated by social learning processes; and even though it can be catalyzed around personal frustration, it is vitally important to recognize that the crime occurs because men have learned to think and act violently regardless of whether or not they are experiencing any deprivation at all. The validation of personal "manhood" through violence is conditioned by the social experiences underlying sexual inequality and by the sexual fetishism of violence. Its expression is not necessarily restricted to frustrating conditions and defense mechanisms. Furthermore, as we shall see, the degree to which this fetishism is actually used by individuals to justify rape is strongly influenced by personal motives that are created by definable sets of social and political conditions.

Finally, in some men, sexual violence cannot be clarified adequately by frustration-aggression hypotheses because individual violence can be the result of a socially learned predisposition that is catalyzed by any source of emotional arousal (Zillman, 1971). Albert Bandura (1973: 56) clarifies the theory and highlights some of the research leading to this conclusion. For example, a series of experiments by P. H. Tannenbaum demonstrates that even nonaggressive sources of arousal enhance aggressive behavior under certain conditions. In an experiment conducted by R. G. Geen and E. C. O'Neal (1969), a mere arousing though nonirritating noise increased individuals' punitiveness *especially if they had prior exposure to aggressive models.* Violence can be a learned response to environmental conditions that have nothing to do with frustration; furthermore, studies show that aggressiveness in some people may be determined more by level of arousal than by its source.

Motives of Rapists: Patriarchal and Beyond

There are rapists who are indeed psychotic. In our opinion, the social and psychobiological causes of their behavior have not been adequately clarified by the current state of scientific theory and research. However, the large majority of rapists are driven by rational motives and thinking processes even if these are, in some cases, affected by acute neurotic and other psychological instabilities. Included here are men who were physically and sexually abused as children (although the conditioning of violence itself can occur without such abuse). Alcohol use also plays an important role in sexual assaults, even though this violence can occur independently of drunkenness. Some men abuse women violently when they are drunk because alcohol strips away the shallow feelings of guilt that inhibit existing positive sentiments toward certain kinds of violence. Alcohol also impairs the judgment of the consequences of violence and makes men willing to take risks they would otherwise not take, even though they harbor positive sentiments toward punitive violence.

Such sentiments can be learned in social contexts that should not be oversimplified as mere examples of male domination or patriarchal relationships. For example, previous chapters have highlighted the qualitative differences in rape in changing economic and political contexts. Such differences characterize the violent relations between classes — for example, between slave owners and slaves. They are manifested whenever rape is justified by an imperial conqueror, colonial guard, and feudal mercenary. Since these relationships add new and different dimensions to its motivated character, we conclude that sexual aggression can support colonialism, slavery, and so forth, and therefore not male domination alone.

These multidimensional relationships underscore the complexities of the rapist's motivation. Instead of expressing singular motives of sex, power, or status, the rapist's contempt for certain women may be fused with racial, class, religious, or national chauvinism. These chauvinisms match male supremacy and rape to definite social contexts, and they refer to women who are held in even greater contempt because they represent and epitomize a particular social group. Thus, in recent times, as we have seen, imperialist standards combined with sexism to select Bangladesh victims in the Pakistani-Bangladesh War. In the Vietnam War, racist standards were conjoined with sexist standards. Such mergers of ideological standpoints again suggest that the motivational dynamics of sexual assault link rapists and victims to the political economy as a whole.

Political ideologies may also determine the sexual aggressor's choice of victims. A good example is the fascist use of rape as an instrument of torture. Fascism is created by dictatorships of the most reactionary elements of capital to counteract socialist and national liberation movements. It developed among the Axis powers in the 1920s and 1930s. Since then, in the face of ensuing revolutions and collapse throughout the world capitalist system, in South America, for example, fascists have continued to justify sexual violence, torture, and other forms of brutality as instruments of state policy. These justifications are based on fascist ideologies.

After the coup against Salvador Allende in Chile, for instance, female political prisoners and their children were systematically tortured. "Torture in Chile," Rose Styron (1975: 258) reports, "is not isolated sadism but state policy, fashioned cleverly to create conformity by terrorization, dehumanization and destruction of the will through prolonged, incalculable pain." The tortures of women included the agony of scorching their nipples and genitals, the blind terror of applying shock treatments to all parts of their bodies, and, of course, gang rape. "An unknown number of women have been raped; some of them pregnant after rape have been refused abortions. Women have had insects forced up their vaginas; pregnant women have been beaten with rifle butts until they have aborted" (Styron, 1975: 259-256). This torture is motivated by an overriding contempt for basic human rights as well as the rights of women, especially women who are members of political and social groups that are objects of fascist repression.

The motives that drive such torture are not aimed at women alone. Men as well as women were reported by Styron (1975: 207): "Prisoners [male and female] have been forced to witness or participate in sexual depravities. . . . Prisoners have been forced to eat excrement, have been plunged endlessly into ice-cold water, have had their bones smashed, have been left to stand naked in the sun for many hours."

Fascism attacks even the most sacred religious principles. Recently, in El Salvador, three Mary Knoll women missionaries from the United States were sexually abused and killed by soldiers maintaining a fascist regime.

Sexual assault under such exploitative conditions can also be committed by individual men who are not state agents and who are not fully controllable by social policy. Some men under fascism, while being molded into general instruments of oppression, become immeasurably more brutal. Even highly oppressed men emulate their oppressors. Activated by a variety of political and chauvinistic sentiments, they affirm their own worth by degrading another's. Functioning willingly in totalitarian settings, they develop opportunistic motives, smouldering hatreds, envious feelings, and thoughts of revenge. Rape is but one expression of this brutalizing process, and it may be inflicted regardless of whether it is explicitly condoned by official policy at any given moment.

But rape is also a problem in the absence of such political extremes. The brutalization of men is not confined to fascism, nor does it necessarily involve overt oppression. Competitive and exploitative relations in capitalist societies generate an amoral individualism, and followers of this individualistic orientation, in all social classes, objectify and exploit people as things. They adopt a callous and instrumental indifference to suffering.

Moreover, these social relationships cultivate persons whose violent behavior is so egotistic in its motivation that it offends even the social standards upheld by established forms of domination. Rape is an example of a crime that offends the vast majority of people, including those who subscribe to patriarchal standards.

The egotistic perspectives that justify this crime, therefore, bring added layers of meaning to motivations based on hatred or contempt for women — for certain women or women in general. Such meanings come easily to persons who really do not care who is being victimized, so long as it is personally advantageous. Although difficult to see at first glance, there is a fine distinction between the *contempt* for others and the *indifference* to other people's welfare that reflects ways of thinking focusing only on egotistic satisfaction.[2]

In our research with juvenile and young-adult offenders, for example, we have noted the degree to which definitions of human beings can be stripped of all humanistic or conventional sentiment. Some criminals depict and live in a world of *givers* and *takers;* and the *takers* are accorded superior status. These criminals assume that successful persons justifiably achieve their positions in life primarily through the manipulation of less powerful beings. They are convinced that people are at each other's throats unceasingly in a game of life that has no moral rules. Society is seen as a jungle in which the powerful and exploitative individual has a greater chance of survival. Such a view can be expressed in combination with or apart from chauvinist standpoints. The exploited may be other males as well as females, white as well as black.

The emergence of this perspective can initially be observed on a large scale during adolescence, when highly delinquent youth begin to use typical kinds of victim terms to catalogue and stereotype others. The frequent adoption of "stereotypes of probable victims" — of words that refer to people as "punks," "pigeons," "chumps," "boxes," and "cunts" — signifies the victimizer's amoral attitudes toward victims.[3] Such stereotypes are generated by complex social processes that occur within peer formations: as adolescence merges with adulthood, they are associated eventually with maxims and adages that recreate society as one vast assemblage of instrumentally defined persons. Young hoodlums often express cynical yet pithy views of the nature of this social reality. They say:

It's *fuck-your-buddy-week*, fifty-two weeks of the year.

Do unto [exploit] others as they would do unto you — only *do it first.*

If I don't cop [steal] it, somebody else will.

You know, man, *everybody's* got their little game.

Significantly, it is often young men, who are active in subterranean economies in slums and ghettos, who adopt this cynical standpoint. Nevertheless, it would be wrong to consider their standpoint a simple survival ethic for coping with social deprivation and poverty. In actuality, such a cynical view intensifies the problems of survival, adding to the massive destruction of communal life created by economic and political conditions.[4]

Within slums and ghettos, peer groups such as clubs and gangs also contribute to the forms of sexual violence — for example, gang rape — as well as the incidence of sexual assaults in these communities. Within some groups, individual members conform overtly to instrumental and sexist norms, at least when they are in the company of peers. Thus, even though a member may vary in his personal commitments, group pressure, on occasion, demands evidence of loyalty to exploitative standards. We suspect that group assaults are less frequent on other social class levels; however, they do occur among middle-class youth, especially among those 14- to 19-year-olds who are organized into certain kinds of upper- and middle- class peer groups.[5] For example, middle-class males may be contemptuous of "indiscriminate" rapes by strangers; yet, under particular conditions, they themselves may regard some women as "fair game." A group of fraternity boys may consider it a lark to abduct and violate a woman who cannot defend herself or who has a "bad reputation" — that is, who has a reputation for promiscuity. At a party, a pair of exploitative males may see a young woman who has become drunk as having stepped beyond the pale and therefore as a legitimate target, a worthless being.

For the most part, fertile soil for the development of this perspective exists whenever the rapacious individualism of capitalism is combined with long-term economic instability, the repression of working-class consciousness, and the reorganization of everyday social relations around undisguised forms of exploitation.[6] Since these conditions are concentrated among marginal members of the labor force, studies find that a higher incidence of rape is committed by marginally employed or totally unemployed younger men.[7] In the Philadelphia study by Amir (1971: 71), as many as 90 percent of the sexual aggressors for both races were at the lower end of the occupational scale.

In Chapter 14 we point out that, in victimization studies, the most economically deprived women reported a far greater incidence of rape than any other group. This finding will be related to the social dynamics that induce higher crime rates among young males, especially in ghetto and slum communities.

Notes

1. Social learning theory emphasizes that people act on the basis of learning experiences, how they think, and what perceived relationships mean to them. Aggressive behavior is regulated by antecedent inducements, response feedback influences and cognitive processes that guide and regulate action. For understanding how this theoretical perspective is applied to the study of violence, see Bandura (1973).

2. Contempt often implies moral condemnation; however, if it devalues persons to justify exploitation simply because they have no power to determine their destiny, then it reflects amoral rather than moral meanings. Egotistic individuals use any kind of justification so long as it deals with situational constraints; consequently, psychoanalytic treatment often merely provides them with added justifications for their conduct. Since the motives that actually regulate their conduct cannot be identified on the basis of any given justification, we propose identifying "models of moral and amoral rhetoric" to evaluate consistency in their justifications. A discussion of these models and their theoretical interrelationships is contained in a forthcoming work by the authors on delinquency.

3. Such metaphors symbolize egotistic, instrumental perspectives toward probable victims. For a discussion of the concept of "stereotypes of probable victims," see Schwendinger and Schwendinger (1967). For an original application of this concept to the crime of rape, see Weis and Borges (1973).

4. The vast majority of young people do not aid their own survival by adopting such an ethic; moreover, their own survival is certainly not enhanced by rape, assault, or even theft from other people, most of whom are equally destitute. Since this ethic, in practice, makes life even more exploitative, calling it "a survival ethic" takes for granted its own standards for survival.

5. Schwendinger and Schwendinger (1976: Chapters 4, 5).

6. Such undisguised forms include the exploitation in subterranean markets which are partly based on illegal goods and services. For instance, in the United States today the enslavement of women for prostitution does not exist on a scale comparable to past centuries. Nevertheless, recent cases of adolescent prostitution indicate its persistence. These cases involve older adolescent girls who run away from homes in the Midwest and elsewhere to large cities such as New York. In the cities they are "befriended" by deceptive pimps who first win their confidence and then subject them to repeated rapes by acquaintances in order to break their will and condition them for prostitution.

7. For the concept of marginalization, see Schwendinger and Schwendinger (1976: Chapters 1-3). Also, studies of police reports find distributions that are similar to other street crimes. Rapists, too, are predominantly young, from 15 to 29 years of age, and their socioeconomic status tends to be low. Blacks are disproportionately represented in these distributions because racism in the United States continues to expose them more than other groups to the political and socioeconomic conditions that generate street crime.

CHAPTER 14

IMMEDIATE PRIORITIES FOR RAPE PREVENTION

In Chapter 13 we noted that many men learn to fetishize violence sexually; however, this does not mean that most men will engage in rape. The fact is that the majority of men in the United States do not violate women. Nonrapists come from all classes, and most are also imbued with patriarchal attitudes. In fact, the dominant patriarchal ideologies in countries like the United States place certain limits on violence. Even though they contain double standards and are frequently applied hypocritically, these ideologies do incorporate moral criteria for evaluating violence. Rape is usually considered an evil and unnatural perversion, presumably offending the laws of nature and God.

Still, we know that patriarchal attitudes are qualified by sexist conceptions that hold certain kinds of women in contempt or that objectify women instrumentally as mere things. We also noted that under certain circumstances, these conceptions are converted into stereotypes of probable victims. In war, where male behavior is especially conditioned by high levels of violence, such stereotypes are buttressed by racial and national chauvinisms that generate enormous increases in sexual victimization by soldiers.

Further, within the United States, the stereotyping of probable victims and the level of interpersonal violence in urban ghettos and slums merit very special consideration. The level of violence in these communities conditions the relations between the sexes, especially among men whose main sources of income are unstable and low-wage jobs or illegal economic activities. With persistent underemployment, some of these men go through a series of dependent relationships, relying for income and resources on family, other relatives, and friends. Some finally turn to thievery and hustling in illegal markets where the exploitation of sexuality has no bounds.[1]

Within these populations, women sometimes provide more stable sources of economic assets than men because of their own earnings, their access to welfare payments, or their role in extended family relationships where they govern the redistribution of whatever resources are available among sisters, brothers, in-laws, and children. Under these conditions, the importance of manipulating and controlling women, by violence if necessary, is elevated among those men who accept capitalism's premises yet who develop extremely cynical and parasitic adaptations to their class situations. A ramified instrumental ideology emerges among men who make these adaptations, and this ideology negates the moral standards supported even by traditional patriarchal standpoints.

Furthermore, under these conditions, we find a greater proportion of peer groups subscribing to violent macho ideals. Sexual attacks by groups of two or more males accounted for as much as 24 percent of the rapes found by a victimization study of twenty-six cities.[2] Such rapes can also be attributed largely to the long-term effects of male supremacy, racism, and adverse economic conditions on family, school, and community life. Since these violent peer groups develop prior to labor market engagement and are secondary products of class conditions, they are relatively impervious to short-term economic fluctuations.

Responding to Rape

We have emphasized socioeconomic conditions because their theoretical significance has generally been ignored by people interested in creating crime-fighting policies helpful to women in our society. In the context of such policymaking, it is well to recall that the struggle for women's rights at the turn of the 1970s made rape a symbol for virtually all the social harms generated by sexual inequality. Consequently, for many women, the response to this crime went beyond the harms done to sexual assault victims alone. The response became infused with a moral outrage so intense, it flared up against every form of violence inflicted by men upon women.

On the other hand, while this kind of outrage is very important, it cannot substitute for an adequate social theory. Without a realistic understanding of society, outrage invites utopianism and eventually disillusionment. Furthermore, without an emphasis on the socioeconomic factors contributing to violence, this outrage is easily captured by demogogic appeals to repressive crime control. It is readily absorbed by political movements that locate the fundamental causes of crime within individuals rather than the social conditions under which individual criminals thrive.

Thus, whether or not moral outrage catalyzes people around effective crime-fighting policies depends on how the causes of crime are interpreted. Is sexual violence a crime that erupts from individual characteristics alone or from the sordid nature of men in general? Or does it essentially express complex causal patterns due to the nature of society? The answers to these questions are extremely important. If social relationships are the fundamental causes, then the repression of individual rapists will never provide anything beyond a short-term, temporary solution to the reduction of rape. For every imprisoned rapist, unchanged social conditions will create other rapists to take his place from the population at large.[3]

In addition to the anthropological evidence shown in previous chapters, there are victimization studies that support a broader policy perspective on sexual assault. These studies are especially valuable because they are based on interviews of women and therefore measure the incidence of sexual victimization independently of the police. The rape rates in victimization studies are higher than official rates and they are more representative of rape incidents especially by strangers, ac-

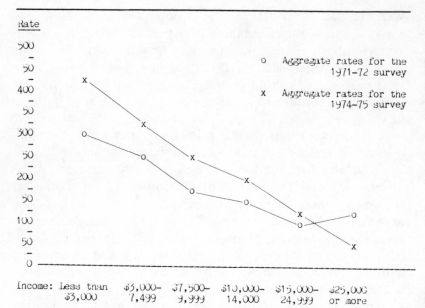

NOTE: Rates are based on numbers of attempted and completed rapes per 100,000 females 12 years of age and older. The cities are: Atlanta, Baltimore, Cleveland, Dallas, Denver, Newark, Portland, St. Louis. Source of data: *Criminal Victimization Surveys in Eight American Cities,* U.S. Department of Justice, LEAA, NCJ Information and Statistics Services, November 1976.

Figure 1: **Estimated Rape Rates, by Family Income of Victim, for 1971-1972 and 1974-1975 (8-cities aggregates)**

quaintances and friends. Some of these crimes such as rape by strangers are particularly terrifying to the population at large.

How do victimization studies support a broadened outlook on crime prevention policies? Just like most other violent "street crimes," sexual assault by nonfamily members is not committed equally in all parts of the population. It is committed primarily by older adolescents and young adults. In addition, the social class of both rapists and their victims is skewed toward one end of the income scale. Figure 1 is derived from two victimization studies conducted 3 years apart in the same 8 cities. Both studies found that victims from low-income groups had the highest rape rates.

Larger victimization studies demonstrate that the relationship between family income and victimization is neither accidental nor due to unreliable responses in other studies.[4] Each small diagram in Figure 2 represents rape rates found by victimization studies of selected large cities or the nation as a whole. Figure 1 has been reduced in size and is represented in the top (left-hand) small diagram in Figure 2. Each of the other small diagrams in Figure 2 shows a tendency similar to that in Figure 1, for different years and different populations. These other diagrams illustrate findings from a 1973 survey of 13 large cities[5]; a 1974-1975 survey of 26 large cities; and two studies of nationwide samples in 1977 and 1978.[6] All discovered the same relationship between victims of rape and family income.[7] Survey after survey has found that the *overwhelming* majority of women who experienced rape or attempted rape have had annual family incomes of less than $10,000.[8]

As indicated, this systematic trend is not the only one showing the importance of social class relationships for the study of this crime. Rapists usually (but not always) pick victims with economic backgrounds that are similar to their own (Amir, 1971: 70, 91-92). When this choice is compared with the disproportionate number of poorer victims, the implications are equally significant. Furthermore, it is likely that the socioeconomic status of most rapists is fairly similar to the status of most apprehended offenders in all the other violent index crime categories. In other words, the poor are highly overrepresented.

This likelihood becomes stronger when we consider the sexual assaults that are accompanied by theft. In the victimization study of 26 cities, victims who were subject to completed rape reported that the attacker stole money or other items of value or tried unsuccessfully to steal something.[9] Only 20 percent of the completed rapes of victims in the lowest income category were accompanied by theft, presumably because these victims possessed little of value. On the other hand, an analysis of this data shows that as many as 40 percent of the attacks on women with incomes of $10,000 and more were

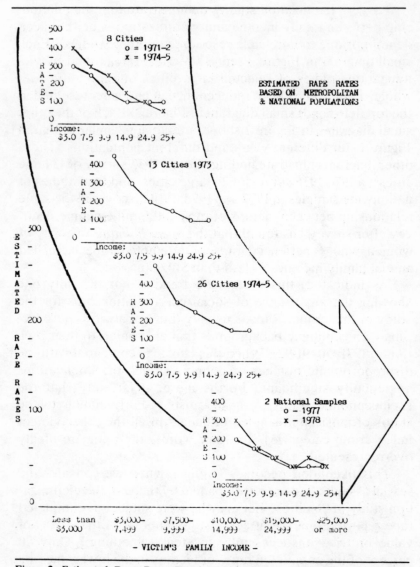

Figure 2: Estimated Rape Rates Based on Metropolitan and National Populations

accompanied by theft.[10] Since robbers are hardly likely to be wealthy, a substantial minority of women in higher income categories were assaulted by men from poorer segments of society.

The personal resources and social conditions that enable women to foil rapists are also structured by class relationships. There are more "attempted rapes" than completed ones. Yet, the 26-city victimization study shows that while 65 percent of the attacks on women in the lowest income category were not completed, as many as 92 percent of the sexual assaults against women in the highest income category were not completed. As a result, when the *completed* rapes found by that survey are isolated, they show the effect of class relationships to an even greater degree. That effect is shown in Figure 3.

The findings of victimization studies, therefore, provide support for social policies that target familiar socioeconomic conditions. Obviously, these studies emphasize the importance of the same racial and social class relationships that affect other violent Index crimes, such as ordinary assault and robbery. They also provide evidence that the *prevention of rape* in the United States is significantly tied to the *prevention of most* "*street crimes.*"

Thus, to prevent rape, social policies must be aimed at changing the conditions that generate higher incidences of direct interpersonal violence among marginal members of the labor force as well as among men whose livelihoods are at least partly based on illegal activities such as pimping and robbery. Sexual assaults by strangers and other nonfamily members, that is, rape as "street crime," can be reduced enormously by changing the conditions of life in poorer working-class communities.[11]

Although we have emphasized rape by lower status men, we are certainly aware that this crime as well as sexual extortion is committed by middle- and upper-class males and known assailants, such as employers, work superiors, husbands and other family members. (We have said that it also erupts in

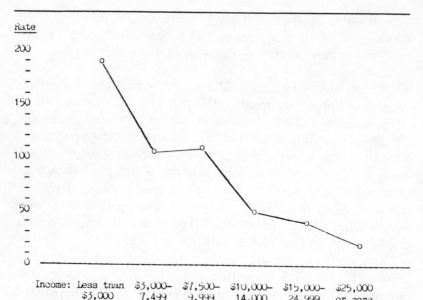

NOTE: Rates are based on completed rapes per 100,000 females 12 years of age and older. The cities are: Atlanta, Baltimore, Boston, Buffalo, Chicago, Cincinnati, Cleveland, Dallas, Denver, Detroit, Houston, Los Angeles, Miami, Milwaukee, Minneapolis, New Orleans, Newark, New York, Oakland, Philadelphia, Pittsburgh, Portland, San Diego, San Francisco, St. Louis, and Washington. Source of data: M. Joan McDermott, *Rape Victimization in 26 American Cities,* U.S. Department of Justice LEAA, NCJ Information and Statistics Service, 1979.

Figure 3: Estimated Rates of Completed Rapes Only, by Family Income of Victim, 1974-1975 (26-cities aggregate)

wartime among men from all classes, especially when these men are infused with racial and national chauvinisms.) Since personal dependency relations, workplace subordination, and chauvinistic standards are causally significant, the reduction of sexual violence requires a variety of measures. Such measures include meaningful full employment legislation to generate jobs for women as well as men; legislative and trade union reforms that enhance the power and status of women in the workplace; movement activity that opposes the use of sexist stereotypes by commercial establishments, especially when those stereotypes are combined with violence; and passing laws that prohibit rape in marriage and that make divorce an inexpensive and feasible alternative for abused wives.

The reduction of female dependency at home and in the labor market is extremely important because it provides individual women with the power to dictate the basic terms on which men must relate to them. In this connection, our analysis of housewives and their personal dependency relations is supported by Russell's (1982: 329) findings regarding wives who stop violence against themselves. Her research found that wives who were primary breadwinners when their husbands first raped them were more likely to take effective action. Her study further showed that 100 percent of the wives who were providing the total family income when they were first raped were no longer married to their rapist husbands. Economic independence and workplace experience give wives greater strength to assert their own rights against abusive men. Also, research by Pauline Bart and Patricia O'Brien (1980) and others would suggest that assertiveness training can usually help prevent rape inside or outside of family relationships, whether or not women are economically independent.[12]

Sexist stereotypes also need special attention because sexual aggression, and aggression in general, are socially learned rather than biologically determined behavior. How, then, can society stop *teaching* men to rape? Reducing the patterns of violence that can be acquired through direct experience and reducing the models for such violence provided in the home, by the mass media, and by other commercial establishments would be helpful.[13] Research indicates that influential models for violent behavior are found in the home (intrafamilial aggression or parents explicitly teaching children to use violence outside the home), among peers, and in the media.[14]

The mass media are extremely important because they provide models for children's behavior. Sexual aggression on the screen either must be replaced or, at least, must be identified with negative consequences that reinforce proper moral attitudes and that cultivate an unambiguous sense of aversion to sexual violence.[15] A number of individual feminists and women's groups have focused on this issue.[16] However, strategies for change in this area would be helped enormously by the development of guidelines for political action that distinguish between erotic symbolism that has no effect on sexual violence and symbolism, such as sadomasochistic pornography, that has such an effect.[17] On the other hand, these guidelines must not conflict with the First Amendment (the "free speech" amendment) to the Constitution, or they will do more harm than good.[18]

Measures for reducing the cultivation of violence among children are implicated in any policy that increases the power of wives to determine their relations with husbands. However, such efforts as Family Anonymous and women's shelters for battered women are also vitally important in this context. Avenues emphasizing prevention would be educational courses in parenting for high school students and/or couples planning to have children. These programs could emphasize the profound effects that family violence has on children. Women's groups could also encourage governmental support for the development of educational research and programs that combat family violence through education and the mass media.

The political times and the theoretical understanding of violence makes it especially imperative that broader strategies for the prevention of violence are adopted by *independent* women's groups. It should be recalled that the strategies pioneered by these groups to defend victims in their contacts with law enforcement agencies, medical institutions, and communities, and their encouragement of self-defense measures originally put women on the offensive against the crime of rape. The antirape movement was also one of the most powerful and effective rallying cries of the women's movement of the 1970s; it gave an activist thrust to women's organizing that had begun merely as consciousness raising. Women were politicized and a large number of people were educated about rape myths and victim rights. The need for autonomous women's groups to fight for women's issues was clearly established.

However, today people like Betty Friedan (1981) feel that an independent women's movement is no longer necessary, even though the struggle for women's rights in certain areas has hardly begun. Friedan's recommendation is difficult to take seriously when we consider that policies directed toward the prevention of sexual harassment on the job or policies confronting attacks by relatives and acquaintances, if they exist, are rarely enforced. Few other organizations will fight for women's rights in these relationships with men. Some unions have fought against sexual harassment, but most still must be convinced that such a fight is important. Legislative changes in rape laws that remove references to the husband's prerogatives are still being urged almost exclusively by women's groups.

Also, there are other struggles for women's rights that have yet to attain their minimum goals. The fight for jobs at equal pay for women is one of them. The struggle for the Equal Rights Amendment was lost by a narrow margin. An ERA and jobs with decent wages will not only decrease women's dependency on men but also will enable more women to establish mutually beneficial relations with men.

The necessity for independent women's groups, however, does not mean that such groups alone will automatically produce policies that will significantly prevent sexual assault. Antirape groups have produced few policies concerning criminal assaults by strangers or relative strangers that go beyond individualistic solutions to crime control. Women as well as men still have to be convinced that self-defense strategies such as carrying whistles, developing street-fighting skills, being alert to dangers and locking doors and windows, although desirable, have limited effects — that they enable some women to avoid attack but do not work for others. Also, no matter how well rape crisis centers deal with victims, their services for victims hardly affect the overall incidence of sexual violence.

Antirape groups have rightfully insisted that rapists should receive swift and certain punishment; and they have proposed policies concerning the apprehension, conviction, and punishment of these criminals. Today, however, women's groups must avoid being seduced by simpleminded law-and-order policies that deceptively promise far more than they can deliver, especially without broader social changes.[19] The women who have joined the law-and-order bandwagon in recent years have made matters worse because they have contributed to a political climate that is benefiting the same untraconservative movements that have been attacking women's gains over the last decade.

Today, these conservative movements and their representatives in political office are directing attention away from serious consideration of crime-fighting policies aimed at improving the conditions of life that especially oppress poor people — black, Hispanic, and white. We have seen only a small part of the solid body of evidence that relates "street crimes" to social and economic conditions. There is also evidence that public policies can decrease unemployment and deterioration of working-class communities through urban planning and the expansion of public-sector jobs in such areas as mass transportation, community development, housing, and health care. However, today government officials and legislatures are ignoring such policy alternatives and are, instead, effecting a massive transfer of public funds from the poor to the rich, even though evidence also shows that this transfer will increase both class inequality and crime.

Within the United States, the incidence of sexual assault cannot be significantly affected without also considering the causes of violence in general and violent crime in particular. It is equally clear that the prevention of rape today means fighting back to reverse long-term government policies that create new generations of violent men. The impoverishment of the working class and the widening of the gap between rich and poor, which is the bottom line of current federal policies, will lead to worse living conditions for the poor and a continued high incidence of sexual violence. Other recent government policies are an even greater threat, because they will escalate violence against women enormously by supporting fascism abroad and by fostering a worldwide arms race leading to new wars. Viewed in this way, the fight against rape must make common cause with the growing resistance to right-wing developments.

In the years ahead, it will not be inappropriate to question whether the moral panics that are raised by people who are outraged by rape will do more to prevent this crime than will working-class and antiwar movements. Whether or not they are explicitly concerned with crime, such movements may accomplish more for rape prevention by struggling politically against the present mobilization for a new war and by resisting the steady deterioration of family, work, and communal life.

It is time to recognize that rape is distributed in our social structure in predictable ways and that sexual assault as well as other violent crime is influenced by political, economic, and ideological conditions. It is time to integrate this recognition into our most significant standards for evaluating whether women's groups are doing enough to prevent violence against women. Surely such groups can raise the consciousness of the people regarding the *political and economic foundations* of rape. They can also forge political coalitions between women's organizations and other progressive movements that are equally interested in developing genuine crime prevention policies.

Notes

1. These relationships are spelled out in greater detail in our forthcoming *Delinquency and the Collective Varieties of Youth*.

2. There are data indicating that these multiple rapes are frequently committed by adolescents and young adults. McDermott (1979: 13) reports that such rapes involve a disproportionate number of younger victims and rapists. Almost one-half of the victims of multiple rapes were between 12 and 19 years old, and 43 percent of the total rapes and attempted rapes committed by multiple offenders included rapists perceived to be under 21 years of age.

3. In addition, those who maintain that crime can be controlled by increasing the amount of time that men spend in prison might consider that imprisonment increases the amount of homosexual rape enormously and that it conditions men to become

violent, even though the large majority of prisoners are not convicted for violent crimes.

4. Because of low frequency, there are reliability problems with rape victimization data. However, for the purposes at hand, these problems are less relevant because the same socioeconomic trend is found repeatedly by different victimization surveys.

5. The 13 cities are Boston, Buffalo, Cincinnati, Houston, Miami, Milwaukee, Minneapolis, New Orleans, Oakland, Pittsburgh, San Diego, San Francisco and Washington, D.C. Source of data: U.S. Dept of Justice (1975). The cities covered by the other surveys mentioned in this chapter are listed in Figures 1 and 3.

6. The national survey has lower rates because it includes in its average rural, small urban, and suburban areas that have markedly fewer rapes.

7. Since many women do not work or work part-time, total family income is a better indicator of the income of rape victims than their personal income.

8. The surveys may seem to undercount rapes involving personal acquaintances because victims are reluctant to report such rapes to interviewers as well as the police. However, estimates from the San Jose study indicate that this undercount involves only a small proportion of the rapes that are counted by the surveys (Mc Dermott, 1979: 3-4). When we also consider that any undercount is distributed among the various income groups, then the likelihood of finding actual distributions that are not skewed socioeconomically is small. On the other hand, Russell (1982) found no difference in income groups when she studied rape in marriage.

9. The rate of theft for the attempted (but not completed) rapes was only 9 percent but Mc Dermott's (1979: 25) report suggests that this low rate occurs because "it is easier for the offender to steal something when the rape is completed and the victim is less capable of offering resistance. The reasons rape attacks are not completed — reasons such as effective resistance, fighting or flight — may also be the reasons for the smaller proportion of thefts in attempted rape."

10. Mc Dermott (1979: 28-29) found that "the proportion of rapes in which something was stolen increases from roughly 2 out of 10 victims with an income of less than $3,000 to a little over 4 out of 10 of the victims with incomes of $10,000 and more."

11. Recent evidence from studies of metropolitan communities suggests that crime rates (including violent crimes such as rape) may be significantly dependent on economic inequality and social disorganization within a population (Blau and Blau, 1982: 114).

12. Self-defense training can be very effective in preventing rape for the individuals who undergo the training. It is also well to keep in mind that Bart's exploratory research found that multiple strategies such as screaming, struggling, and fleeing were associated with avoiding rape while talking or pleading, as the only strategy, was associated with being raped. In a small study of women who were personally interviewed by Julia Schwendinger, it was also found that screaming and struggling helped discourage rape, during an attack. However, individual women must consider the advisability of a physical confrontation when it appears that they can be seriously injured or killed.

13. See Bandura (1973: 144ff.) for a thoughtful evaluation of research indicating that exposure to televised violence promotes aggressiveness in children.

14. The influence of peers on rape and sexual assault is very important, but this influence is less widely understood than the influence of the family and media. We explore this complex topic in *Delinquency and the Collective Varieties of Youth*.

15. Such possibilities are also suggested by research. Again, in this regard, see Bandura (1973: 155ff.).

16. For feminist debates about pornography, see Friedman, and Friedman and Yankowski (1981: 44-52).

17. Feshbach (1978), in "Mixing Sex With Violence — A Dangerous Alchemy," concludes: "The depiction of violence in pornography can have decided negative effects." Recent studies by Feshbach, Neil Malamuth, and others (1980) suggest that "males, in particular, are prone to use violent erotica to reinterpret expressions of pain on the part of female rape victims as indications of sexual excitement."

18. The development of such guidelines should be informed by research that distinguishes the effects of different kinds of sexual symbolism on individual behavior. Such research, for instance, suggests that erotic symbolism per se does not encourage sexual violence (Bandura, 1973: 154). On the other hand, pornographic presentations that depict the violent victimization of women do reinforce violent behavior positively (Feshbach, 1978, 1980). Finally, such guidelines do not have to conflict with First Amendment rights, because these rights were formulated to protect political rights and not the rights of corporate executives to make money by exploiting sexually violent pornography.

19. The feminist periodical *Aegis,* which is dedicated to combatting crimes against women is a very good source of critical ideas and information about crime control and prevention. (An *Aegis* subscription can be obtained by writing to Feminist Alliance Against Rape, Box 21033, Washington, D.C. 20009.) *Crime and Social Justice* is more professionally oriented, but it is a superb periodical which is now publishing theoretical and policy articles helpful to social movements. Two additional periodicals that we recommend highly (because they regularly feature articles that groups interested in social justice and the prevention of crime will find useful) are *Contemporary Crisis* and *Crime and Delinquency.*

BIBLIOGRAPHY

Adler, Freda (1975) SISTERS IN CRIME: THE RISE OF THE NEW FEMALE CRIMINAL. New York: McGraw-Hill.

Afonja, Simi (1981) "Changing Modes of Production and the Sexual Division of Labor among the Yoruba." SIGNS 7 (Winter).

Amir, Menachem (1971) PATTERNS IN FORCIBLE RAPE. Chicago: University of Chicago Press.

Attenborough, F. L. [ed. and trans.] (1963) THE LAWS OF THE EARLIEST ENGLISH KINGS. New York: Russell & Russell.

Babcock, Barbara A., Ann E. Freedman, Eleanor H. Norton, and Susan Ross (1975) SEX DISCRIMINATION AND THE LAW. Boston: Little, Brown and Company.

Ball-Rokeach, Sandra J. (1973) "Values and Violence: A Test of the Subculture of Violence Theory." AMERICAN SOCIOLOGICAL REVIEW 38 (December).

Ball-Rokeach, Sandra J. (1975) "Reply to Magura: Issues and Non-Issues in Testing a Subculture Thesis." AMERICAN SOCIOLOGICAL REVIEW 40 (December).

Bandura, Albert (1973) AGGRESSION: A SOCIAL LEARNING ANALYSIS. Englewood Cliffs: Prentice-Hall.

Bart, Pauline B. and Patricia O'Brien (1980) "How to Say No to Storaska and Survive: Rape Avoidance Strategies." Presented at the Annual Meetings of the American Sociological Association: New York.

Bateson, Gregory (1958) NAVEN (2nd ed.). Stanford, CA: Stanford University Press.

Bell, Diane (1981) "Women's Business Is Hard Work: Central Australian Aboriginal Women's Love Rituals." SIGNS 7 (Winter).

Blau, Judith R. and Peter M. Blau (1982) "The Cost of Inequality: Metropolitan Structure and Violent Crime." AMERICAN SOCIOLOGICAL REVIEW 47 (February).

Bloch, Marc (1966) FEUDAL SOCIETY. Chicago: University of Chicago Press.

Boehringer, Gill H. and Donna Giles (1977) "Criminology and Neocolonialism: The Case of Papua New Guinea." CRIME AND SOCIAL JUSTICE 8 (Fall/Winter).

Brain, James L. (1978) " Down to Gentility: Women in Tanzania." SEX ROLES 4.

Brown, Judith (1975) "Iroquois Women: An Ethnographic Note." In Rayna R. Reiter (ed.) TOWARD AN ANTHROPOLOGY OF WOMEN. New York and London: Monthly Review Press.

Brown, Julia S. (1952) "A Comparative Study of Deviations from Sexual Mores." AMERICAN SOCIOLOGICAL REVIEW 17 (April).

Brownmiller, Susan (1975) AGAINST OUR WILL: MEN, WOMEN AND RAPE. New York: Simon and Schuster.

Brundage, James (1978) " Rape and Marriage in the Medieval Canon Law." REVUE DE DROIT CANONIQUE 28.

Buenaventura-Posso, Elisa and Susan E. Brown (1980) "Forced Transition from Egalitarianism to Male Dominance: The Bari of Colombia." In Etienne, Mona and Eleanor Leacock (eds.) WOMEN AND COLONIZATION. New York: Praeger.

Burgess, Ann Wolbert and Lynda Lytle Holmstrom (1974) RAPE: VICTIMS OF CRISIS. Bowie, Maryland: Robert J. Brady Company.

Burgess, Ann Wolbert and Lynda Lytle Holmstrom (1976) " Rape: Its Effect on Task Performance at Varying Stages in the Life Cycle." In Marcia J. Walker and Stanley L. Brodsky (eds.) SEXUAL ASSAULT: THE VICTIM AND THE RAPIST. Lexington, MA: Lexington Books.

Cason, Hulsey (1943) "The Psychopath and the Psychopathic." JOURNAL OF CRIMINAL PSYCHOPATHOLOGY 4 (January).

Cason, Hulsey (1946) "The Symptoms of the Psychopath." PUBLIC HEALTH REPORTS 61 (December 20).

Catterall, Helen T. (1932) JUDICIAL CASES CONCERNING AMERICAN SLAVERY AND THE NEGRO (Vol. 3). New York: Octagon.

Caulfield, Mina Davis (1977) "Universal Sex Oppression? — A Critique from Marxist Anthropology." CATALYST 10/11 (Summer).

Caulfield, Mina Davis (1981) "Equality, Sex and Mode of Production." In Gerald D. Berreman (ed.) SOCIAL INEQUALITY: COMPARATIVE AND DE-VELOPMENTAL APPROACHES, New York: Academic Press.

Clark, Alice (1968) WORKING LIFE OF WOMEN IN THE SEVENTEENTH CENTURY. New York: Augustus M. Keller.

Clark, Lorenne M. G. and Debra J. Lewis (1977) RAPE: THE PRICE OF COER-CIVE SEXUALITY. Toronto: Women's Educational Press.

Clark, J.H. and M.X. Zarrow (1971) "Coitus-induced Ovulation Tied to 'Rhythm' Failures." OBSTETRICAL GYNECOLOGY NEWS 6 (June).

Cohen, Albert (1955) DELINQUENT BOYS: THE CULTURE OF THE GANG. New York: Free Press.

Cohen, Murray and Richard Boucher (1972) "Misunderstandings about Sex Criminals." SEXUAL BEHAVIOR (March).

Comment (1968) "Police Discretion and the Judgment That a Crime Has Been Committed — Rape in Philadelphia." University of Pennsylvania Law Review 117 (December).

Conway, Carol Coe (1979) "Letter." URPE: NEWSLETTER OF THE UNION FOR RADICAL POLITICAL ECONOMICS 11 (June/July).

Coote, Anna and Tess Gill (1975) THE RAPE CONTROVERSY. London: National Council for Civil Liberties.

Creel, George (1944) WAR CRIMINALS AND PUNISHMENT. New York: R. M. McBride.

Cressey, Donald (1974) CRIMINOLOGY (9th ed.). Philadelphia: Lippincott.

CRIMINAL VICTIMIZATION SURVEY OF THIRTEEN AMERICAN CITIES. (1975) Department of Justice, Washington, DC: United States Government Printing Office.

CRIMINAL VICTIMIZATION SURVEYS IN EIGHT AMERICAN CITIES. (1976) Department of Justice, Washington, DC: United States Government Printing Office.

CRIMINAL VICTIMIZATION IN THE UNITED STATES-1977. (1979) Department of Justice, Washington, DC: United States Government Printing Office.

CRIMINAL VICTIMIZATION IN THE UNITED STATES-1978. (1980) Department of Justice, Washington, DC: United States Government Printing Office.

Daily, Joyce (1980) FAMILY VIOLENCE RELATING TO CHILD ABUSE CASES ENCOUNTERED IN PROBATION WORKS. Tucson, AZ: Pima County Adult Probation Department.

Davis, Alan J. (1968) "Sexual Assaults in the Philadelphia Prison System and Sheriffs' Vans." TRANSACTION 8 (December).

Davis, Angela (n.d.) "JoAnn Little — The Dialectics of Rape." In SAVE JOANN LITTLE. Oakland, CA: Women's Press Collective. (No publication date for this pamphlet; because it was used to raise funds for JoAnn Little's defense, it was probably published in Spring, 1975.)

Davis, Kingsley and Wilbert E. Moore (1945) "Some Principles of Stratification." AMERICAN SOCIOLOGICAL REVIEW 10 (April).

Debris, Jean-Pierre and Andre Menras (1973) WE ACCUSE. Santa Monica: Indochina Mobile Education Project, Indochina Peace Campaign.

DeFrancis, Vincent (1969) "Protecting the Child Victim of Sex Crimes Committed by Adults." Denver: The American Humane Association.

Diamond, Stanley (1971) "The Rule of Law Versus the Order of Custom." SOCIAL RESEARCH 38 (Spring).

Dixon, Marlene (1978) WOMEN IN CLASS STRUGGLE. San Francisco: Synthesis.

Draper, Patricia (1975) "!Kung Women: Contrasts in Sexual Egalitarianism in Foraging and Sedentary Contexts." In Rayna R. Reiter (ed.) TOWARD AN ANTHROPOLOGY OF WOMEN. New York: Monthly Review Press.

Dubois, Rene (1943) "Obstetrical Cases in Wartime." In MORALS IN WARTIME. Victor Robinson (ed.) New York: Publishers Foundation. (Originally published in 1916.)

Dupre, Georges and Pierre-Phillipe Rey (1980) "Reflections on the Pertinence of a Theory of the History of Exchange." In Harold Wolpe (ed.) THE ARTICULATION OF MODES OF PRODUCTION: ESSAYS FROM ECONOMY AND SOCIETY. London: Routledge & Kegan Paul.

Edwards. Allison (1976) RAPE, RACISM, AND THE WHITE WOMEN'S MOVEMENT: AN ANSWER TO SUSAN BROWNMILLER. Chicago: Sojourner Truth Organization (P.O. Box 8493, Chicago, IL 60680).

Eisenberg, Sue E. and Patricia L. Micklow (1977) "The Assaulted Wife: 'Catch 22' Revisited." WOMEN'S RIGHTS LAW REPORTER 3 (Spring/Summer).

Eisen-Bergman, Arlene (1974) WOMEN OF VIETNAM. San Francisco: People's Press.

Engels, Frederick (1975) THE FAMILY, PRIVATE PROPERTY AND THE STATE. New York: International.

Estioko-Griffin, Agnes and P. Bion Griffin (1981) "Woman the Hunter: The Agta." In Frances Dahlberg (ed.) WOMAN THE GATHERER. New Haven, CT: Yale University Press.

Farley, Lin (1978) SEXUAL SHAKEDOWN, THE SEXUAL HARASSMENT OF WOMEN ON THE JOB. New York: McGraw-Hill.

Feshbach, Seymour (1980) "Mixing Sex with Violence — A Dangerous Alchemy." New York Times August 3: Section 2.

Feshbach, Seymour and Neal Malamuth (1978) "Sex and Aggression: Proving the Link." PSYCHOLOGY TODAY 12 (November).

Finer Report (1974) REPORT OF THE COMMITTEE ON ONE PARENT FAMILIES (Vols. 1, 2). Cmnd. 5269. London: Her Majesty's Stationery Office.

Fisher, Seymour and Robert P. Greenberg (1977) THE SCIENTIFIC CREDIBILITY OF FREUD'S THEORIES AND THERAPY. New York: Basic Books.

Flexner, Eleanor (1970) CENTURY OF STRUGGLE, THE WOMAN'S RIGHTS MOVEMENT IN THE UNITED STATES. New York: Atheneum.

Fogel, Robert W. and Stanley L. Engerman (1974) TIME ON THE CROSS: THE ECONOMICS OF AMERICAN NEGRO SLAVERY (Vols. 1, 2). Boston: Little, Brown.

Friedan, Betty (1981) THE SECOND STAGE. New York: Summit Books.

Friedman, Deb (1981) "Pornography — Cause or Effect?" AEGIS 31 (Winter/Spring).

Friedman, Deb and Lois Yankowski (1981) "Ban Porno?" AEGIS 31 (Winter/Spring).

Gager, Nancy and Cathleen Schurr (1976) SEXUAL ASSAULT: CONFRONTING RAPE IN AMERICA. New York: Grosset and Dunlap.

Geen, R. G. and E. C. O'Neal (1969) "Activation of Cue-Elicited Aggression by General Arousal." JOURNAL OF PERSONALITY AND SOCIAL PSYCHOLOGY 11.

Geis, Gilbert (1978) "Rape in Marriage: Law and Law Reform in England, the United States, and Sweden." ADELAIDE LAW REVIEW 6 (June).

George, Margaret (1973) "From 'Goodwife' to 'Mistress,' the Transformation of the Woman in Bourgeois Culture." SCIENCE AND SOCIETY 38 (Summer).

Genovese, Eugene D. (1974) ROLL, JORDAN, ROLL: THE WORLD THE SLAVES MADE. New York: Pantheon Books.

Goebel, Julius, Jr. (1976) FELONY AND MISDEMEANOR: A STUDY IN THE HISTORY OF CRIMINAL LAW. Philadelphia: University of Pennsylvania Press.

Godelier, Maurice (1981) "The Origins of Male Domination." NEW LEFT REVIEW 127 (May/June).

Goode, William J. (1969) "Violence Among Intimates." In D. J. Mulvihill, Melvin M. Tumin, and Lynn A. Curtis (eds.) CRIMES OF VIOLENCE. Washington, DC: United States Government Printing Office.

Griffin, Susan (1971) "Rape: The All American Crime." RAMPARTS 10 (September).

Groth, Nicholas (1979) MEN WHO RAPE. New York: Plenum Press.

Hall, Stuart, Charles Critcher, Tony Jefferson, John Clarke, and Brian Roberts (1978) POLICING THE CRISIS: MUGGING, THE STATE, AND LAW AND ORDER. London: Macmillan.

Hamilton, Roberta (1978) THE LIBERATION OF WOMEN. London: Allen & Unwin.

Harris, Marvin (1975) CULTURE, PEOPLE, NATURE. New York: Crowell.

Hanawalt, Barbara A. (1979) CRIME AND CONFLICT IN ENGLISH COMMUNITIES: 1300- 1348. Cambridge, MA: Harvard University Press.

Herrick, Allison, Saone Baron Crocker, Sidney Harrison, Howard John, Susan MacKnight, and Richard Nyrop (1969) AREA HANDBOOK FOR UGANDA. Washington, DC: Government Printing Office.

Hewitt, Patricia (1975) "Introduction." In Anna Coote and Tess Gill, THE RAPE CONTROVERSY. London: National Council for Civil Liberties.

Higginbotham, Leon Jr. (1978) IN THE MATTER OF COLOR: RACE AND THE AMERICAN LEGAL PROCESS — THE COLONIAL PERIOD. New York: Oxford University Press.

Holstrom, Nancy (1981) "Women's Work and Capitalism." SCIENCE AND SOCIETY 45 (Summer).

Hunter, Monica (1961) REACTION TO CONQUEST (2nd ed.). London: Oxford University Press. (Originally published in 1936.)

Inglis, Amirah (1975) THE WHITE WOMEN'S PROTECTION ORDINANCE, SEXUAL ANXIETY AND POLITICS IN PAPUA. London: Sussex University Press.

Johnston, James H. (1970) RACE RELATIONS IN VIRGINIA AND MISCEGENATION IN THE SOUTH, 1776-1860. Amherst: University of Massachusetts Press.

Jordan, Winthrop D. (1968) WHITE OVER BLACK: AMERICAN ATTITUDES TOWARD THE NEGRO, 1550-1812. Chapel Hill: University of North Carolina Press.

JUDGMENT OF THE INTERNATIONAL MILITARY TRIBUNAL FOR THE FAR EAST (Vol. 2). (1948) Tokyo: International Military Tribunal.

Kanowitz, Leo (1971) WOMEN AND THE LAW, THE UNFINISHED REVOLUTION. Albuquerque: University of New Mexico Press.

Keiser, L. (1968) THE TRAUMATIC NEUROSIS. Philadelphia: J. B. Lippincott.

Kenny, Mary (1973) "Women as Chattels." AGENOR 35 (May/June).

Kinsie, Paul M. (1950) "Sex Crimes and the Prostitution Racket." JOURNAL OF SOCIAL HYGIENE 36.

Kline, Paul (1972) FACT AND FANTASY IN FREUDIAN THEORY. London: Methuen.

Kohl, Philip and Rita Wright (1977) "Stateless Cities: The Differentiation of Societies in the Near Eastern Neolithic." DIALECTICAL ANTHROPOLOGY 2 (November).

Krige, E. Jensen and Krige, J.D. (1943) THE REALM OF A RAIN QUEEN. London: Oxford University Press.

Kuhn, Annette and AnnMarie Wolpe [eds.] (1978) FEMINISM AND MA-TERIALISM: WOMEN AND MODES OF PRODUCTION. London: Routledge & Kegan Paul.

Lacey, W. K. (1968) THE FAMILY IN CLASSICAL GREECE. Ithaca: Cornell University Press.

Lafitau, Joseph F. (1724) MOEURS DES SAUVAGES AMERIQUAINS, COM-PAREES AUX MOEURS DES PREMIERS TEMPS (4 vols.). Paris: Saugrain l'aine.

LaFree, Gary D. (1979) DETERMINANTS OF POLICE, PROSECUTION AND COURT DECISIONS IN FORCIBLE RAPE CASES. Doctoral Dissertation, Indiana University.

Lang, Daniel (1969) CASUALTIES OF WAR. New York: McGraw-Hill (Originally appeared in the NEW YORKER October 18, 1969.)

Largen, Mary Ann (1981) "Grassroots Centers and National Task Forces: A Herstory of the Anti-Rape Movement." AEGIS 32 (Autumn).

Leacock, Eleanor Burke (1975) "Introduction." In Frederick Engels, THE ORI-GIN OF THE FAMILY, PRIVATE PROPERTY AND THE STATE. New York: International.

Leacock, Eleanor (1977) "The Changing Family and Levi Strauss, or Whatever Happened to Fathers?" SOCIAL RESEARCH 44 (Summer).

Leacock, Eleanor Burke (1981) MYTHS OF MALE DOMINANCE, COL-LECTED ARTICLES ON WOMEN CROSS-CULTURALLY. New York: Monthly Review Press.

Leacock, Eleanor and Jacqueline Goodman (1976) "Montagnais Marriage and the Jesuits in the Seventeenth Century: Incidents from the Relations of Paul Le Jeune." WESTERN CANADIAN JOURNAL OF ANTHROPOLOGY 6.

Lerner, Gerda (1973) BLACK WOMEN IN WHITE AMERICA, A DOCUMENTARY HISTORY. New York: Vintage.

Lichtman, Richard (1970) "Symbolic Interactionism and Social Reality." BERKE-LEY JOURNAL OF SOCIOLOGY 15.

Magura, Stephen (1975) "Is There a Subculture of Violence? Comment on Ball-Rokeach." AMERICAN SOCIOLOGICAL REVIEW 40 (December).

Marx, Karl (1959) CAPITAL (Vol. 1). Moscow: Foreign Languages.

Mason, Herbert (1970) GILGAMESH. New York: New American Library.

McCahill, Thomas W., Linda C. Meyer, and Arthur M. Fischman (1979) THE AFTERMATH OF RAPE. Lexington, MA: D.C. Heath.

McDermott, Joan M. (1979) RAPE VICTIMIZATION IN 26 AMERICAN CITIES. Washington, DC: United States Government Printing Office.

Mcintosh, Mary (1978) "The State and the Oppression of Women." In Annette Kuhn and Ann Marie Wolpe (eds.) FEMINISM AND MATERIALISM. London: Routledge & Kegan Paul.

Mead, Margaret (1963) SEX AND TEMPERAMENT. New York: Dell.

Mead, Margaret (1969) MALE AND FEMALE: A STUDY OF THE SEXES IN A CHANGING WORLD. New York: Dell.

Medea, Andra and Kathleen Thompson (1974) AGAINST RAPE. New York: Farrar, Straus and Giroux.

Meillassoux, Claude (1972) "From Reproduction to Production: A Marxist Approach to Economic Anthropology." ECONOMY AND SOCIETY 6.

Meillassoux, Claude (1975) FEMMES, GRENIERS ET CAPITAUX. Paris: Maspero.

Meillassoux, Claude (1980) "From Reproduction to Production: A Marxist Approach to Economic Anthropology. " In Harold Wolpe (ed.) THE ARTICULATION OF MODES OF PRODUCTION: ESSAYS FROM ECONOMY AND SOCIETY. London: Routledge & Kegan Paul.

Mellaart, James (1967) ÇATAL HÜYÜK: A NEOLITHIC TOWN IN ANATOLIA. New York: McGraw-Hill.

Merton, Robert K. (1938) "Social Structure and Anomie." AMERICAN SOCIOLOGICAL REVIEW 3 (October).

Miller, Walter (1958) "Lower Class Culture as a Generating Milieu of Gang Delinquency." JOURNAL OF SOCIAL ISSUES 14 (Summer).

Moynihan, Daniel Patrick (1969) MAXIMUM FEASIBLE MISUNDERSTANDING. New York: Free Press.

Murphy, Robert F. (1960) HEADHUNTER'S HERITAGE. Berkeley: University of California Press.

Murphy, Yolanda and Robert F. Murphy (1974) WOMEN OF THE FOREST. New York: Columbia University Press.

Nagel, Ernest (1959) "Methodological Issues in Psychoanalytic Theory." In Sidney Hook (ed.) PSYCHOANALYSIS, SCIENTIFIC METHOD AND PHILOSOPHY. New York: New York University Press.

Nance, John (1975) THE GENTLE TASADAY. New York: Harcourt Brace Jovanovich.

Parsons, Talcott (1954) "Psychoanalysis and the Social Structure." In ESSAYS IN SOCIOLOGICAL THEORY. New York: Free Press.

Paxton, John D. (1833) LETTERS ON SLAVERY, ADDRESSED TO THE CUMBERLAND CONGREGATION. Lexington, MA: Abraham T. Skilman.

Perkin, H. (1969) THE ORIGINS OF MODERN ENGLISH SOCIETY, 1780-1880. London: Methuen.

Phillips, Ulrich (1929) LIFE AND LABOR IN THE OLD SOUTH. Boston: Little, Brown.

Ploskowe, Morris (1962) SEX AND THE LAW. New York: Ace.

Preu, P. W. (1944) "The Concept of the Psychopathic Personality." In J. V. Hunt (ed.) PERSONALITY AND THE BEHAVIOR DISORDERS (Vol. 2). New York: Ronald Press.

Radelet, Michael L. (1981) "Racial Characteristics and the Death Penalty." AMERICAN SOCIOLOGICAL REVIEW 46 (December).

Rapp, Rayna (1977) "Gender and Class: An Archaeology of Knowledge Concerning the Origin of the State." DIALECTICAL ANTHROPOLOGY 2 (November).

Rapp, Rayna (1978) "Family and Class in Contemporary America: Notes Toward an Understanding of Ideology." SCIENCE AND SOCIETY 42 (Fall).

REDBOOK (1976) November.

Reich, Michael, David M. Gordon, Richard C. Edwards (1973) "Dual Labor Markets, a Theory of Labor Market Segmentation." AMERICAN ECONOMIC REVIEW 63 (May).

Reid, John Phillip (1970) A LAW OF BLOOD: THE PRIMITIVE LAW OF THE CHEROKEE NATION. New York: New York University Press.

Rohrlich, Ruby (1980) "State Formation in Sumer and the Subjugation of Women." FEMINIST STUDIES (Spring).

Rohrlich-Leavitt, Ruby, Barbara Sykes, and Elizabeth Weatherford (1975) "Aboriginal Woman: Male and Female Anthropological Perspectives." In Rayna R. Reiter (ed.) TOWARD AN ANTHROPOLOGY OF WOMEN. New York: Monthly Review Press.

Roscoe, John (1965) THE BAGANDA (2nd ed.). London: Frank Cass. (Originally published in 1911.)

Roy, K.K. (1975) "Feelings and Attitudes of Raped Women of Bangladesh Towards Military Personnel of Pakistan." In Israel Drapkin and Emilio Viano (eds.) VICTIMOLOGY: A NEW FOCUS (Vol. 5). Lexington, MA: D.C. Heath.

Rubin, Gayle (1975) "The Traffic in Women: Notes on the 'Political Economy' of Sex." In Rayna R. Reiter (ed.) TOWARD AN ANTHROPOLOGY OF WOMEN.

Ruggiero, Guido (1944) VIOLENCE IN EARLY RENAISSANCE VENICE. New Brunswick, NJ: Rutgers University Press.

Russell, Diana E.H. (1975) THE POLITICS OF RAPE, THE VICTIM'S PERSPECTIVE. New York: Stein & Day.

Russell, Diana E.H. (1982) RAPE IN MARRIAGE. New York: Macmillan.

Ryan, Cornelius (1966) THE LAST BATTLE. New York: Simon & Schuster.

Sacks, Karen (1975) "Engels Revisited: Women, the Organization of Production, and Private Property." In Rayna R. Reiter (ed.) TOWARD AN ANTHROPOLOGY OF WOMEN. New York: Monthly Review Press.

Sacks, Karen (1979) SISTERS AND WIVES: THE PAST AND FUTURE OF SEXUAL EQUALITY. Westport CT: Greenwood Press.

Sanders, William B. (1980) RAPE AND WOMAN'S IDENTITY. Beverly Hills, CA: Sage.

Schechter, Susan (1979) "Towards an Analysis of the Persistence of Violence Against Women in the Home." AEGIS (July/August).

Schneier, Miriam (1972) FEMINISM, THE ESSENTIAL HISTORICAL WRITINGS. New York: Random House.

Schuessler, Karl and Donald Cressey (1950) "Personality Characteristics of Criminals." AMERICAN JOURNAL OF SOCIOLOGY 55 (MARCH).

Schwendinger, Herman and Julia Schwendinger (1967) "Delinquent Stereotypes of Probable Victims." In Malcolm W. Klein (ed.) JUVENILE GANGS IN CONTEXT. Englewood Cliffs, NJ: Prentice-Hall.

Schwendinger, Herman and Julia Schwendinger (1974) THE SOCIOLOGISTS OF THE CHAIR. New York: Basic Books.

Schwendinger, Herman and Julia Schwendinger (1976) "Delinquency and the Collective Varieties of Youth." CRIME AND SOCIAL JUSTICE 7 (Spring-Summer).

Schwendinger, Herman and Julia Schwendinger (forthcoming) DELINQUENCY AND THE COLLECTIVE VARIETIES OF YOUTH.

Schwendinger, Herman and Paul Takagi (1976) Prepared Statement. In U.S. House of Representatives, HEARINGS BEFORE THE SUBCOMMITTEE ON

CRIME OF THE SUBCOMMITTEE ON THE JUDICIARY. Washington, DC: United States Government Printing Office.

Schwendinger, Julia (1978) "Women's Resource Center: Jail Census Report." Introduction by Herman Schwendinger. In United States House of Representatives, HEARINGS BEFORE THE SUBCOMMITTEE ON CRIME OF THE COMMITTEE ON THE JUDICIARY. Washington, DC: United States Government Printing Office.

Schwendinger, Julia and Herman Schwendinger (1974) "Rape Myths: In Legal, Theoretical and Everyday Practice." CRIME AND SOCIAL JUSTICE 13 (Summer).

Schwendinger, Julia and Herman Schwendinger (1976) "A Review of the Rape Literature, A Review Essay." CRIME AND SOCIAL JUSTICE 6 (FALL/WINTER).

Schwendinger, Julia and Herman Schwendinger (1978) "Studying Rape: Integrating Research and Social Change." In Carol Smart and Barry Smart (eds.) WOMEN, SEXUALITY AND SOCIAL CONTROL. London: Routledge & Kegan Paul.

Schwendinger, Julia and Herman Schwendinger (1980) "Rape Victims and the False Sense of Guilt." CRIME AND SOCIAL JUSTICE 13 (Summer).

Schwendinger, Julia and Herman Schwendinger (1982) "Rape, the Law and Private Property." CRIME AND DELINQUENCY 28 (April).

Smith, Cyril J. (1974) "History of Rape and Rape Laws." WOMEN LAWYERS' JOURNAL 60.

Smith, Paul (1978) "Domestic Labour and Marx's Theory of Value." In Annette Kuhn and Ann Marie Wolpe (eds.) FEMINISM AND MATERIALISM: WOMEN AND MODES OF PRODUCTION. London: Routledge & Kegan Paul.

Smole, W. J. (1976) THE YANOAMA INDIANS: A CULTURAL GEOGRAPHY. Austin: University of Texas Press.

Stone, Merlin (1978) WHEN GOD WAS A WOMAN. New York: Harcourt Brace Jovanovich.

Styron, Rose (1975) "Special Report on Chile." In AMNESTY INTERNATIONAL: REPORT ON TORTURE. New York: Farrar, Straus and Giroux.

Suarez, Susan D. and Gordon G. Gallup, Jr. (1979) "Tonic Immobility as a Response to Rape in Humans: A Theoretical Note." THE PSYCHOLOGICAL RECORD 29.

Svalastoga, Kaare (1962) "Rape and Social Structure." PACIFIC SOCIOLOGICAL REVIEW 5 (Spring).

Tannenbaum, P. H. (1972) "Studies in Film-and-Television Mediated Arousal and Aggression: A Progress Report." In G. A. Comstock, E. A. Rubenstein and J. P. Murray (eds.) TELEVISION AND SOCIAL BEHAVIOR, Vol. 5: TELEVISION EFFECTS: FURTHER EXPLORATIONS. Washington, DC: United States Government Printing Office.

Tormes, Yvonne M. (1968) "Child Victims of Incest." Denver: The American Humane Association.

Toure, I. Nkenge (1981) "Black Focus." AEGIS, MAGAZINE ON ENDING VIOLENCE AGAINST WOMEN (Winter/Spring).

Toynbee, Arnold J. (1943) "Violation of Women in War." In Victor Robinson (ed.)

MORALS IN WARTIME, Part II: MORALS IN THE FIRST WORLD WAR. New York: Publishers' Foundation.

TRIAL OF THE MAJOR WAR CRIMINALS BEFORE THE INTERNATIONAL MILITARY TRIBUNAL (Vol. 7). (1947) Nuremberg: International Military Tribunal.

Turnbull, Colin (1965) WAYWARD SERVANTS. Garden City, NY: Natural History Press.

Turnbull, Colin (1981) "Mbuti Womanhood." In Frances Dahlberg (ed.) WOMAN THE GATHERER. New Haven, CT: Yale University Press.

Ullman, Leonard and Leonard Krasner (1969) A PSYCHOLOGICAL APPROACH TO ABNORMAL BEHAVIOR. Englewood Cliffs, NJ: Prentice-Hall.

Viet Nam Veterans Against the War (1972) WINTER SOLDIER INVESTIGATION. Boston: Beacon Press.

von Hentig, Hans (1951) "The Sex Ratio." SOCIAL FORCES 30.

Wallerstein, Immanuel (1976) "American Slavery and the Capitalist World Economy: A Review Essay." AMERICAN JOURNAL OF SOCIOLOGY 5 (March).

Walker, Marcia J. and Stanley L. Brodsky (1976) SEXUAL ASSAULT: THE VICTIM AND THE RAPIST. Lexington, MA: Lexington Books.

Ward, Lester (1883) DYNAMIC SOCIOLOGY (Vols. 1, 2). New York: Appleton.

Washington, William J. (1972) "Roundtable: Rape and Its Consequences." In Charles M. Hayman, (ed.) MEDICAL ASPECTS OF HUMAN SEXUALITY 6 (February).

Weis, Joseph G. (1976) "Liberation and Crime: The Invention of the New Female Criminal." CRIME AND SOCIAL JUSTICE 6 (Fall/Winter).

Weis, Kurt and Sandra Borges (1973) "Victimology and Rape: The Case of the Legitimate Victim." ISSUES IN CRIMINOLOGY 8 (Fall).

Werth, Alexander (1964) RUSSIA AT WAR. New York: Dutton.

West, Jackie (1978) "Women, Sex, and Class." In Annette Kuhn and Ann Marie Wolpe (eds.) FEMINISM AND MATERIALISM: WOMEN AND MODES OF PRODUCTION. London: Routledge & Kegan Paul.

Weidemann, Thomas (1981) GREEK AND ROMAN SLAVERY. Baltimore: Johns Hopkins University Press

Williams, Eric (1944) CAPITALISM AND SLAVERY. Chapel Hill: University of North Carolina Press.

Wolfgang, Marvin E. and Marc Riedel (1975) "Rape, Race, and the Death Penalty in Georgia." AMERICAN JOURNAL OF ORTHOPSYCHIATRY 45 (July).

Wolfgang, Marvin E. and Franco Ferracuti (1967) THE SUBCULTURE OF VIOLENCE: TOWARD AN INTEGRATED THEORY IN CRIMINOLOGY. London: Social Science Paperbacks.

Wolpe, Harold [ed.] (1980) THE ARTICULATION OF MODES OF PRODUCTION: ESSAYS FROM ECONOMY AND SOCIETY. London: Routledge & Kegan Paul.

Yaley, Barbara and Tony Platt (forthcoming) CONTAGION OF MISERY: LABOR AND PENAL POLICY IN CALIFORNIA 1850-1940. Chicago: University of Chicago Press.

Zaretsky, Eli (1976) CAPITALISM, THE FAMILY AND PERSONAL LIFE. New York: Harper and Row.

Zillman, D. (1971) "Excitation Transfer in Communication-Mediated Aggressive Behavior." JOURNAL OF EXPERIMENTAL SOCIAL PSYCHOLOGY 7.

INDEX

ABOUT THE AUTHORS

JULIA R. SCHWENDINGER is Adjunct Assistant Professor of Sociology at the State University of New York at New Paltz and was an Assistant Professor of Criminal Justice at the University of Nevada, Las Vegas. She received her doctorate in criminology from the University of California, Berkeley, and a master's degree in social work from Columbia University. In the San Francisco Sheriff's Department, she was a Deputy Parole Commissioner and the Director of the Women's Resource Program. She was a founder of Bay Area Women Against Rape (BAWAR) in Berkeley, the first rape crisis center in the world.

HERMAN SCHWENDINGER is Associate Professor of Sociology at the State University of New York at New Paltz. He received his doctorate in sociology from the University of California, Los Angeles, and a master's degree in social work from Columbia University. He taught for ten years at the School of Criminology, University of California, Berkeley.

The Schwendingers are also founders of the journal, *Crime and Social Justice*. They co-authored *The Sociologists of the Chair* (1974) and have published widely in journals of criminology and sociology and in anthologies in the United States and England. They are on the editorial advisory boards of such journals as *Crime and Social Justice* and the *International Journal of the Sociology of Law*.